BIOGRAPHICAL ESSAYS

1790–1890

BIOGRAPHICAL
ESSAYS,
1790—1890

By

Sir EDWARD BOYLE, Bt.

Essay Index Reprint Series

Originally published by:
OXFORD UNIVERSITY PRESS

BOOKS FOR LIBRARIES PRESS
FREEPORT, NEW YORK

First Published 1936
Reprinted 1968

Reprinted from a copy in the collections of
The New York Public Library
Astor, Lenox and Tilden Foundations

LIBRARY OF CONGRESS CATALOG CARD NUMBER:

68-54331

MANUFACTURED
BY
HALLMARK LITHOGRAPHERS, INC.
IN THE U.S.A.

MATRI DILECTAE
PER VITAM SOCIAE
FILIUS

PREFACE

·❦══════════❦·

THE essays which make up this volume put forward no claim to be based on original research. Such title as any of them may have to publication must rest on other grounds.

Although some of them are concerned with personalities of eminence, the particular matters with which they deal are comparatively unfamiliar. Little has been written in English about Chateaubriand and hardly anything about *Le Génie du Christianisme*. Goethe and Victor Hugo have received, as they deserve, more attention than Chateaubriand, but there is not much in English about the former's Italian Journey; and a study of Victor Hugo's oratory may claim to throw fresh light on his character. Rogers and Miss Martineau are hardly more than names to the present generation, and the same is certainly true of Paoli and Hawkins. The paper on Byron is a sort of *addendum* to Mr. Harold Nicolson's book on the Last Journey, and the sketch of Miss Rossetti is perhaps justified because the writer is one of a dwindling number who have been personally acquainted with some of the later survivors of the Pre-Raphaelite circle.

It may also be claimed as a feature common to most of the essays that the descriptions of the various journeys or cities or homes are based on personal knowledge. There are, indeed, few places mentioned in the book which the writer has not visited. In most cases they are not merely known to him but familiar.

The number of works which have been consulted is inevitably very considerable, and a book of this kind should not be overburdened with references; but where the writer feels himself to be indebted in a special degree, the books are mentioned by name in the text. He hopes this general acknowledgement may be accepted as sufficient.

The article on Byron appeared in *The Times* on the centenary of his funeral, and those on Hawkins and Rogers in the *National*

PREFACE

Review. Thanks are due to the Editors in each case for courteously permitting their appearance here. The paper on Paoli was read before the Johnson Club.

The extracts from the speeches of Victor Hugo are taken from Messrs. Nelson's edition of *Actes et Paroles*. The copyright of the speeches of Victor Hugo is now owned by the Librairie Delagrave, 15 Rue Soufflot, Paris, who have themselves published the speeches of Victor Hugo in three volumes. I am greatly obliged to them for allowing me to make the quotations given in the text.

I am indebted also to personal friends who kindly read some of the essays in manuscript: Lady Grogan, my sister Mrs. Halahan, Dr. R. W. Chapman, Mr. A. P. Fachiri, Mr. W. F. Fox, and Mr. E. S. P. Haynes. My thanks are due to Mr. F. W. Hirst for much constructive criticism and for his constant encouragement, and also to my secretary, Mr. R. J. Field; nor must I omit to express my gratitude to Sir Humphrey Milford and to the readers and printers of the Oxford University Press. Not least, I have to thank my wife for helpfulness which has always been at my command throughout.

The book was read in proof by the late Mr. Henry Broadbent of Eton during the last days and almost the last hours of his life. That he should have volunteered for the task will always remain a proud memory to one who was his pupil nearly forty-five years ago.

E. B.

JANUARY 1936

CONTENTS

CHATEAUBRIAND AND *LE GÉNIE DU CHRISTIANISME*

·❮══════❯·

I

*L*E *Génie du Christianisme* is the greatest book of the greatest French writer of his day. It is written in language of
unsurpassed beauty and dignity. If, as is generally conceded,
the French language is one of the most musical of tongues, that
language is nowhere seen to greater advantage than in this book.
Its influence spread from France throughout Europe, and writers
in every country drew their inspiration from its source. It had
a political importance in the circumstances of its appearance
which cannot be over-estimated. Its influence in the world of
thought was as great as in the world of affairs. Indeed, the
influence of *Le Génie du Christianisme* on the writers of the
succeeding generation, and through them upon their successors
until the present time, is immense. For all that, it is unfamiliar to
the general reader in France except in selections as a text-book,
and hardly read at all in England or Germany or Italy. It is
famous, but it is little known. And yet on the day of its issue,
April 15th, 1802, the whole edition was sold out. Jules Lemaître
calls *Le Génie du Christianisme* 'the greatest success in the whole
history of our literature, even from the point of view of sales,
taking into account the period, the character of the work, its
size and its price'.

At the moment of its appearance Chateaubriand was thirty-four.
The younger son of a noble Breton family, he had been trained
originally for the Church, but after contemplating for a moment
a naval career, he joined the regiment of Navarre at Cambrai.
His proud, independent, adventurous spirit, however, could
neither then nor at any time during his life submit to authority.
In 1791, therefore, he left France for America with the avowed
purpose of discovering the North-West Passage, but more probably impelled by a desire for travel and for solitude and by his
disgust at the progress of the Revolution. The following year

he returned, and while fighting alongside the émigrés was wounded at the siege of Thionville; there followed long years of exile and want in Jersey, in Belgium, and in England, which are described with great charm, though with something less than complete accuracy and candour, in the *Mémoires*. During his exile he composed his *Essay on Revolution*, a mere fragment of the gigantic scheme he had set before himself, which was to deal with ancient and modern revolutions in their political and their moral aspect and to consider them in connexion with the French Revolution. It is no longer read in any quarter, and its only interest consists in the part which it plays in the mental development of Chateaubriand himself. Of the two volumes published, the first dealt with the revolutions which mark the history of Greece, and the second with the career of Philip and of Alexander. It is sometimes spoken of as if it were anti-Christian in tone. This is a mistake. 'The Essay', as Chateaubriand said himself later on, 'was not an irreligious book, but a book of doubt and sorrow.' He had nothing in common with the philosophical ideas of Diderot and the Encyclopédistes. Following his own line of thought he came to much the same conclusions as they did, that there was no future for Christianity, and he put the question: 'What will be the religion which will replace it?'—a question to which he fails to find a reply. Apart from this, the outstanding feature of the work is the comparison of the personalities and the events of ancient Greece with the personalities and the events which marked the recent history of France. The conclusion which the reader is invited to draw is the trite one that the more things change, the more they are the same thing. The whole Essay was pessimistic, non-Christian, essentially of the eighteenth century. But it was not anti-Christian. It has, indeed, been called a *Génie du Christianisme* according to the Savoyard Vicar, and nobody will question the influence of Rousseau on Chateaubriand. Chateaubriand always had belief in God: he never doubted the immortality of the soul. The Essay ends on a note of interrogation: *Le Génie du Christianisme* supplies the answer. Chateaubriand's story of the origin of the book is well known. On July 1st, 1798, his sister, the Comtesse de Farcy, wrote to him: 'My dear, we have just lost the best of Mothers. If you knew how many tears your errors have caused your revered Mother to shed, it would perhaps help to open your eyes and to induce you to give up writing.' There is a moving account in the *Mémoires* of his grief. He recalls his mother's sufferings, the break-up of her home, her imprisonment at seventy-two, her son's execution, almost everything she held dear ruined. By the time the letter reached him Madame de Farcy was dead also, owing to her privations in prison. 'These two voices from the tomb affected me deeply', he says. 'I became a Christian . . . my conviction came from the heart : I wept and I believed.'

The *Mémoires* are at once a great help and a great stumbling-block to anybody who seeks to deal with Chateaubriand. Writing many years later, he sets out not necessarily what happened, but what he would have us believe had happened, and what it is possible he had himself come to believe had happened; and it is quite certain that the story given in the preface to *Le Génie* is incorrect, for at the time his mother and his sister died the book was already in an advanced state. Sainte-Beuve, it is true, believed the story on the strength of a letter written by Chateaubriand to the wife of his loyal friend Fontanes, but the dates are against him. His mother died on May 31st, 1798, and Madame de Farcy on July 22nd, 1799. The first sheets were in the hands of the printer on August 19th.[1] Chateaubriand is able to say in a letter to Bandus, through whom he communicated with Fontanes as early as October 25th, that the work would be in two octavo volumes of 350 pages. But there was truth in the statement, even if the statement was not true. For years past Chateaubriand had been writing and carrying his manuscripts about with him in France, in America, in Belgium, and in England: he has himself described how he even wrote on the battlefield. At the time of his mother's death much of the great mass of material which made up what finally appeared as *Atala*, *René*, and *Les Natchez* was already in existence :

[1] The book of August 1779 would have been in one volume. When the work finally appeared in 1802 in four volumes, it had been entirely recast.

indeed, at that date they were part of a whole, and though in fact they appeared as independent works and at different times, Chateaubriand was undecided at the time of his mother's death how best to make use of his material. Her death decided him. *Atala*, intended as an 'illustration' for *Le Génie*, appeared separately in 1801. *Le Génie* appeared itself in 1802, with *René* included. It remained included until 1805. *Les Natchez*, the manuscript of which had long been lost, did not appear until 1826.

Chateaubriand returned to France on May 8th, 1800, with the manuscript and some of the proofs of *Le Génie*, thanks to Fontanes, who induced the First Consul to strike his name out of the list of émigrés. He has described his emotions on seeing Paris once again after nine years. Fontanes introduced him at once to Joubert, a man whose name, at the time when Matthew Arnold published his famous essay, was hardly known in th's country. The debt owed by Chateaubriand to these two was immeasurable, and he never failed to acknowledge it. Joubert lived a semi-invalid life in his modest apartment in the Rue St. Honoré, in close touch with everybody in the literary world of Paris worth knowing (with the important exceptions of Benjamin Constant and Madame de Staël), and enjoyed the confidence of the First Consul. He received Chateaubriand with open arms and introduced him to Madame de Beaumont, the woman who perhaps more than any other won his devotion, whose memory remained with him to the last. Joubert took him to call upon Lucien Bonaparte. Fontanes meanwhile found him work on the *Mercure de France*. Their joint influence induced Chateaubriand to publish *Atala* separately and in advance of *Le Génie* in order to test the public taste. The experiment succeeded beyond their hopes. 'It is from the publication of *Atala*', says Chateaubriand truly enough, 'that there dates the stir I have made in the world.'

Atala is what we should call nowadays a prose poem. The frontispiece to the second edition of Biré's excellent edition of the *Mémoires* is an engraving of Philippoteaux's picture of 'Chateaubriand with the army of Condé' and shows him sitting by himself on a ruin, his hat and his arms cast aside, with his haversack on his lap, a manuscript in one hand and a pen in the other, absorbed in composition. Under some such circumstances, it may well be believed, was *Atala* read over and improved. In the preface Chateaubriand relates that his intention in going to America was to discover the North-West Passage, and how he was prevented from doing so only by the Revolution. *Atala*, he says, was written in the desert in the huts of savages. This is probably a gross exaggeration. The greater body of critical opinion seems to be agreed that he saw few Red Indians and saw them only during a short period. All that can be said with certainty is that *Atala* was always with Chateaubriand during his travels, while the bulk of the manuscript of *Les Natchez* was for many years mislaid. The story of *Atala* is concerned with Chactas, an Indian of the Natchez tribe. Chactas, an old man and blind, had visited France in the time of Louis XIV and had personally known Fénelon. He still loved France though he had little reason to do so, and he relates his experiences to René, a young man who has fled from civilization, the victim of suffering and misfortune. The stage is romantically set: a moonlight night with Chactas and René together in a canoe on the vast Mississippi. The recital of Chactas is in four parts. The first part, 'The Hunters', tells how Chactas was taken to the war against the Muscogulges, the enemies of his tribe. His side was defeated, he fled to Saint Augustin, fatherless, where a Castilian named Lopez and his sister took pity on him. But he is restless and yearns for the desert life. In trying to reach his own people, however, he is captured by the Muscogulges and condemned to be burnt. While a prisoner he meets a young girl, Atala, who believes herself to be the daughter of Simoghan, the chief of the tribe, but she is in fact the daughter of Lopez and a Christian woman. Atala comes secretly to Chactas, unbinds him, and stanches his wounds. They flee together, and as they sail down the stream on a raft she tells him of her life. Chactas soon becomes perplexed at what he calls the contradiction between the 'abandon of her tenderness and the chastity of her conduct'. The second part—'The Workers'—introduces Father Aubry the missionary, who receives the fugitives. Part III—'The

Drama'—deals with the passion of Chactas and Atala for one another and with the suicide of Atala as the only way in which to keep the vow of chastity which she had made to her mother. The story concludes with the burial of Atala by the two men and an epilogue in which Chactas gives rein to his grief.

There appear to be three reasons why this short story intended for incorporation into *Le Génie* was published separately. First, the reader cannot fail to realize the fact that the physical passion which, however subdued and however artistically expressed, is its main, and indeed its only, theme, would render it ill suited to find a place in a work which sets out to restate the case for Christianity. The moral of the story, the good effect of Christianity on the lovers, impresses itself less on the reader than the descriptions which Chateaubriand gives of their love. But there was another reason which, no doubt, was more important, the fact that some of the proofs had gone astray and Chateaubriand had good cause to fear that unauthorized editions might be published. 'I feared', he says, 'they had stolen my romance.' The chief reason, however, was frankly set forth in the preface. 'I do not know whether the public will like this story which deviates from the usual channels, and presents habits and customs entirely unknown to Europe. There is no adventure in *Atala*: it is a sort of poem, half descriptive, half dramatic: it consists entirely of the account of two lovers who walk and talk in solitude, and in the delineation and turmoil of love amid the calm of the desert and the calm of religion.' Thus we have a clear admission as to why the book appeared before *Le Génie*. Chateaubriand did not lack friends, and on this occasion they rallied to his support. His supporters in the press in fact served him well, and M. Yves Le Fèbvre justly remarks in his book on *Le Génie* that it was one of the most ably launched works of the nineteenth century. Fontanes, who edited the *Mercure de France* and was critic as well as friend, induced Chateaubriand to excise or to amend passages where the thin line between the sublime and the ridiculous had been overstepped. '*Atala* was one of those little trial balloons which are sent up before the big one in order to test the atmosphere.' The success was immediate among all classes and Chateaubriand found himself famous. Parody and caricature (and the story lent itself to both) only added to its fame. There was just enough criticism among those who clung to older and more severe styles in writing, to many of whom, no doubt, the underlying purpose of the book was unacceptable, to stimulate to yet greater heights the general chorus of appreciation. Nor is the reason far to seek. Chateaubriand had adopted new subjects and had developed them in a new way. He never wrote anything more melodious than whole passages of *Atala*. It was not what was said that mattered or the purpose which lay behind the writing. What mattered and what attracted the public was the writing itself. In his book which claims to collect *Les meilleures pages de Chateaubriand* by M. Charles Defossez, it is noticeable that the editor includes the greater part of *Atala*. Chateaubriand also, it must be remembered, opened out a new world to his public, a world of which Europe knew little or nothing. His standpoint towards Nature was something unfamiliar and stimulated new attitudes of mind in his readers towards things around them. And not least there was the figure of René as they were to know him under one name or another for half a century to come : Chactas in *Atala*, and something too in the character of his listener, René in *Les Natchez* and in the episode of that name, Eudore in *Les Martyrs*—under whatever alias, always Chateaubriand himself.

The little work has been analysed and criticized more, perhaps, than any other book of the same size. There is much in it that is obviously youthful and immature, something in it of the absurd. And it should be remembered that if immorality is sinful, so is suicide. At least the figure of the priest, Father Aubry, is attractive and his work and character as drawn by the writer are calculated to inspire reverence for the creed he served. The book showed Christianity in a lovable light, and that, after all, was its main purpose.

Everything, indeed, conspired to draw attention to *Le Génie*, even the delay in its appearance. There were the articles in the *Mercure* and the *Journal des Débats*. There was the moral

support which he received from the literary coterie in which he
found himself, and the highly critical attitude which he adopted
towards Madame de Staël's book on *Literature*. 'Your talent is
only half developed,' he told her, 'your philosophy stifles it.' No
wonder their relations were not easy. There was the fact that
portions had already been read and were almost well known in
circles of political no less than literary importance. There can
be no doubt that the First Consul was aware that the book was
in preparation and aware also of its general tenor and political
value to his policy of reconciliation with the Holy See. The
labours of composition were finally completed by six months'
intensive work under the roof of Madame de Beaumont. Even
when the book was ready, it was not immediately published.
The signature of the Concordat was celebrated at the same time
as the Peace of Amiens by a solemn Te Deum in Notre Dame, at
which all the high officials of the State attended. France and
the Catholic Church were formally reconciled. The years of
revolution were at an end; the nation was making a fresh start.
The date was April 18th, 1802. Four days previously there
had appeared in five octavo volumes *Le Génie du Christianisme*.

II

The general reader of to-day will wonder how it was that such
a book upon such a topic should have attracted notice at all.[1]
That it should have attracted such wide and eager interest, that
it should be of such immense importance in the history of French
literature, seems at first sight an almost inexplicable phenomenon. Nevertheless, the reasons are not obscure. The moment
of its appearance was, as has been already indicated, well timed.
As to this, Sainte-Beuve refers to the Te Deum at Notre Dame
on April 18th, which marked at once the inauguration of international peace and the re-establishment of public worship. 'It

[1] Macaulay deals with it in characteristic style. Reading it towards the end of his
life, he is 'astonished at the utter worthlessness of the book both in matter and
manner. The French may be beautiful as far as mere selection and arrangement of
words go. But in the higher graces of style . . . there is a lamentable deficiency. . . .
As to the substance, it is beneath criticism. [Chateaubriand] was simply a great
humbug.'

was', he says, 'on the occasion of this ceremony that *Le Génie* appeared, and that its semi-religious, semi-secular tone became audible, like festive music heard within or like an organ listened to from outside.' Théophile Gautier remarked that Chateaubriand 'has revived the Gothic cathedral'. This remark lends itself to misinterpretation and goes to explain why so much attention has been drawn to the particular chapter which deals with the subject. The phrase is merely a picturesque and epigrammatic way of saying that the book was by far the greatest influence in bringing about the change which marked the attitude of educated men and women towards religion. Sentimental deism and agnosticism had long had it all their own way. With the discredit of the Revolution there followed the discredit of the philosophy which lay behind it. The old-fashioned Christian apologetics would have had no chance; they would have continued to meet with derision. But in *Le Génie* Chateaubriand forged a new weapon. He sought to show that Christianity was true because it was beautiful and that it was beautiful because it was true. The weapons, literary, historical, philosophical, scientific, which had made up the armoury of its opponents, he adopted on behalf of the Faith. The faults of the book are manifest. Many of its arguments are ridiculous, much of its history is incorrect, its science was out of date even in 1802. It was, indeed, regarded purely as an apology for Christianity, hardly Christian. But Chateaubriand wrote as a poet, and as a poet he appealed to old memories of men's childhood, he appealed to national pride: quite frankly he appealed to the emotions. Logic had led the world astray and he eschewed logic. A right instinct induced his readers to fasten upon his picture of the Gothic cathedral because the cathedral symbolized his main contention, that Christianity was not ridiculous but noble, not hateful but to be revered. The eighteenth century had based itself architecturally on Greco-Roman models: Chateaubriand appealed to the national pride in the style which had been evolved by its own consciousness. Joubert frankly regarded Chateaubriand's theology as negligible, as indeed it was. 'Let him stick to his own business,' he said, 'let him enchant us.'

Chateaubriand was the Rousseau of the reaction, as Frederic Harrison has admirably described him. The fire of the Revolution had burnt itself out, and here was a young prophet with eloquence and enthusiasm, with strong convictions and boundless ambitions, to give expression to the mood of the moment and to the vague yearnings of the public. He made irreligion unfashionable.

But whatever the book may have effected in this direction did not last and could not last. Its importance is not that Chateaubriand was the standard-bearer of a religious teaching, but that *Le Génie* is the forerunner of the Romantic movement. Chateaubriand drew attention once again to old traditions and to the Middle Ages. His work stimulated not merely to new ideas but to a new habit of mind. In drawing the many pictures which are contained in *Le Génie* he is less concerned to describe the scenes themselves than to describe the impressions they left upon his mind. He has his models: Homer, Virgil, Dante, Milton, and he does not disguise his admiration for them. The reader of *Les Martyrs* may sometimes wonder whether Chateaubriand does not at the back of his mind cherish the notion that his own work can stand comparison with theirs. Chateaubriand, as has more than once been emphasized, was not consciously and deliberately sounding a new note. *Le Génie* was not a gage thrown down in any such spirit as that of Victor Hugo when he surprised and enraged the classical taste by producing *Hernani*. Chateaubriand, on the contrary, shows much of the classical spirit. His praise of great renaissance churches and of the Invalides and the Hôtel-Dieu rings more true, even if it be less eloquent, than his passage on Gothic cathedrals. He quotes the classical masters—Corneille, Boileau, Molière (more rarely), and his two favourites, La Fontaine and Racine—with evident relish: indeed, it is of the essence of his case that they are in no sense inferior to the masters of antiquity. When he writes a play—*Moïse*—its form is classic, and its observance of the unities is strict. The importance of the book is not that it breaks away from tradition, but that in addition to reverting to an older tradition it opens the way to a new attitude towards Nature.

It is Chateaubriand's descriptions of Nature that are really the outstanding feature. Nature is not as heretofore merely a background in front of which we watch the actions of characters. Chateaubriand does not trouble himself so much with the interplay of ideas between men and women: he was not read in his own day, and he is certainly not read to-day, for his dramatic power. But in describing Nature he opened a new field to poetry. He found beauty in great things and in small, men and women, rare or common, at home or abroad. How far his exile in England may have influenced him raises an interesting question which has never been looked into, and as to which he himself is silent. His debt to Milton he never disguises, and the debt is patent to any reader of *Les Martyrs* (he called him the Christian Homer). But what of other influences? Chateaubriand was in England between 1793 and 1800. We know he was acquainted with the works of Young and of Gray and Beattie. The very frequent references to the Ossian poems throughout his book sufficiently testify to the impression they had made upon him. But there are other writers whom he does not mention. *The Seasons* had been completed in 1730, and though Pope lived and wrote for some fourteen years to come, Thomson sounded the early notes of the Romantic revival. As much as any one man he led the Return to Nature. His attitude was not that which in a later generation characterized Tennyson, who filled notebooks with careful and detailed observations ready to be worked up: he made the pageant, as it were, pass before him and noted at one moment the general effect, and at another the significant detail. He was, in fact, a careful observer of Nature at a time when it was the fashion to worship Art. The influence of Thomson on Collins and Gray descended to Cowper and Goldsmith, to Burns and to Blake. The movement so marked in France away from the stiff and conventional, back to simple nature, was hardly less marked in England: and it is at least worth noting that when Chateaubriand was at Beccles between 1795 and 1797 Cowper was at East Dereham: and although Crabbe had already left his native Aldeburgh, where he had been curate, *The Village* had appeared some twelve years before Chateaubriand arrived

in the neighbourhood. The new attitude for which Chateaubriand stood and the new type of picture that he drew certainl'
had its counterpart in England. What makes *Le Génie* stand out
so prominently is partly its substance, partly its political time-
liness, partly—as Chateaubriand later admitted—the attitude
of mind which he adopted towards Christianity, and partly the
leading part it played in the early stages of the Romantic movement. At a later date Chateaubriand would have written a
different book. He would have made his apology for Christianity
perhaps more conventional and, no doubt on that account, less
effective. Although he mentions slavery in part four, he says
in 1837 that had he written the book at that date he would
have emphasized the liberal element in Christianity. In 1837
Chateaubriand would have been appealing to another generation, and his political career would have been behind him and
not ahead. In 1802 his chief purpose was to stimulate regret
for the past and to appeal not so much to the intelligence as
to the imagination of his readers. In this he brilliantly succeeded.

III

As to the influence of the work on Chateaubriand's subsequent
career, Jules Lemaître has said that he was the prisoner of the
book for the rest of his literary life. And this is true, for the success of *Le Génie* induced him to write *Les Martyrs*, and to justify
Les Martyrs and its local colour he undertook the journey which
is described in the *Itinéraire de Paris à Jérusalem* (1811), which
remains, after *Les Mémoires*, by far the most readable of his
works, though Lemaître does not think so. Chateaubriand
returned through Spain. *Les Aventures du dernier Abencérage*
is said to have been composed before *Les Martyrs* and appeared
only in 1826. It was in Spain that by arrangement he met his
friend Madame de Noailles, and there can be no doubt that the
little book in the form in which it finally appeared owed much
to their romantic association which marked the climax of his long
journey. Many of Chateaubriand's later books were no more
than sections taken out of the enormous mass of manuscript

which he accumulated during his youth, material which was
e gerly welcomed by the public in the years of his fame. Just
as first *Atala* and later *René* were detached from *Le Génie*, so *Le
Voyage en Amérique* (1827) contains material which had remained
over after the appearance during the previous year of *Les
Natchez*. *Les Natchez* was indeed the mine itself out of which
Atala and *René* had already been quarried. His imaginative
work thus all hangs together. His *Essai sur la littérature anglaise*
(1836) accompanied his translation of Milton. In old age he
returned again to the works of a poet whose influence upon
him was great in his youth and who figures prominently in
Le Génie.

It is indeed clear, therefore, that the book permeated his whole
literary life. But much more than that: its influence is apparent
no less in his whole public career. The life of Chateaubriand
clearly divides into two portions. The literary life closed in
1811 with the publication of *L'Itinéraire*. Thereafter he continued to produce books and pamphlets, but his imaginative
activity was at an end, and such work as he published in later
years apart from political and historical books and essays was what
remained over from his youth. After 1811 he is the public man,
the politician, and it is not too much to say that in this capacity
also it is the influence of *Le Génie* which gives to his career its
unique character. Chateaubriand the statesman no less than
Chateaubriand the writer is always René. Chateaubriand, indeed,
never hid the fact that he regarded himself as René. He was
René in his egoism, in his supreme interest and confidence in
himself. He was capable of giving to a cause whole-hearted and
unselfish devotion. He would throw himself into a cause irre-
spective of its chances if the cause appealed to him, and in fact
during his long career he was the champion both of causes which
succeeded and of causes which failed, though one may suspect
that he was happier under the latter than under the former conditions. Perhaps it will be truer to say that he was indifferent
whether a cause succeeded or failed so long as he played his part
as a prominent figure. If all went well, then he was always
ready to enjoy the limelight of success. If things went ill, he

could resign or retire with a large and noble gesture. His pride
was immense. He spoke of 'Bonaparte and I' and about 'my'
war in Spain. His self-pity was on a similar scale. René could
never get away from himself. His sorrows and his griefs were
greater in scale than those of ordinary people: he personifies in
his melancholy *l'enfant du siècle*. To return to our metaphor, the
scenery might change—indeed, during his long and strange career
it did change more often than in the life-drama of most other men;
but whatever the backcloth, whoever may have figured in the
cast, Chateaubriand had to occupy the centre of the stage,
whether for the moment the stage represented the court of
a grateful monarch or the deathbed of a beloved friend in a
modest room under Italian skies; whether it was a public reception in a foreign country to the Ambassadors of the Great Powers,
or an interview by candlelight with an aged king in exile;
whether it showed an international Congress of plenipotenti-
aries, or a few admiring listeners gathered together in a Paris
flat. This amazing egoism, which revelled like René in sorrow
no less than in success, explains what at first sight appear to be
the public inconsistencies in the career of the author of *Le Génie*.
In 1803 Napoleon repaid his services to the policy of the Concordat by nominating him as first secretary to the Embassy at
Rome under his uncle, Cardinal Fesch, an uneasy conjunction.
Chateaubriand was then 35: the Royalist émigré found his
foot on the ladder. In March 1804 he reached a step higher,
and found himself nominated Minister in the Valais. Within
a week there occurred the execution of the Duc d'Enghien, and
Chateaubriand thereupon wrote to the First Consul throwing
up the post for reasons of health, though Napoleon realized
clearly enough that by this gesture he had gone over to the ranks
of his enemies. This, it is now certain, was merely an excuse.
Chateaubriand wished to be an Ambassador, he was dissatisfied
with Napoleon's personal attitude towards him, he was not
content to serve in what almost amounted to banishment under
the orders of Talleyrand. There followed happy years—so far
as a man like Chateaubriand could ever be happy—of retirement
at the property, La Vallée-aux-Loups, which he delighted to

develop with trees grown from seedlings collected during his travels, and especially with trees from his beloved Brittany. There he wrote *Les Martyrs* and there in 1811 he began the *Memoires*. In this year occurred the incident at the Académie Française, for membership of which Chateaubriand had become a candidate with the approval of Napoleon. His Reception Address contained veiled attacks on the Emperor, and when it was returned to the writer with Napoleon's own excisions he refused to accept them or to attend the meeting. As a result, the relations of the two men, who alternately attracted and repelled each other, became worse than ever. The Russian campaign showed the beginning of the end. Chateaubriand moved to Paris, and in April 1814 appeared the pamphlet *De Buonaparte et des Bourbons*, of which Louis XVIII is reported (by Chateaubriand) to have said that it was worth an army to him. Certainly its influence was immense, and he looked for that appreciation of his services from the King which he had not obtained from the Emperor. But history repeated itself. Louis never liked him, feared his abilities, and was perhaps jealous of his fame. He was appointed Ambassador to Sweden, but the Hundred Days came before he could take up his post, and again Chateaubriand found himself on the losing side, only to return once more to Paris after Waterloo with the victorious Bourbons and to find himself face to face with the hated Talleyrand. Again his pride, his self-concentration, his rigidity stood in his way: he was the antithesis of Talleyrand and Fouché, who could quite shamelessly adjust themselves to new conditions and who, it must in fairness be remembered, sought to serve the State as well as themselves in circumstances of extraordinary difficulty and complexity. In *La Monarchie selon la Charte* (1816) Chateaubriand shows that the Bourbons, if only they are wise, will be willing to forget some things and will be willing to learn from experience. It is a protest against the fierce reactionary tendency of the first parliament of the restored Monarchy, and it was calculated to please nobody; for while admitting on the one hand that the eighteenth century could not be restored and the Government must be representative, which enraged the reactionaries, he attacked as an ultra-royalist the men who were round the King. His name was struck off the list of Ministers of State, he lost his pension, and he was compelled to sell his property and his books. It was the Duc de Richelieu who brought a new turn to his fortunes when, in 1820, as part of a policy of general appeasement, he appointed Chateaubr and Minister in Berlin, which post he held until July 1821, when he resigned with Villèle from the Ministry. It was undoubtedly his hope to obtain the office of Foreign Minister in the Coalition which followed, but again he had to suffer disappointment. He was sent to London, and though he found pleasure in the contrast between his earlier situation as a penniless émigré and his present post as Ambassador, he remained dissatisfied. He still felt himself banished and not wanted in Paris, which was indeed the truth. At the Congress of Vienna he was one of the delegates, but not, as he had hoped, the sole one, and only in 1823 was his ambition at last satisfied, when he became Minister of Foreign Affairs in the Villèle government. There followed the short war with Spain. In retrospect that war seems to have been merely designed to force an eminently undesirable king on an unwilling country, though no doubt it also served the purpose of so many other wars, of distracting attention from difficulties at home. And then, close on success, came ruin. He quarrelled with Villèle. Beginning with some misunderstanding about foreign decorations the trouble grew, and finally, on the ground that his silence in the Chamber had manifested disloyalty to the Government, Chateaubriand was dismissed. He refers to the occasion in the *Mémoires* with proud and conscious dignity: 'Feeling keenly the insult,' he says, 'it was impossible for us to forget that we were the restorer of religion and the author of *Le Génie du Christianisme.*' He turned to journalism, and in the *Journal des Débats* he attacked Villèle as he had previously attacked Richelieu and Decazes, and he finally brought him down. In all his long career, as Sainte-Beuve has remarked, there were only two years during which he was not in opposition. But the opposition to Villèle opens a new phase in Chateaubriand's political development, the liberal phase. He became the centre of the Liberal Royalist movement, advocating, above all, the freedom of the press, which, no doubt, went far to prepare the way for the Revolution of 1830. He hailed Charles X with enthusiasm on his coronation, and attempts by the Court to conciliate him were not lacking, even though the King himself liked Chateaubriand no better than had Louis XVIII. When at the end of 1827 Villèle fell, it was Montignac who became President of the Council and La Ferronays who went to the Foreign Office. Once again and for the last time Chateaubriand was sent abroad, on this occasion as Ambassador to Rome. There he remained, eager to play his part in the efforts to secure the election of a Francophil Pope, until, when home on leave, he resigned his post as a protest against the dangerously reactionary policy of Polignac. Chateaubriand's public career was at an end. He lived another eighteen years. Characteristically he had, as a Liberal, thrown up his career, and at the same time, as a Royalist, he refused to have any dealings with the Liberal Monarchy of Louis-Philippe. He had no love of the Bourbons and had no reason to love them, but he was loyal to them in their exile: he did what he could to reconcile Charles X with the Duchesse de Berri after her pitiful failure to raise La Vendée against the Government, and he showed the attitude of a wise old courtier towards the Comte de Chambord, who lived on into our own day. Apart from that, the later years evoke a picture of the old man working and writing as long as he had the strength, with financial resources no more than adequate, reading his memoirs at l'Abbaye au Bois to the chosen friends assembled around him, a picture so admirably drawn for us in the book on Madame Récamier by M. Herriot. The end came on July 4th, 1848, the day of the Revolution, and the guns sounded in his ears as he died. To some men their tomb is a matter of indifference, to Chateaubriand it was, on the contrary, a matter which had exercised his mind for years. He is buried on a rock in the open sea off his native St. Malo. The rock, the Grand Bé, is approachable only at low water, and on its seaward side there is the grave, visible from the ramparts, a stone and cross which bear no name. No more romantic spot can be imagined: the picturesque town with its medieval walls and its little tidal harbour, the broken, bare, hilly coastline extending on either side as far as the eye can see. Such a tomb suggests pride and at the same time humility, loneliness, and romance. Silhouetted against the sky-line it is a constant witness to the thesis which *Le Génie* was written to prove. It is, in fact, an epitome of Chateaubriand.

LE GÉNIE DU CHRISTIANISME: AN EXAMINATION

·❨══════════❩·

I

*L*E *Génie du Christianisme* has a certain symmetry of structure. It is divided into four parts, and each part as originally planned contains six books, each book consisting of a
number of chapters. Part I is concerned with dogmas and doctrines. It deals with the Christian mysteries and sacraments and
with the truth of Scripture. It finds in the marvels of Nature
proof of the existence of God, and claims that conscience in mankind is itself the best evidence of immortality. Parts II and III go
together and deal with what Chateaubriand calls the 'Poetry of
Christianity'. Part II deals in the strict sense with poetry. It
compares the Christian epics with the best work of the classical
writers to the advantage of the former, and in this part of the
book Chateaubriand endeavours to show how superior are the
characters portrayed by Christian writers to the best and most
famous characters to be found in Greek and Roman literature.
Part III deals with the Arts, Philosophy, History, and Eloquence.
Part IV treats of what he calls Worship—churches, ceremonies,
the clergy, missions, and it concludes with a general view of the
services which Christianity has rendered to the world. It is to be
noted, however, that the symmetry of structure in the original
plan of the book is not carried out in its entirety. Whereas
Parts I and IV are divided into six books, Parts II and III con-
sist of five only. This is because *René* was originally intended to
follow on Book III, Part II (the chapters dealing with the Passions), and *Atala* was intended to follow Book V of Part III as
an example of the influence of Christianity on the emotions of the
human heart. *Atala*, as we know, appeared before *Le Génie* was
published, and *René* was withdrawn at an early stage, so that the
book lacks the balance which Chateaubriand originally intended
it to have. In any case, however, it is a symmetry in appearance
only. The author wanders over a very wide field. Many of the

matters upon which he touches could be dealt with equally well under one head as under another. Sometimes the same topic is dealt with under more than one head. Chateaubriand's title fully justifies him in taking this course. The word *Génie* means essence or essential nature. The book is, in fact, an essay on the spirit of Christianity. Chateaubriand's first intention was to call his book the *Beauties of the Christian Religion*, but in the Introduction he admits frankly that the old type of Christian apologetics would be utterly useless. 'Who would now read a work of theology? A few saintly men who are already convinced, a few true Christians who are already persuaded.' In taking this view of course he was right. The general public has never been disposed to read theology as such, while on the other hand there has never been a time when the ordinary man has not been ready and eager to listen to any well-qualified teacher who has a message to give and who can state his case clearly and well.

It is said with truth of *Le Génie* that it is neither a treatise on dogma, nor a poem, nor an essay on moral philosophy, and yet something of each. Its manner is often erudite, but it is not in any real sense scholarly. It is constantly to be borne in mind that the book was addressed to a generation who had grown up in an age which considered not merely that Christianity was out of date but that it was utterly ridiculous. In a sense the book is directed more against the Encyclopédistes than against Voltaire. Again and again Chateaubriand refers to Voltaire with appreciation. The same is true, though in a less degree, of Rousseau; but the Encyclopédistes are rarely mentioned and never with approval. The Encyclopédie had directed itself not to attacking Christianity as such, but to attacking sacerdotalism. The religious attack, as Lord Morley puts it, was prompted and guided by the same social feeling that inspired the economic articles. Priests are held in contempt not because they are priests but because they are oppressors. And if freedom of opinion lay at the root of the teaching of Diderot, the same is true of Holbach. His argument was directed not against religion but against the organization of Church and State as they were in eighteenth-century France. He stood for something not merely critical but constructive in the sense that his system of nature sought to provide a substitute for the teaching of the Church: the sovereignty of physical laws, evolution, a sort of foretaste of the Religion of Humanity. Helvétius, again, was a precursor of Bentham and of utilitarianism, for he, too, sought the greatest good of the greatest number, and he found in education a panacea for social and moral evils. In considering the work of Chateaubriand, it is therefore important to remember that he set himself against all such teachings as these quite as resolutely as against the sentimental deism of Rousseau and the humanitarian deism of Voltaire. The value of the book to-day consists in two things only—in the beauty of the sketches it contains of scenery or of character, and in the underlying conception of Christianity as one of the richest sources of the Beautiful and of the Bible as an outstanding masterpiece of literature.

The Introduction sets out clearly and defiantly the author's point of view. Society must no longer base itself upon conceptions which derive from Greece and Rome. Politics, literature, and art in all its manifestations have been permeated with the ideas and the ideals of the ancients. The moment has now come to have done with imitations of the past and to look ahead, to find inspiration in ideas which the previous generation had spurned, and to expose the fallacies and the emptiness by which they had allowed themselves to be deceived. Chateaubriand throws down the gauntlet.

Ce n'était pas les sophistes qu'il fallait réconcilier à la religion, c'était le monde qu'ils égaraient. On l'avait séduit en lui disant que le christianisme était un culte né du sein de la barbarie, absurde dans ses dogmes, ridicule dans ses cérémonies, ennemi des arts et des lettres, de la raison et de la beauté; un culte qui n'avait fait que verser le sang, enchaîner les hommes et retarder le bonheur et les lumières du genre humain: on devait donc chercher à prouver au contraire que, de toutes les religions qui ont jamais existé, la religion chrétienne est la plus poétique, la plus humaine, la plus favorable à la liberté, aux arts et aux lettres; que le monde moderne lui doit tout, depuis l'agriculture jusqu'aux sciences abstraites, depuis les hospices pour les malheureux jusqu'aux temples bâtis par Michel-Ange et décorés par Raphaël.— Vol. i. 13.[1]

[1] The quotations are from the Édition Flammarion, in two volumes.

Part I, then, deals with dogmas and doctrine. There is in it much that is interesting, much eloquence, some learning, and it must be allowed, some nonsense. There are in Part I numerous passages which generally find a place in any collection of the 'Beauties of Chateaubriand', though Sainte-Beuve is no doubt right in saying that it is the weakest portion of the work. It would be easy to overweight this essay with quotations, and the endeavour must be made to limit them to such cases as those in which it is right that Chateaubriand should be allowed to speak for himself or where the form in which the writer clothes his thoughts is recognized as being of exceptional interest or beauty. Chateaubriand deals first of all with the Christian mysteries, the Trinity, the Redemption, the Incarnation. He approaches the doctrine of the Trinity in a manner which must have been surprising to the Church of which he had constituted himself the defender. He quotes Plato, the beliefs of Hinduism, the Tibetans, the natives of Otahiti, the myths of polytheism, as each in their own way affording support to the doctrine. He quotes the argument of Tertullian, that God created the world by His Word, His Reason, and His Power. That which proceeds from God is God, and the two together with their Spirit are one. The Son has his own origin but is nevertheless in no sense separate from God. The Word is Spirit of a Spirit and God of God, just as one light may be lit from another. This explanation of the Trinity, says Chateaubriand, perhaps rather optimistically, 'can be understood by the simplest minds'. In speaking of the Redemption Chateaubriand, as so often in *Le Génie*, adopts a logical form of argument. Man is born perfect: the end for which he was created must therefore itself be perfect. Man has fallen by reason of his disobedience, but the purpose of his creation remains. In his state of imperfection he cannot attain his perfect ends. He cannot redeem himself, and nothing less than God can redeem him. Chateaubriand turns to deal with the sacraments and shows himself much more the poet than the theologian. This is very marked when he deals with the Communion. He speaks of the bread and wine as the 'gifts of the fields ready to harvest', he recalls the Jewish Passover and regards the ceremony as marking the end of sacrifices of blood, and as uniting men in one great family. Only at the close does he speak of 'the Real Presence of God in the consecrated bread'. If the book was meant as a serious contribution to religious thought it was justly objected at the time it appeared that the poetical style of the writing was a disadvantage. If, on the other hand, the book was intended to show how helpfully modern poetry could look to the Christian faith for inspiration, the purely dogmatic part is redundant. Chateaubriand's friend Joubert saw this clearly enough, and sets out his view in the often quoted letter to Madame de Beaumont: 'The public', he says, 'will bother itself little enough with his quotations, but much with his thoughts: people are more interested in his genius than in his learning: we shall seek in his book beauty rather than truth: his own personality and not his doctrine will make its fortunes.' This was written at the time when Chateaubriand was putting the finishing touches to the work under the roof of Madame de Beaumont. The whole letter is full of the wisest advice. 'Hide your knowledge,' he says, 'true art is to conceal art': advice which Chateaubriand, who liked to make a parade of his learning, was unwilling to follow. In these chapters on the Sacraments there is no little evidence of study, both in the text and in the notes. The classical writers, the Christian Fathers, the canon law, medieval history, all are brought under contribution. The greater part of two chapters is devoted to the praise of virginity. It was such passages that go to explain why it was that the relations of Chateaubriand with Madame de Staël were never easy. Madame de Staël had an abundance of a quality which Chateaubriand woefully lacked—humour. In his *Mémoires* it is clear that, though their acquaintance covered a long period, it was never intimate. Joubert, who in his day knew everybody in the world of letters, refused to know her. He considered, he said, that she had more vehemence than truth, more heat than light. Chateaubriand as a young man was content to follow Joubert's lead. Indeed, his first appearance in print after his return from exile had been an intervention in the *Mercure* 'assez peu courtoise', as he himself admits, in a literary controversy between Madame

de Staël and Fontanes. This she had taken in good part, even
handsomely. All through his life he was anxious neither to
offend her nor to develop friendship with a woman who would
have little sympathy with humbug or pose, whose standpoint,
moreover, differed so widely from his own. When she died in
1817 he remarked that her death induced in him a certain
'mysterious astonishment', but it is significant that on the same
page he dwells rather on the fact that at her table and in her
absence (she was dying in another room) he met again after
twelve years Madame Récamier. Passing from the Sacraments,
Chateaubriand proceeds to deal with Faith, Hope, and Charity.
Here we arrive at the first of the many instances where the
author adopts a line of argument which was rare in his day. He
compares the Decalogue with other ancient codes, and the ideas
as to the origin of the world put forward by Thales and Plato,
Aristotle and Zeno, the Scandinavians, the Red Indians, the
Peruvians, and others, with the Mosaic cosmogony. Remarks
on the Fall of Man suggest the serpent, and the serpent suggests
his own experiences in America. When Chateaubriand is
writing something based on his own knowledge, nothing can be
more admirably vivid. In this chapter there is an account of the
charming of an angry snake most dramatically and convincingly
told; but the writer has to keep in mind that he is dealing with
the Fall, and in the same chapter we come across a statement like
the following: 'We have not failed to recognize in [the serpent]
that detestable temper and that subtlety which Scripture attributes to him.' Chateaubriand asks himself the question: how is
it that, while animals remain the same in their intelligence and
their passions, mankind is always aware of a struggle between
conscience and inclination? Herein he finds new proof of original
sin. He raises the question, how could the world have gone
on if mankind had been immortal, and he can find no solution
except that with God everything is possible. Chateaubriand
then proceeds to show to his own satisfaction that there is
nothing in the chronologies of Egypt or Persia or Greece and
no argument based on either history or astronomy or geology
which can upset that of Moses. In chapters to which excep-

tionally full references are attached he sets himself to prove
that we need not trouble because there have been civilizations
which appear to be inconsistent with the story in Genesis. His
answer to this is in effect that science is wrong in its dates and
that people became civilized in a very short period of time.
When he comes to astronomy he appears, as it were, to play off
one system against another. He points out, as he continues to do
again and again in the course of his work, how much astronomy
has owed to the Church. In all the long years of disorganization
which followed the dissolution of the Roman Empire it was
the Church that provided a sanctuary for scientific study. He
remarks that in the century between Copernicus and Newton
astronomy made more strides than in three thousand years
before. To the comment that the world is millions of years old
and not merely six thousand, he makes the rhetorical answer that
because astronomy has remained four thousand years in its
middle age we are not entitled to conclude that it remained
myriads of centuries in its cradle. What Chateaubriand says
under this head is indeed quite valueless and negligible, and the
same is true of his remarks on geology. When he is asked to
explain fossils, the structure of mountains, the implications of
rock strata, he replies majestically: 'This difficulty has been a
hundred times solved by this reply: God has no doubt seen fit
to create the world with all the marks of age upon it, just as we
see it.'

Chateaubriand then argues that the wonders of the natural
universe are in themselves the best evidence of the existence of
God. Here the author begins to be more at home: the poet and
the traveller get their chance, and perhaps the romancer too.
Book V is called *The Existence of God proved by the Marvels of
Nature*. There are at this point relegated to the notes what
he considers the metaphysical arguments for the existence of
God. He finds them under three heads, matter, movement, and
thought, and from each he draws the conclusion favourable to his
contention. Under 'matter', the first of the three heads, he argues
that something must always have existed, something independent and unchangeable. This something cannot be mere matter:

it is of necessity unique and cannot be quite a blind agent. It possesses infinite power and is infinitely good. It is God. Secondly, he speaks of movement, and suggests that movement is not essential to matter. There are bodies which are static: universal movement would be the same as universal immobility: and the irregular movement of matter can never be considered as creator of the universe. A cause can never create an effect of which it is not itself the origin, which would mean an effect without a cause. From this it follows that there is a chief agent of movement outside matter. This again is God. Thirdly, there is thought. Thought exists only after man is created: it is produced by something outside matter which must be something finer and stronger than the thought itself. If a thought being indivisible is immortal, this must be true of what produced the thought. Arguments along these lines all satisfy Chateaubriand that there is beyond everything a First Cause infinitely powerful, infinitely good: God.

The argument in the text is less arid, and indeed, the last two books of Part V are perhaps the most eloquent portion of *Le Génie*. He finds evidence of a Creator in the mere existence of the universe. The very heavens declare the glory of God. He finds it, too, in the law of adaptation to environment, in the marvels of the physical structure of animals, birds, and fishes, in the blossoming of trees and flowers. Apart from and in addition to the organization of beings, there is the marvel we call instinct: the beaver that builds his dam, the hen who will violently attack the enemy, whoever he be, of her chickens, the migratory birds. Then follows a passage of outstanding beauty on the songs of birds.

On voit accourir de savants artistes avec des sonates merveilleuses, de vagabonds troubadours qui ne savent chanter que des ballades à refrain, des pèlerins qui répètent mille fois les couplets de leurs longs cantiques. Le loriot siffle, l'hirondelle gazouille, le ramier gémit: le premier, perché sur la plus haute branche d'un ormeau, défie notre merle, qui ne le cède en rien à cet étranger; la seconde, sous un toit hospitalier, fait entendre son ramage confus ainsi qu'au temps d'Évandre. Le troisième, caché dans le feuillage d'un chêne, prolonge ses

roucoulements semblables aux sons onduleux d'un cor dans les bois.
Enfin le rouge-gorge répète sa petite chanson sur la porte de la grange,
où il a placé son gros nid de mousse; mais le rossignol dédaigne de
perdre sa voix au milieu de cette symphonie: il attend l'heure du
recueillement et du repos, et se charge de cette partie de la fête qui
se doit célébrer dans les ombres.—Vol. i. 98.

The two chapters which follow, on the nests and on the migration of birds, are frequently quoted as showing the style of
Chateaubriand at its best, the style that paints a picture in words
which make that picture live to the imagination in all its colour
and form.

From migration of birds he turns to migration of animals.
A passage on the migration of the buffalo across the plains of
Louisiana and New Mexico reads, and is clearly meant to read,
like that of an observer. How much of America Chateaubriand
visited is still very much debated, but the dates of his arrival and
departure make it quite certain that he saw much less of the
country than he would have us believe. It is quite impossible
that he visited New Mexico; it is equally unlikely that he should
have visited Florida, though his remarks about crocodiles and
serpents suggest that he wrote from his own recollections of
travel. On the other hand, in the chapter which follows, on
plants and the movement of plants, he quotes what we know to be
his own experience in exactly the same manner. The descriptions of the ocean and the neighbourhood of Niagara in Chapter
12 may well be considered among the finest in *Le Génie*.

Dieu des chrétiens! c'est surtout dans les eaux de l'abîme et dans les
profondeurs des cieux que tu as gravé bien fortement les traits de ta
toute-puissance! Des millions d'étoiles rayonnant dans le sombre azur
du dôme céleste, la lune au milieu du firmament, une mer sans rivage,
l'infini dans le ciel et sur les flots! Jamais tu ne m'as plus troublé de ta
grandeur que dans ces nuits où, suspendu entre les astres et l'Océan,
j'avais l'immensité sur ma tête et l'immensité sous mes pieds!—
Vol. i. 119.

And again:

Une heure après le coucher du soleil, la lune se montra au-dessus
des arbres à l'horizon opposé. Une brise embaumée, que cette reine

des nuits amenait de l'orient avec elle, semblait la précéder dans les forêts comme sa fraîche haleine. L'astre solitaire monta peu à peu dans le ciel : tantôt il suivait paisiblement sa course azurée ; tantôt il reposait sur des groupes de nues qui ressemblaient à la cime de hautes montagnes couronnées de neige. Ces nues, ployant et déployant leurs voiles, se déroulaient en zones diaphanes de satin blanc, se dispersaient en légers flocons d'écume, ou formaient dans les cieux des bancs d'une ouate éblouissante, si doux à l'œil, qu'on croyait ressentir leur mollesse et leur élasticité.—Vol. i. 120.

There can be little doubt that Chateaubriand saw Niagara, and yet this fine passage might well have been written by a poet who had never been nearer to it than the banks of the Suffolk Yare or the rocky coast of Brittany. All that can safely be said about these descriptions is that they are deliberately intended to mystify us as to how far they are the results of experience and how far those of imagination.

Chateaubriand finds evidence of an immortal soul in man's instinct of patriotism. But for this, he argues, the whole population of the world might well endeavour to concentrate itself in special areas where the climate was good and the soil fertile, whereas in fact the savage is as content with his hut and the highlander with his cot as the prince with his palace. The Eskimo, lacking the mere elements of civilization, is content to brave incredible hardships ; the Arab, under scorching suns, knows where to water his camels. Love of home inspires them all, but Christianity shows this love at its best, because whereas love of country inspired the ancients to excesses, Christianity has made it, though more than ever a dominating impulse in mankind, no longer, as it used to be, exclusive. Those who have lived through the orgy of nationalism which has characterized the present age and who bear in mind the intense nationalism evoked by the Revolution will hardly be impressed by Chateaubriand's arguments on this point. He is on surer ground when he claims that the existence of God can be inferred from that hope which is innate in every man. The animal creation is satisfied easily enough: 'A little grass for the sheep, a little blood for the tiger.' The only creature which seeks, however

blindly, something outside himself, who does not live for himself
alone, is man. He is always seeking happiness ; even amid the
worst miseries, he hopes. His sorrows may be certain, his
pleasures uncertain, his work hard, his repose uneasy. But just
as a mother holds out something to her child in order to distract
its attention from what makes it unhappy, so Providence holds
out hope for us at the end, beyond the tomb. This line of
thought is very similar to that of Dr. Inge in his Romanes
Lecture. 'The ancients were not pessimists,' he says, 'but they
mistrusted hope. . . . Whether the human type itself is capable of
further physical, intellectual, and moral improvement we do not
know. It is safe to predict that we shall go on hoping, though
our recent hopes have ended in disappointment.'

Conscience, according to Chateaubriand, is another proof of
immortality : whereas a tiger kills and sleeps, a murderer kills
and suffers.

A third proof of immortality Chateaubriand finds in respect
for the dead and for their tombs, a strange line of thought, for he
must have known that ancestor-worship can be entirely independent of such belief. The chapters which follow were directed
against the widespread atheism of his day. Whether they were
likely to convince any but those who were ready and anxious
to be convinced may be doubted. He claims, what is perhaps
broadly speaking true, that the greatest generals have been
religious-minded men and that religion is based on men's
sensitiveness of soul, on the warmest attachments of life, and
that it gives (what atheism cannot give) comfort in grief and
hope in a life to come. These chapters contain one curious
and interesting line of thought. Nature, he says, is strongest in
the tropics or in the arctic zone. It is there that are to be found
the highest mountains, the largest animals, birds, rivers, flowers ;
and he asks how it is that man has not grown to the size of the
elephant on the Line, or the whale near the Pole? He gives the
answer that man fails to follow what appears to be a general law
of nature because there is something in him which finds itself
in direct opposition to mere passive nature, his immortal soul.
God, he maintains, has seen to it that the soul should assert itself

where matter is least active, and that man diminishes where the
brutes augment. Chateaubriand concludes by arguing that if the
existence of God and the immortality of the soul are conceded it
must follow that there is a future life of punishment or recom-
pense, and he points out that most of the great religious systems,
however widely they disagree, are at one as to this. In two
chapters of sonorous rhetoric on the Last Judgement and the
happiness of the just, the book ends. Chateaubriand, no doubt
with relief, ceases to write as a scholar and a metaphysician, ill
equipped as he was in either capacity, and becomes again the
poet. It was the poetry of *Le Génie du Christianisme* that stirred
his contemporaries, and it is as a poem that it continues to hold
its high place in the history of French literature.

II

The second and third parts of the book are concerned with
what Chateaubriand calls the poetry of Christianity. He includes in the term not merely poetry itself but the fine arts,
philosophy, history, and oratory. Chateaubriand was no theologian. But he was a critic, an artist, an historian, an orator, and a
philosopher, and it is as such that he writes about Christianity,
not as a Catholic, and indeed hardly as a Christian. M. Victor
Giraud considers that he was certainly a communicant in 1799
and almost as certainly ceased to be so for many years after
1801; and that he was again a practising Catholic for some years
before he died. Lemaître consulted a theologian on the matter
and quotes him at length. This authority is of opinion that while
Chateaubriand never had the explicit faith of a Bossuet, he
nevertheless had 'implicit' faith which thoroughly understood
the dogmas of the Church and was yet content to leave their
expression, so far as he personally was concerned, to those
qualified to expound and declare them.

He begins by some general remarks on the Christian epics,
Dante's *Inferno*, Tasso's *Gerusalemme Liberata*, and the *Paradise
Lost* of Milton. Chateaubriand's attitude towards Dante is
almost patronizing. 'The beauties of this strange production',
he says, 'flow almost entirely from Christianity: its faults belong

to the century and to its author's lack of taste.' But he admits that
in the portrayal of the pathetic and the terrible Dante has perhaps equalled the greatest poets, and he quotes elsewhere the
famous lines so beautiful in their monotonous cadence which
suggest 'the eternal cry of anguish which rises from the bottom
of the abyss':

> Per me si va nella città dolente;
> Per me si va nell'eterno dolore;
> Per me si va tra la perduta gente.

He considers that the New World awaited (as it awaits to this
day) its poet, but the Crusades, the other modern subject for an
epic, have given birth to the *Gerusalemme Liberata*, 'a perfect
model of composition'. Chateaubriand's enthusiasm is easy to
understand, for Tasso's poem was in its day the challenge of
revived Catholicism in the face of infidelity. Tasso had done
what he himself was hoping to do. Much that attracted Chateaubriand in the poem—its sentiment, its discursiveness, what
Frederic Harrison has called its symmetry of imagination—
render it as little readable by the general public as *Le Génie du
Christianisme* itself. Nobody wants to read about the loves of
Rinaldo and Tancredi. It is at first sight surprising that Chateaubriand has nothing to say about *Orlando Furioso*, but the reason
is clear. Although Ariosto wrote about chivalry he had little
belief in it. He wrote on the same topic as Tasso, the defence of
European civilization against the Saracens, but the spirit of the
work is very different. There is no warm expression of admiration for the Church, while on the other hand justice is done to the
Saracens. Above all, it has humour which even degenerates into
burlesque. Side by side with *Gerusalemme Liberata* is placed
Paradise Lost. In the vast critical literature which the work
of Chateaubriand has brought into being, there is a growing
interest in his group of studies which are concerned with English letters. It has been said that nothing more important than
the *Essai sur la littérature anglaise* of 1836 was published in
France before Taine. Chateaubriand's knowledge of English
literature and of the English language qualified him as a guide

to his compatriots, who knew little of either. In this portion of the work, and indeed all through it, Chateaubriand quotes extensively from *Paradise Lost*. Milton, it must be admitted, has for the most part found little appreciation in France. To speak plainly, he is not infrequently regarded as something of a bore. Chateaubriand's admiration of him is described roundly as a strange weakness. During thirty years, from the time of his exile in Norfolk and his idyll with Charlotte Ives, Chateaubriand read, studied, and translated *Paradise Lost*. His complete and literal translation appeared in 1836. It is easy to understand why Milton made so strong an appeal to Chateaubriand, and how it was that he is so frequently used to support the arguments put forward in *Le Génie*, for the book shows just the combination of the classical and the modern, the Christian and the Pagan, that are to be found in the English poet. The freedom with which Milton deals with the Old Testament, the daring with which he supplemented its stories with the eloquence of his own imagination, was bound to appeal to Chateaubriand. He appreciated also the majestic beauty of the language, for it is a feature of *Le Génie* that the writer goes out of his way frequently to draw attention to the qualities of form inherent in the quotation he is making, be it English or Italian, Latin or Greek or French. In *Paradise Lost* he was conscious of a unity of scheme comparable with that which underlay *Le Génie*. Above all, the work is inspired by high moral purpose which places it in a category with the greatest masterpieces of the epic, with the *Iliad*, the *Æneid*, and the *Inferno*. Homer, Virgil, and Dante together with Milton are therefore the main sources to which again and again Chateaubriand turns for example and comparison.

To Dante and to Milton Chateaubriand adds rather surprisingly *La Henriade*. He considers it had most of the ingredients of a great epic: it even contained some element of the miraculous, which he deemed an essential feature. But it lacked religion. The attraction which Henry of Navarre had for Voltaire lay in the fact that he stood for toleration. The idea of toleration underlies the whole poem. In twelve cantos it describes

Henry's early years, his adventures in England, the St. Bartholomew massacres, and the wars of the League. In a dream Henry is transported to Heaven and is shown by St. Louis a vision of the heroic figures of French history past and future. Then follows the battle of Ivry, and a meeting with Gabrielle d'Estrées; and the work concludes with Paris opening her gates to a King Henry who has been converted to Catholicism. Chateaubriand notes, as succeeding generations have done, the contradictory elements in Voltaire which enable everybody to find in him much to admire and much to hate. He speaks of him fairly, even generously, but the prominence he gives to one of the least read of Voltaire's works remains a puzzle, and is to be explained only by his admiration of a French hero who combated fanaticism, and who in his hour of victory remembered the Church.

He turns next to poetry in its bearing first on the character and then on the passions of man. Various characters are taken as types, and much of the argument in these chapters strikes the reader as being very far-fetched. He begins with husbands and wives, and his examples are Ulysses and Penelope and Adam and Eve, and he compares the work of blind Homer with the work of blind Milton. What strikes him as beautiful in the story as told by Homer is its essential truth; but quite apart from the majesty of Milton's verse, he finds the figures of Adam and Eve infinitely more to be admired because 'true religion alone can show a tenderness so holy, so sublime'. Here again Chateaubriand is perilously near writing nonsense. Adam and Eve had as little to do with his ideas of religion as Milton had to do with his ideas about Christianity. He next takes the idea of the father, and compares Priam, the pre-Christian type, with Lusignan, the Father in Voltaire's *Zaïre*. In this play Voltaire for the first time brought French characters upon the tragic stage. The story is one of the struggle between passionate love and filial duty. Lusignan is descended from the Kings of Jerusalem and Zaïre is ignorant that she is his daughter. They are both held captive by Orosmane, who loves Zaïre and is about to marry her. A young Christian knight, Nérestan, arrives with their ransom, and Zaïre recognizes in him her brother, and that Lusignan is her father. She is ready to be baptized and to throw over Orosmane. Orosmane, unaware of the facts, suspects her of infidelity with Nerestan and kills her. On realizing his mistake he kills himself. 'I shall try', wrote Voltaire, 'to put into this work everything that is most interesting and most pathetic in the Christian religion', and Lusignan's passionate appeal to Zaïre to accept Christianity has no parallel elsewhere in Voltaire's dramatic work. 'The misfortunes, the blood, the suffering of Lusignan', says Chateaubriand, 'mingle with those of Christ. Zaïre could not renounce her Redeemer on the very spot where he had given himself for her.' And Chateaubriand points out how weak an appeal Lusignan would have made by comparison, had he merely been able to invoke the joys of Olympus and the banquets of the Gods.

Andromache typifies the mother. Homer's Andromache is, he notes, more wife than mother. This applies even more to Virgil's, while as drawn by Euripides the character, in Chateaubriand's estimation, shows no maternal instinct at all. Racine's Andromache, on the other hand, is essentially a mother and talks like a Christian woman. Chateaubriand's preference few Englishmen are likely to share. Englishmen are always supposed to be unappreciative of Racine. It was Matthew Arnold who wrote of the 'exaggerated French estimate' of him, a judgement which at least has the support of Chateaubriand's own friend Joubert, who calls him 'Le Virgile des ignorants'. Gusman —Chateaubriand turns once again to Voltaire—the Peruvian Governor who loves Alzire, represents the character of the son. Alvarez, exercising paternal authority at the same time that he obeys his son as his lawful superior, shows that the Christian morality is as great an advance on that of the ancients as are the Gospels in comparison with Plato. Finally, Iphigenia stands for the daughter, and once again the same subject is compared as treated by Euripides and by Racine. As drawn by Racine she is the Christian daughter. 'Her Father in Heaven has spoken, it remains only to obey.' Chateaubriand claims that Christianity takes nothing from the poetic value of characters drawn by the ancients for our admiration, and offers in addition the special influence it can itself bring to bear. He proceeds to compare the position of the priest in classical ages with his greatly enlarged influence in Christian times; and he claims that the soldier who is truly imbued with knightly virtues can only be a Christian. The book concludes with a fine passage:

Le soleil vient de se lever : les armées sont en présence ; les bannières se déroulent aux vents ; les plumes flottent sur les casques ; les habits, les franges, les harnais, les armes, les couleurs, l'or et le fer étincellent aux premiers feux du jour. Monté sur un coursier rapide, Godefroi parcourt les rangs de son armée ; il parle, et son discours est un modèle d'éloquence guerrière. Sa tête rayonne, son visage brille d'un éclat inconnu, l'ange de la victoire le couvre invisiblement de ses ailes. Bientôt il se fait un profond silence ; les légions se prosternent en adorant celui qui fit tomber Goliath par la main d'un jeune berger. Soudain la trompette sonne, les soldats chrétiens se relèvent, et, pleins de la fureur du Dieu des armées, ils se précipitent sur les bataillons ennemis.—Vol. i. 200.

When he comes to deal with the passions Chateaubriand claims disinterested friendship as a virtue characteristic of Christianity. The end of Paganism, he says, is a few ashes mixed in an urn. Christian love has a certain warmth peculiar to itself. Christianity gives men hope. He then proceeds to tell the story of Dido's hopeless passion as set out in the fourth Aeneid and to compare her with Racine's Phèdre whom he describes as a Christian wife—Christian because she would have faced willingly an eternity of suffering if she had enjoyed a moment of happiness. This is certainly a surprising statement, which would, one imagines, have amused and bewildered nobody more than Phèdre herself. Héloïse is also, we learn, in spite of her fault, a Christian type. Instead of burning on her funeral pyre like Dido, she was content to burn slowly on the altar of her religion. The next comparison is between country tales, between an idyll of Theocritus and *Paul et Virginie*. Chateaubriand chooses No. 11,[1] in which Polyphemus describes his love for Galatea. He praises its delicacy, its naïve simplicity, and the art that can make something beautiful and touching out of what

[1] He translates from line 19 onwards, ᾿Ω λευκὰ Γαλάτεια, τί τὸν φιλέοντ᾿ ἀποβάλλῃ.

is in fact repulsive; but he claims that in the romance of Bernardin de Saint-Pierre there is more. He finds in it what he calls a 'moral melancholy', something sad and tender such as is to be found in the Gospels; he finds resignation to the Will of God, obedience to parents, charity to the poor, in short, a Christian atmosphere. Chateaubriand's preference is not difficult to understand though it may not be easy to share. In *Paul et Virginie*, a story told by an old man living a solitary life among the mountains, we have something that reminds us of *Atala*. Bernardin de Saint-Pierre was, in fact, a precursor of Chateaubriand. He then goes on to speak of the strong emotions which Christianity has aroused in such men as Thomas à Kempis and St. Augustine. He quotes from the *Imitatio Christi* passages of passionate mysticism. He does not quote, as he might have been expected to do, from the sayings of St. Francis. He makes his points from writers of his own choosing and he makes them in his own way. This attitude of mind is characteristic of Chateaubriand, both in his writings and in his public career. He is always the individualist.[1]

This portion of the work concludes with a passage on what Chateaubriand calls the 'surge of the emotions', based clearly on his own youthful experience. He speaks of those moments when the imagination is stimulated at the same time that life seems dull and unattractive. The ancients, he thinks, can have known nothing of this, or, if they did, it was not in their power to balance the fleeting sorrows of the world with the lasting joys of the world to come. It was Christianity which for the

[1] Chateaubriand quotes as representing the passions inspired by Christianity a passage which is a fine example of Corneille's power of dramatic concision. Félix urges Polyeucte to sacrifice to false Gods. Polyeucte refuses.

> *Félix.* Enfin ma bonté cède à ma juste fureur:
> Adore-les, ou meurs.
> *Polyeucte.* Je suis chrétien.
> *Félix.* Impie!
> Adore-les, te dis-je, ou renonce à la vie.
> *Polyeucte.* Je suis chrétien.
> *Félix.* Tu l'es? O cœur trop obstiné!
> Soldats, exécutez l'ordre que j'ai donné.
> *Pauline.* Où le conduisez-vous?
> *Félix.* A la mort.
> *Polyeucte.* A la gloire.

first time gave mankind a true sense of proportion and the power to face the troubles of existence and, as in the monastic life, to renounce its joys. The point is, of course, a false one, as Chateaubriand very well knew. Monasticism is no more peculiar to Christianity than is belief in a future state. Perhaps the real purpose of this short chapter was to link up the preceding line of argument with what followed in the original edition of the book and remained until 1805, the episode of *René*, originally inserted as illustrative of Chateaubriand's remarks on the passions. René, a youth filled with sadness, depressed and introspective, has escaped from the world after much travel and many experiences to live among the Natchez tribe of Indians. His adopted father, Chactas, and a missionary, Father Souel, induce him at length to lay open his heart to them. He explains to them why he has fled to America and tells how his sister, who was dearer to him than anybody in the world, has taken refuge in a convent. Much of *René* is certainly autobiographical; how much will always remain a matter of controversy. It is to be remembered that *René* was written before *Le Génie* and, indeed, before the *Essay on Revolution*, which lends colour to the belief in its autobiographical character. *René* is merely the tale of the love of a sister for a brother, in which one party finds refuge in taking the veil and the other flees from civilization and seeks peace of mind with the Noble Savage. This is, in its main lines, the story of Chateaubriand and his sister Lucile. It is this that explains his sudden journey to America and the anxiety of Madame de Farcy to get him married immediately on his return to France. It would have been well for Lucile if, like Amélie in the story, she had accepted the life of the cloister. It was, on the contrary, her fate to marry unhappily, to leave her husband, to be placed by Chateaubriand in the care of kindly people, to attempt suicide, to escape from her friends, to be found wandering about without anything to identify her, and to die and be buried almost as a pauper during her brother's absence from Paris. It would be incorrect to suggest that the state of mind for which René stands—the pessimist, the dreamer, the romantic tired with life, the youth sated with experience—is an

invention of Chateaubriand. Chateaubriand himself admits that
it is not the case. The type is to be found already in writers of
the time of Louis XIV. Chateaubriand used him, as he said, in
order to show the effect of Christianity on the modern mind, and
also the usefulness of monasteries.[1] But nevertheless René is
very much of his time, the very symbol to his contemporaries of
romantic love. Nor can it be denied that the subject which lies
behind *René* had a great interest for the writers of the period.
The Byron literature of the last few years gives rise even to-day
to bitter controversy among those who are at once fascinated
and repelled by a personality so outstanding. Like Werther,
René considers that because his desires are limitless he is himself a superior being. In fact there is nothing superlative about
either of them except their imagination. Nothing is more
characteristic of both of them than their admiration for Ossian,
whose inflated rhetoric was taken both in this country and on
the continent for the poetry of nature. Dr. Johnson, who saw
through the fraud from the first, said bluntly to Reynolds: 'Sir,
a man might write such stuff for ever, if he would *abandon* his
mind to it.' On the other hand, Werther is weaker than René.
We may doubt whether René would have killed himself for a
hopeless love. It may rather be suspected he would be likely
(as in the case of Chateaubriand himself) to discover that the
weapon was out of order. If there is something of Chateaubriand in René, a little of Goethe in Werther, there is more of
Byron in Manfred. Manfred is another lonely figure, self-con-
centrated, always seeking relief from eternal suffering and failing
to find it. He will surrender only to death.

> The mind which is immortal makes itself
> Requital for its good or evil thoughts.

We may smile at René to-day, but his importance can hardly be
overlooked. The type may disappear for a time, but it recurs. His
state has been called justly *le mal du siècle*. Chateaubriand himself
had no illusions about it. Father Souel says frankly, almost
brutally, to René: 'Nothing in this story calls for the pity which

[1] His actual words are: 'de montrer quelle sagesse a dirigé les institutions
chrétiennes'.

we show you here. I see a youth infatuated with idle fancies, never satisfied, who has withdrawn himself from the responsibilities of life in order to give himself up to useless dreaming. There is no superiority, Sir, in seeing life only under a hateful light.' Whatever the measure of responsibility which rests on Chateaubriand for having introduced this tiresome and rather ludicrous figure to the public, he himself had to pay a heavy penalty. Just as in all his subsequent writing he was never allowed to go far away from *Le Génie*, so for all his days to come he continued to be identified in the mind of the public with his hero René.

Chateaubriand next proceeds to argue that classical writers did not understand nature; that strictly speaking there is no descriptive poetry before Christianity. The contention aroused considerable criticism when the book first appeared, as well it might. He endeavoured to develop his ideas in a note, in which he explains that though Virgil may describe a country house and Theocritus a farm, these descriptions are merely backgrounds for the action of characters. Only in our own times, he asserts, have writers been content to write about mountains and forests and streams for themselves alone. The book appeared at a time when admittedly a change of attitude towards nature was manifesting itself as a reaction from the classical formalism of the eighteenth century, and it is perfectly true that the modern attitude towards nature which dates from that time is something essentially new. But in what he says about the classical writers he greatly overstates his case. No men ever appreciated more warmly or more discerningly the charms of country life than did those Roman writers who generation after generation describe them with loving care. Lesbos, Rhodes, Samos were visited for their climate and beauty. Mitylene, Ephesus, Smyrna, and later Egypt had their tourist traffic. Pliny's villas at Como, which he has described with such unaffected delight, were the homes of a man who loved the country quite apart from terraced gardens.[1] A similar feeling lies

[1] It is worth noting that in his descriptions Pliny mentions two flowers only, roses and violets.

behind the more stately prose of Cicero's letters and the Odes
even of such a *mondain* as Horace. Catullus loved the country
if ever man did. Mr. George Sargeant in his brilliant essay
on the landscape of Virgil makes clear the measure in which
Chateaubriand's generalization is correct.

Virgil was a lover of the country as well as a 'landscape lover' to use
Tennyson's phrase, and it is the combination of these two qualities that
gives the Georgics their peculiar fascination. . . . The landscape is never
out of relation to man. It is little more than a background shown in
the briefest manner and strictly relevant to the action of the subject,
yet always suggesting like the backgrounds in the work of the central
Italian painters the infinite space in which the actions of life occur, the
overhanging sky, the intense heat of the summer, the sweep of clouds,
wind over the fields, the serenity of cloudless evening, the influence of
sunlight and moonlight.[1]

The structure of the Greek city state, the need for its defence,
the character of much of the soil of Greece, the economic pressure
to utilize it to feed the urban areas, the natural bent of the Greek
mind, all these factors tended, no doubt, to prevent the development of enjoyment of a country life in a modern sense. When
it came to Greece it came late, through the influence of Rome
and Egypt. At least we may admit with Chateaubriand that
the visions of Pan and Priapus and the dryads romping about
among the trees compare ill with that other vision of God
walking in the Garden in the cool of the evening, even though
the one is as little Christian as the other. Christianity, according
to Chateaubriand, taught mankind the charms of solitude and
peopled those solitudes with beings which are free from the
weaknesses and vices which make the pagan gods so absurd.
God can love and hate, can change His mind, can show anger and
remorse. The Saints and the Angels can pity our suffering.
Childish memories of St. Malo may well have inspired the
passages which follow:

Un vaisseau est prêt à périr: l'aumônier, par des paroles qui délient
les âmes, remet à chacun la peine de ses fautes; il adresse au ciel la
prière qui, dans un tourbillon, envoie l'esprit du naufragé au Dieu des

---

[1] *Classical Studies*, by G. M. Sargeant, Chatto & Windus, 1929.

orages. Déjà l'Océan se creuse pour engloutir les matelots; déjà les
vagues, élevant leur triste voix entre les rochers, semblent commencer
les chants funèbres; tout à coup un trait de lumière perce la tempête;
l'Étoile des mers, Marie, patronne des mariniers, paraît au milieu de la
nue. Elle tient son enfant dans ses bras, et calme les flots par un
sourire: charmante religion, qui oppose à ce que la nature a de plus
terrible ce que le ciel a de plus doux! Aux tempêtes de l'Océan, un
petit enfant et une tendre mère!—Vol. i. 243.

The Heaven of the Christian, he tells us, is no mere Olympus,
but is something unimaginable and limitless, peopled with beings
perfect indeed yet not devoid of feeling; and the writer then
turns to describe the character of Satan in *Paradise Lost*.

The rest of the second part of the work consists of a comparison between the Bible and Homer. Chateaubriand notes
three separate styles in the Bible: first the historic, secondly
the poetic, and thirdly the didactic. This division, it will be
generally agreed, is neither scientific nor complete. Under the
first head he comprises not merely the strictly historical Books
but also what he calls 'elegies', such as the Book of Job, and
also what he calls 'pastorals'. In his second category he includes the Psalms and the Prophets. The third is the New
Testament. The comparison with Homer is carried out under
six headings. First of all he finds the Bible 'simpler'. 'It is like
an aged priest who, full of all knowledge, sets it forth with
certainty and precision, whereas Homer is like an old traveller
describing to a host the experiences of a long life.' He notes
in the second place that the habits and customs of the patriarchs,
their lives as described to us, are more to be admired than the
lives described by Homer. It is more simple. Where Homer
speaks of a stranger (which suggests politics and local customs)
the Bible speaks of a traveller (which suggests a moral idea and
is of universal application). Next, and here he is unquestionably correct, the Bible has none of the digressions characteristic of Homer; the story is told clearly and rapidly. Fourthly,
there are in the Bible few long descriptions such as interrupt
Homer's narrative. The picture is made to live by one or two
vivid touches. Fifthly, the Bible is free from Homer's tedious

comparisons. Finally, the sublime is more strikingly delineated. Chateaubriand gives instances in support of his contentions. He considers that the first scenes in the *Iliad*, such as the scene where Achilles stands in the Greek trenches after the death of Patroclus and terrifies the Trojan host with his cries, cannot compare with the splendour of passages from the Book of Isaiah. Ulysses hiding his face when Demodocus at the feet of King Alcinous sings of the Trojan war and the sorrows of the Greeks is finely drawn, but the story compares ill, he considers, with the story of Joseph who wept at the sight of Benjamin when he received his brethren in Egypt. Ulysses argues long to prove his identity to Telemachus. In the story of Joseph, the climax where he says merely, 'I am Joseph', brought tears of admiration, so Chateaubriand asserts, to the eyes of Voltaire. He sums up his argument as to the superiority of the poetry of Christianity by quoting the famous passage from the Book of Ruth beginning 'Intreat me not to leave thee' and translating it into Homeric form.

La belle Ruth répondit à la sage Noémi, honorée des peuples comme une déesse: Cessez de vous opposer à ce qu'une divinité m'inspire; je vous dirai la vérité telle que je la sais et sans déguisement. Je suis résolue de vous suivre. Je demeurerai avec vous, soit que vous restiez chez les Moabites, habiles à lancer le javelot, soit que vous retourniez au pays de Juda, si fertile en oliviers. Je demanderai avec vous l'hospitalité aux peuples qui respectent les suppliants. Nos cendres seront mêlées dans la même urne, et je ferai au Dieu qui vous accompagne toujours des sacrifices agréables.—Vol. i. 286.

On this note Part II closes, after the comparison between the Bible and Homer has been worked out in great detail and at considerable length. Though to the reader of to-day it may seem a strange and valueless line of argument, it has certainly to be borne in mind that to 1802 it was not merely something new, but a ringing challenge. The argument was something which ran counter to all the ideas of the eighteenth century. It gave to the policy of the Concordat a welcome support on the philosophical side. Friends and supporters were forced to realize from the first that what was opening was not merely a new

chapter in politics. With the Revolution was gone also the
philosophy which had inspired it.

III

Part III Chateaubriand calls 'Art and Letters', and perhaps
more than any other portion of the work it displays that combination of the important and the trivial which is so marked a
characteristic of *Le Génie*. No other section of the book dates
as this does. *Le Génie* in many respects sounded a new note. It
was a work of novelty which turned its back on the past, yet
with one very important exception (its attitude towards Gothic
architecture) its artistic judgements are conventional and essentially of its day. Chateaubriand has little to say about music.
He remarks that the Gregorian chant descends from the music
of Greece, that music and Christianity were closely associated,
and that Christianity invented the organ. This last statement
is, of course, incorrect and is perhaps made metaphorically. The
organ as we know it goes back at least two centuries before
Christ, and the idea of music made by blowing air through a reed
is as old as civilization itself. The only musicians he mentions
by name are Pergolesi and Rameau, who died some sixty and
some thirty years respectively before his book appeared, and it
is to be remembered that in 1802 Beethoven and Haydn were
in their prime. Bach, Handel, Mozart, and Gluck had all died
within the previous half-century. It might appear less surprising
that those names are omitted than that there should be no
mention of Cherubini, who was at the height of his fame in 1802,
did we not remember that his relations with the First Consul
were not good, which may well explain Chateaubriand's silence.
Nor, indeed, do Pergolesi and Rameau come in for more than
very perfunctory praise. 'Pergolesi', he says, 'has unfolded the
riches of his art in the *Stabat Mater*, but has he surpassed the
simple hymn of the Church?'—by which he means the Gregorian
chant. Chateaubriand thereupon goes on to speak with equal
brevity of modern painters, a subject with which he clearly feels
himself ill qualified to deal, although it is one which in other
hands might have been made to support his general thesis more

effectively than do lines of thought on which he expatiates at much greater length. He opens with the pretty Greek legend that the first drawing was made by a young girl who traced the outline of her lover from his shadow on the wall. 'The Christian school', says Chateaubriand, 'has sought another teacher: he recognizes him in that artist who, kneading a little clay in his strong hands, pronounced these words, "Let us make man in our own image."' Chateaubriand points out the importance of pictures and painting in the Eastern Empire before the time of the Iconoclast rulers, and he summarizes shortly the history of art through the times of the Goths and the Lombards. He finds, just as we should do to-day, in Nicholas (Niccolo Pisano) and Cimabue the seeds of that artistic renaissance which reached its full flower in Raphael and Michelangelo. In arguing that modern art works hand in hand with Christianity, Chateaubriand gives a very interesting list of names in proof of his contention: Michelangelo, Raphael, the Caracci, Domenichino, Le Sueur, Poussin, Coustou. Here we have a list put forth in 1802 by a brilliant young Frenchman of those artists who in his view were the outstanding figures from the time of the Renaissance until his own day. Michelangelo would, no doubt, be sure of his place on any list and at any time, Raphael would be on most lists though not on all. It was in the fifties of the last century that his name became a storm-centre; but it must be remembered that the term Pre-Raphaelite was never meant by the leaders of that movement to imply lack of appreciation of Raphael's own work. It was Ruskin who fulminated against the teaching or the implication that nature was full of faults but that Raphael was perfection, and that the more the young student copied him the better. Nor was it contended by Rossetti and Holman Hunt and the young Millais that there was little healthy or good art after Raphael. It was rather that in their view the sincerity and the simplicity which characterized the pictures of earlier masters was no longer to be found. Before Raphael great artists were inspired by reverent study, whereas after his time pictures represented more and more 'lifeless dogma and the corruption of decay'. They painted Christianity no longer, but only Catholicism. 'The medieval principles', says Ruskin, 'led *up* to Raphael and the modern principles lead *down* from him', which is only to say that after Raphael art tended to be sentimental and became insincere and finally commercialized. Herein is the explanation why modern ideas would find no place for any of the other names on Chateaubriand's list. The Caracci were deemed by Reynolds to be models of perfection and were held up as such in his Academy Discourses. To our eyes their work is mechanical and lacking in spontaneity. The theory of eclecticism in art seems to us to be fundamentally erroneous. Types replace portraits, individuality is lost, and instead of combining in themselves the characteristics of all the older masters this school omitted or ignored those very features which modern standards find most to be admired: the exquisite care in painting the thing itself, and not a merely idealized version of it; the love of simplicity and of nature for their own sake. We have indeed travelled far from the preferences of Chateaubriand. Addington Symonds has pointed out that there is a direct line of succession from Ludovico Caracci (the most famous of the three) to the great artist whom the Pre-Raphaelites called 'Sir Sloshua', and it is significant that Domenichino and Poussin each figure in Chateaubriand's list. The 'grand style' which substituted ideal generalities for specific qualities and thereby earned the praise of Reynolds was well calculated to arouse Chateaubriand's enthusiasm. In this he was the child of his century; and as there is nothing final in matters of taste, it may well be that the reaction that has brought other schools back into public favour will one day bring the eclectics out of their long unpopularity. Poussin has been called the Raphael of France; Le Sueur painted in the Raphaelesque manner. They are each representatives of the historical school of France, which explains their presence on the list. Finally there is Coustou the sculptor, an unfamiliar name, responsible with his brother for much work at Marly and Versailles, best known to-day by the 'Horse-tamers' at the lower end of the Champs-Élysées. After some rather trite remarks as to the field of subjects for painting in the New

Testament, the author turns in two short chapters to speak of architecture.

The three masterpieces of modern architecture he considers to be St. Peter's at Rome, Santa Sofia at Constantinople, and St. Paul's in London. He praises the Invalides and Versailles and he speaks of 'grandeur and dignity' very much in the eighteenth-century way. The most famous chapter in the whole work is, perhaps, the chapter in praise of medieval Gothic which follows immediately after. Chateaubriand does not, as is generally supposed, turn his back on contemporary standards. On the contrary, he accepts them, but he regards them as leading up to ideas from which hitherto they had been deemed a reaction. The paragraph which clearly sets this forth runs as follows:

> Le christianisme a rétabli dans l'architecture, comme dans les autres arts, les véritables proportions. Nos temples, moins petits que ceux d'Athènes, et moins gigantesques que ceux de Memphis, se tiennent dans ce sage milieu où règnent le beau et le goût par excellence. Au moyen du dôme, inconnu des anciens, la religion a fait un heureux mélange de ce que l'ordre gothique a de hardi, et de ce que les ordres grecs ont de simple et de gracieux.—Vol. i. 296.

Of Gothic architecture he writes:

> L'ordre gothique, au milieu de ces proportions barbares, a toutefois une beauté qui lui est particulière.
>
> Les forêts ont été les premiers temples de la Divinité, et les hommes ont pris dans les forêts la première idée de l'architecture. Cet art a donc dû varier selon les climats. Les Grecs ont tourné l'élégante colonne corinthienne avec son chapiteau de feuilles sur le modèle du palmier. Les énormes piliers du vieux style égyptien représentent le sycomore, le figuier oriental, le bananier et la plupart des arbres gigantesques de l'Afrique et de l'Asie.
>
> Les forêts des Gaules ont passé à leur tour dans les temples de nos pères, et nos bois de chênes ont ainsi maintenu leur origine sacrée. Ces voûtes ciselées en feuillages, ces jambages qui appuient les murs et finissent brusquement comme des troncs brisés, la fraîcheur des voûtes, les ténèbres du sanctuaire, les ailes obscures, les passages secrets, les portes abaissées, tout retrace les labyrinthes des bois dans l'église gothique; tout en fait sentir la religieuse horreur, les mystères et la divinité. Les deux tours hautaines plantées à l'entrée de l'édifice

su rmontent les ormes et les ifs du cimetière, et font un effet pittoresque
su ʾ l'azur du ciel. Tantôt le jour naissant illumine leurs têtes jumelles;
tai tôt elles paraissent couronnées d'un chapiteau de nuages, ou gros-
sie s dans une atmosphère vaporeuse. Les oiseaux eux-mêmes sem-
bl ent s'y méprendre et les adopter pour les arbres de leurs forêts: des
corneilles voltigent autour de leurs faîtes et se perchent sur leurs
galeries. Mais tout à coup des rumeurs confuses s'échappent de la
cime de ces tours et en chassent les oiseaux effrayés. L'architecte
chrétien, non content de bâtir des forêts, a voulu, pour ainsi dire, en
imiter les murmures; et, au moyen de l'orgue et du bronze suspendu, il
a attaché au temple gothique jusqu'au bruit des vents et des tonnerres,
qui roule dans la profondeur des bois. Les siècles, évoqués par ces sons
religieux, font sortir leurs antiques voix du sein des pierres, et soupi-
rent dans la vaste basilique: le sanctuaire mugit comme l'antre de
l'ancienne Sibylle; et, tandis que l'airain se balance avec fracas sur
votre tête, les souterrains voûtés de la mort se taisent profondément
sous vos pieds.—Vol. i. 299–300.

And yet it may be doubted whether, though he likens the
towers of a Gothic building to the trees of the forest, the sound
of the organ to the whispers of the breeze or the roll of the
thunder, though he understands the mystery and the spirit
which inspired it all, whether in his heart he did not prefer the
Invalides. The devotion which made men bring one by one the
stones of which the cathedral of Amiens was built, the emulation
which induced the men of Beauvais to erect a loftier church even
than Amiens, the enthusiasm which inspired nameless men to
build at Reims for the glory of God, no doubt filled him with
delighted and admiring wonder, for all this was 'Le Génie du
Christianisme' in its most patent and splendid manifestation.
But the book mentions neither Amiens nor Beauvais, Reims nor
Chartres, by name, while the Invalides and Versailles each have
a separate chapter. To say this is not to minimize the interest
and importance attaching to Chateaubriand's attitude towards
architecture. Entrenched as he was in eighteenth-century conceptions, he yet sounded the note for an advance.

The next book, entitled 'Philosophy', begins with a chapter
on astronomy and mathematics. How do they assist in supporting Chateaubriand's thesis? The dogmas of Christianity, he

affirms, are in no opposition to the truths of nature. Its d oc-
trines, he tells us, forbid no special line of study—which, so far
as Catholicism is concerned, is perhaps not strictly true. Chateaubriand is at any rate safe in pointing out that the physicist can
weigh the air in his tube without fear of offending Juno. The
Church has condemned what at other times she has approved:
what does this mean, he asks, except that priests being men
like ourselves have shown progressive enlightenment as time
has passed? This line of argument can hardly have been agreeable to the Church and shows that strain of liberalism and
independence which is so characteristic of Chateaubriand, both
as a writer and as a politician. If Christianity has persecuted
science, he says, so did the ancients. The same ecclesiastical
tribunal which condemned the Copernican system accepted it
as an hypothesis within six years. A pope reformed the calendar,
a friar invented gunpowder: while on the other hand many
philosophers can be quoted who openly took the view that
mathematical study was a danger for the multitude. Newton
refused for years to have anything to do with mathematics.
Descartes can be quoted as decrying them. Condillac despised
them no less than Hobbes. Chateaubriand concludes that before
arranging our ideas it is better to be sure one has ideas at all:
children should learn their moral and religious duties, and
mathematics should come only after there has been real education of the heart and brain. 'An eloquent page of Bossuet on
morality is more useful and more difficult to write than a whole
volume of philosophical abstractions.' Not content with this,
he goes on to remark that nature never meant mathematicians
to play a prominent part: a 'sad obscurity' should be their lot.
Leibnitz, D'Alembert, and Descartes are famous for their metaphysics rather than for their mathematics.

In all this, we may remark, there is certainly much special
pleading. In mathematics mankind has worked steadily and
interruptedly on foundations laid by his ancestors. From the
dawn of civilization to the present day, before Christianity,
within the Church, outside the Church, the study of mathematics
has gone forward. Whatever *obiter dicta* Chateaubriand may

quote, Newton and Leibnitz are each and independently responsible for the differential calculus, a discovery based directly on
the work of Descartes. In this matter the world will probably
accept the view of Comte rather than the view of Chateaubriand.
In his theoretical hierarchy of human conceptions Comte based
morals and sociology on what he called Preliminary Science or
Natural Philosophy, which included biology, chemistry, physics,
and astronomy, all on a foundation of mathematics.

From mathematics our author proceeds to chemistry and
natural history, and he notes that however science sets out to
work, the fundamental secrets of nature continue to elude the
investigator. He enters a gentle protest against systems of
analysis and classification. 'If one may say so,' he remarks,
'it seems a great pity to find to-day the man mammal ranged
in accordance with the Linnaean system with monkeys, bats, and
the sloth.' Such studies lead to materialism, they kill the sense
of beauty. Such a mentality should be content with museum
specimens. Chateaubriand claims that the Church has not been
illiberal. She favoured the beginnings of science and opposed
herself only to the unreasonable and limitless pretensions of
certain scientists. She took, in fact, the only line open to her:
she held the reins tight and loosened them according as circumstances demanded; and, in speaking of metaphysicians, he puts
forward the claim that a religion which could find room within
itself for Bacon, Newton, Leibnitz, Grotius, Pascal, and others
runs no risk of deserving the reputation of hostility to scientific
thought, especially when it can at the same time claim the
allegiance of political philosophers such as Machiavelli, Thomas
More, Bodin (the precursor of Hobbes in his conception of
sovereignty), Pufendorf, and Locke.

Finally, under the head of philosophy come moralists. La
Bruyère has a chapter to himself, important chiefly because in
the course of it Chateaubriand sets out explicitly the idea which
underlies his whole work. Were La Bruyère to return he would
indeed be 'astonished to see' that religion of which the great
men of his day admitted the beauty and excellence treated as dis-
graceful, laughable, and negligible. From La Bruyère he passes

to Pascal, and nowhere else could Chateaubriand have found a better conclusion for this part of his argument than in quoting one who was a scientist and a mathematician and, above all, a thinker overwhelmed with the idea of the insignificance of man and the power of God. If *Le Génie* had come from Pascal, says Chateaubriand (and no man was better qualified to write a book on such a subject), how wonderful a book it would have been! The preparation of an 'Apology for the Christian Religion' was indeed the occupation of Pascal's last days, though we may doubt whether it would have had much affinity with the book produced by Chateaubriand.

From philosophy the author turns to history. His book has been hitherto an implied rather than an explicit attack on the Revolution. In the section which follows the attack is direct: its leaders are mentioned by name. It must also be borne in mind how recent it all was. Chateaubriand was writing in 1802, thirteen years only after the fall of the Bastille, nine years since the execution of the king, eight years since the height of the Terror, seven years since the 13th Vendémiaire when Napoleon first became famous. It was therefore to this part of the work that public notice was in special measure directed. Chateaubriand begins by a chapter on the Christian manner of writing history. He sees the hand of Providence in the Revolution, that while a spirit of ruin is eating up France within, a spirit of preservation is defending her without. Only a writer inspired by religion, he claims, can explain the failure of the coalition against France. Their aim was not merely to bring an end to revolutionary violence, but at the same time to serve their own purposes; and it was God who said, 'Thou shalt not destroy the people of St. Louis.' Religion, he says—i.e. divine intervention —alone can explain the most incomprehensible facts of history. Chateaubriand considers that modern writers of history are less successful than the ancient, and he gives two reasons for this. The first is that the modern historian has not the same material on which to work. Though there may be interesting periods, famous reigns to record, brilliant scenes to describe, there is yet lacking that completeness which enables the historian of ancient

times to draw a really satisfying picture. The nations which
have arisen on the ruins of the ancient world show in their
development a certain uniformity. Little republics become prin-
cipalities, which in turn are absorbed into kingdoms. Art and
science play an important part, but they become increasingly
the interest of a section only among the population, and so their
influence on human destiny is lessened. This is due to Christianity. Christianity has made certain virtues, certain standards
of conduct, widely, if not generally, accepted, and to the extent
to which it has done so, it has made history relatively a drab
affair. Chateaubriand's second reason follows from this: the
ancients have used up, as it were, all the colours. Herodotus
set out before his readers the story of the origins of society and
its primitive organization. Thucydides followed by tracing the
ills suffered by mankind to political dissension, a lesson they are
slow to learn. Xenophon took a road of his own: he paid regard
to the human heart and became the father of the history of
morals. Livy, so Chateaubriand claims, was the orator as Herodotus was the poet of history. Finally we have in Tacitus the
philosophical historian: the causes which Herodotus attributes
to the gods, Thucydides to political constitutions, Xenophon
to morality, Livy to a combination of all three, Tacitus puts
down to the wickedness of human nature. Modern historians,
argues Chateaubriand, can only imitate along one or other of
these lines, and that in fact is what they have done. Hume,
Robertson, and Gibbon have more or less followed Sallust or
Tacitus in their methods. Tacitus has been the model of two
men as great as himself, Machiavelli and Montesquieu, and
Chateaubriand ends with a warning against any attempt to
imitate the style of Tacitus, 'phrases which under the appearance
of brevity amount to obscurity and bad taste'.

Upon these curious chapters which deal with the writing of
history there is much which might be said. Modern readers
may stoutly deny that history, ancient or modern, has anywhere
a more dramatic story to tell than (to take only one instance)
that of the long contest between the Papacy and the Empire,
while no episode in human records can more truly be called

colourful than the Revolution through which Chateaubriand himself had lived. His remarks on the ancient historians are interesting. Critical minds of to-day will certainly not accept his view of Xenophon. There is a general opinion that he is of no importance as a philosopher and hardly a literary figure of the first rank. Professor Gilbert Murray says of him, frankly, that he is an amateur, a man who covered a wide field efficiently and agreeably rather than with distinction. Chateaubriand's remarks about Tacitus are curious. He is justified in bracketing him with Machiavelli and Montesquieu only to the extent that each was a master of concise phrase. It has been said that whole pages of Machiavelli were written with the point of the stiletto. Montesquieu's style was no less vigorous and epigrammatic. But it is surely unnecessary to suggest that either of them, well acquainted though no doubt they were with Tacitus and with Roman literature as a whole, deliberately based themselves upon him. Lord Morley has emphatically combated the notion that the comparison between Machiavelli and Montesquieu can be carried very far. It is more of a contrast than a comparison.

[Montesquieu] launched effectively on European thought the conception of social phenomena as being no less subject to general laws than all other phenomena. Of a fundamental extension of this kind, Machiavelli was in every way incapable, nor did the state of any of the sciences at that date permit it. As for secondary differences, it is enough to say that Machiavelli put the level of human character low, and Montesquieu put it high: that one was always looking to fact, the other to idea: that one was sombre, the other buoyant and an optimist: Montesquieu confident in the moral forces of mankind, Machiavelli leaving moral forces vague, not knowing where to look for them.[1]

These two are also contrasted with one another by Sainte-Beuve. As to the danger of taking Tacitus as a model, Chateaubriand himself certainly ran no risks. Tacitus not merely practised brevity, it was the deliberate purpose behind his writing to compress the largest number of ideas in the fewest possible words. No writer who has ever lived has ever been able not merely to say but to imply so much by one phrase.

[1] 'Machiavelli', in *Miscellanies*, 4th series, by John Morley, Macmillan & Co., 1908.

Chateaubriand says of Gibbon that he followed Tacitus—more or less. It is well for his own critical reputation that he inserted a qualification. The vivid manner in which Tacitus tells his story no doubt had an important influence on Gibbon, and, like Tacitus, Gibbon may have given rein to his prejudices, though, like him, he took care to make his story live.

Chateaubriand then puts the question: How is it that France produces writers of memoirs rather than historians? No other country, it must be admitted, produces so many writers of memoirs. Up to the time that *Le Génie* appeared Rollin and Voltaire alone can be rightly called historians of the first rank, though it so happened that about that same date there were born many historians of the highest distinction. Thierry was born in 1795, Michelet in 1798, de Tocqueville in 1805. In addition there were the historians who played in greater or less degree a part in public life—Thiers, Guizot, Quinet, and Louis Blanc as well as Mignet, Ampère, and others. But in 1802 the contention was broadly true. Chateaubriand's explanation of this state of affairs is certainly one which nobody but a Frenchman would dare to put forward. 'The Frenchman', he says, 'has always been, even when he was a savage, vain, volatile, and sociable. He reflects little upon things as a whole, but he notices detail minutely, and his glance is sharp, sure, and shrewd. He must always have been present himself and he is unwilling, even as an historian, to disappear altogether.' This is an acute judgement and applies truly enough to many of the nineteenth-century historians mentioned above. Chateaubriand develops his generalization by saying that when it came to writing history in which there is no place for small personal details the writing tends to become dry and too formal. The Frenchman does not live the life of study and retirement best fitted for the elaboration of historical works, although Chateaubriand considers that from the point of view of liberty of speech he can have little ground for complaint against a régime which allowed Montaigne, Charron, Montesquieu, and Bossuet to say what they liked. Censorship no doubt there was, but it was occasional and temporary and was tolerant of such books as Voltaire's *Charles XII*

and his *Age of Louis XIV*. It must be the work of modern
historians to show how Christianity has affected society, and
in a fine passage Chateaubriand sums up what he regards as
the outstanding characteristics of the Frenchman:

Fils aînés de l'antiquité, les Français, Romains par le génie, sont
Grecs par le caractère. Inquiets et volages dans le bonheur, constants
et invincibles dans l'adversité, formés pour les arts, civilisés jusqu'à
l'excès, durant le calme de l'État; grossiers et sauvages dans les
troubles politiques, flottants comme des vaisseaux sans lest au gré des
passions; à présent dans les cieux, l'instant d'après dans les abîmes;
enthousiastes et du bien et du mal, faisant le premier sans en exiger de
reconnaissance, et le second sans en sentir de remords; ne se souvenant
ni de leurs crimes ni de leurs vertus; amants pusillanimes de la vie
pendant la paix; prodigues de leurs jours dans les batailles; vains,
railleurs, ambitieux, à la fois routiniers et novateurs, méprisant tout
ce qui n'est pas eux; individuellement les plus aimables des hommes,
en corps les plus désagréables de tous; charmants dans leur propre pays,
insupportables chez l'étranger; tour à tour plus doux, plus innocents
que l'agneau, et plus impitoyables, plus féroces que le tigre: tels furent
les Athéniens d'autrefois, et tels sont les Français d'aujourd'hui.—Vol.
ii. 11–12.

Voltaire he calls the first French historian after Bossuet.
Chateaubriand, like so many other people, finds himself alternately attracted and repelled by that strange genius, and he
quotes one of Voltaire's sayings which perhaps in itself supplies
the explanation. 'J'ai pris les deux hémisphères en ridicule; c'est
un coup sûr.' Commines is compared with Plutarch and Rollin is
called the Fénelon of history. But Bossuet comes first. He
is more than an historian, he is a Father of the Church, and
Chateaubriand compares him with the author of the book of
Maccabees, with Livy, and with Sallust. Later on, when considering his orations, he compares him with Cicero and with
Demosthenes. Nor is the explanation of this full measure of
praise far to seek. Bossuet, apart from the fame of his sermons,
apart from his philosophical standpoint in the writing of history,
was one of the first who wrote not so much to prove a thesis as
to give to the world his conclusions based upon data carefully

collected and collated. He was to be admired for the independence of his soul, as being a man who could never be
tempted by the favour of courts or seduced by the attractions
of power. To the student of Chateaubriand's own career
there need be no surprise that he should have rated Bossuet
so high.

Having spoken of Bossuet, by a natural transition Chateaubriand turns to deal with eloquence. Cicero, he considers, spoke
like a lawyer, Demosthenes as a patriot. Before the Gospels he
finds nowhere any moral eloquence. Eloquence is defined by
La Bruyère as *tristesse évangélique*. Cicero and Demosthenes were
most eloquent when inspired by religion, but he finds nothing
in ancient literature to compare with Bossuet, Bourdaloue, or
Massillon.[1] Chateaubriand clearly anticipates the question 'What
about the orators of the Revolution?', and he replies that their
talents were undeveloped and that they showed merely snatches
of eloquence because they attacked the Faith of their fathers.
Here his partiality clearly overrides his judgement, as is shown
by the fact that he singles out for praise one speech of Vergniaud
because he therein pleaded for Louis XVI. Unprejudiced opinion
will probably admit that the addresses of Mirabeau are, of their
kind—that is to say the kind that is written out by himself or
by others and read—unsurpassed as oratory. Louvet and, in a
different way, Danton, a phrasemaker and extemporizer, were
orators of the highest quality. Chateaubriand is under this
heading at his least convincing.[2]

He then turns to the Fathers of the Church: Saint Ambrose

---

[1] Bourdaloue was a Jesuit, more interested in morality and in conduct than in
dogma. Massillon, his junior by some thirty years, preached the terrors in store for
the wicked like a revivalist. Both he and Bourdaloue seem to have understood the
world better than Bossuet. To posterity Bossuet, both as an orator and champion
of the Gallican Church, stands in a class apart, but this was not the view of many of
their contemporaries, nor the view later of Voltaire.

[2] In a note at the end of Chapter I, Book IV, Part III, Chateaubriand quotes a
passage from a speech of M. de Montlosier, a member of the constitutional Right in
the Constituent Assembly. Speaking of the clergy he said, 'Vous voulez leurs croix
d'or, ils prendront une croix de bois: c'est une croix de bois qui a sauvé le monde.'
This recalls the late Mr. Bryan's famous peroration at the Chicago convention of
1896, no impromptu but, as his biographer has stated, a carefully prepared climax:
'You shall not crucify mankind upon a cross of gold.'

he calls the Fénelon of Latin Christendom and Tertullian the Bossuet. This is perhaps a little obscure. Ambrose was the friend of the Emperor Theodosius who is alleged to have punished the citizens of Thessalonica by wholesale massacre carried out by Rufinus. The friendship of the Bishop and the Emperor was renewed only after the latter had done penance for his crime. Fénelon owed both his tutorship to the young Duke of Burgundy and his Archbishopric of Cambrai directly to Louis XIV, but his disapproval of the King's policy and administration was never disguised. After the publication of *Télémaque* he forfeited the royal favour. This could hardly be otherwise if his contemporaries were right in identifying Sésostris, Calypso, and Protesilaus respectively with the King himself, Madame de Montespan, and Louvois. The careers of St. Ambrose and Fénelon therefore give some ground for the comparison. If the comparison is made as to the style of their oratory, it hardly holds good. Chateaubriand calls Fénelon 'bland, smooth, copious'. St. Ambrose, on the other hand, does not stand out among the Christian Fathers for his eloquence but rather for his immense industry (his figure is associated in art with the beehive) and his activity against heresy, indicated by the scourge in his hand. The relations of Fénelon with the Quietists and Madame Guyon were one of the outstanding features of his life and one which redounded highly to his honour, for he openly and meekly accepted the censure of Rome. But it is difficult to see how he can profitably be compared with the great fighting champion of orthodoxy. As to Tertullian, Chateaubriand finds that the tone and substance of his plea for religion is essentially modern in spirit. He is no mere dialectician but a true evangelist, and, as might be expected in a modern evangelist, he is guilty of errors of style and errors of taste; but his 'Letter to the Martyrs' (by which Chateaubriand probably means his treatise '*About Flight in Persecution*') might well have been addressed to the victims of Robespierre. Here again we may be allowed to think the comparison far-fetched between Bossuet, the courageous, eloquent, and courtly preacher, with his strict standards of theology, and Tertullian with his passionate

nature fighting ceaselessly with his asceticism. Nor does anything in the career of Bossuet compare with Tertullian's lapse
from Catholicism into Montanism, a belief that the Holy Spirit
of God comes directly to all Christians and not as something
that is handed down from Apostolic times, a belief that lies
behind the activities of Puritan sects in every country. The
remarks of Chateaubriand about the Fathers of the Church may
indeed be said to be of little value. There is no reason to believe
that his knowledge of them at the time he wrote the book was
other than very superficial. His point amounts to no more than
this, that Christianity has from the first stimulated its followers
to eloquence.

From the Latins he proceeds to the Greeks and instances
St. Chrysostom, St. Basil, and St. Gregory of Nazianzus. Of
these St. Chrysostom was undoubtedly a supreme orator; the
rhetorical power of St. Basil was the foundation of his influence
in his youth, and it has been said of St. Gregory by Charron
that his sermons combine 'the invincible logic of Bourdaloue, the
unction, colour, and harmony of Massillon, the flexibility, poetry,
grace, and vivacity of Fénelon, the force, grandeur, and sublimity
of Bossuet'. This no doubt overcoloured appraisement of the
sermons of St. Gregory by Charron summarizes a comparison
which may be made between the four, a comparison with which
Chateaubriand would be little disposed to quarrel. Chateaubriand's remarks about the Fathers are really no more than an
introduction to what he has to say about these great pulpit orators.
Once again Chateaubriand compares: he sets Cicero beside
Massillon and Bossuet beside Demosthenes, and once again it is
on Bossuet that he lingers, noting particularly the dignity of the
eloquence, the invariably happy quotation, the wide generaliza-
tions. Bossuet is, in fact, he says, not merely a preacher but a
poet. The author concludes his remarks under this head by
observing that decadence of taste is the result of lack of faith.
A writer who has no belief in God deliberately restricts the
scope within which his genius can operate. The seventeenth
century with Pascal and Bossuet, Molière and La Fontaine (to
say nothing of Racine whose eminence rivals that of Virgil) is,

in his view, far in advance of the eighteenth; and this is due
to religion. Voltaire, had he been a Christian, would, says Chateaubriand, have rivalled Racine. Religion again supplies the
strongest incentive to patriotism. Rousseau himself owed much
to such religion as he had. On the other hand, Buffon lacked
feeling because he had no religion; and Chateaubriand makes it
a matter of complaint against him that in enumerating the different sorts of dog he forgot to mention the blind man's dog.
The greatest name of the century he considers to be that of
Montesquieu, who was a believer. He ends pessimistically.
The present is a period of little men, even of physically small
men: men who lack candour, whose imagination has little room
for love or inspiration: philosophers, logicians, men mathema-
tically minded.

To us to-day much of all this argumentation seems nonsen-
sical, and we can accept but few of Chateaubriand's valuations.
But it must be borne in mind that the book was addressed to the
world of 1802. The case against the eighteenth century is
greatly, even grotesquely, overstated; but Chateaubriand had
a case, and to a people in whose recollection such terrible suffering was still so vivid, he, choosing his moment with consummate art, puts forth his remedy: 'Forward to the new problems
in the old spirit; Le Génie de la Révolution has brought us
sorrow and lost us greatness. Let us turn again to Le Génie
du Christianisme!'

There is no need to linger over the last book of Part III,
called rather pompously 'Harmonies of the Christian religion
with scenes of nature and the passions of the human heart'. Book
V is the last book in this part, because *Atala*, which had originally
followed as Book VI, had already been published separately in
May 1801. In this book Chateaubriand elaborates his conception of the noble savage. The nature and virtue of civilized
men are no more than the perfected instinct and innocence of
primitive mankind. There follow passages describing pictur-
esquely the lonely homes of anchorites, old abbeys hidden away
in forests, convents perched on the edge of chasms, together
with a long poem in alexandrines written by Fontanes. From

picturesque sites it is a natural transition to ruins, so dear to
the taste of the period, and upon this theme Part III concludes.
Chateaubriand writes of the ruins of Palmyra, of Egypt, of the
vale of Tempe, the woods of Olympus, the coasts of Africa.
In speaking of ruins which date from the Christian era, he
singles out for praise those that are to be found in the British
Isles 'beside the Cumberland Lakes, in the mountains of Scotland,
even in the Orcades'. Chateaubriand is no doubt thinking of
Furness Abbey which is in Lancashire, and perhaps of Melrose
or Dryburgh, neither of which is among the mountains. His
love of Fingal and Ossian must be held responsible for the
remark about the Orkneys. Perhaps he was thinking vaguely
about Iona. In these chapters Chateaubriand is the poet and
little else. He is not arguing: he is merely a consummate
musician playing on his instrument. His vignette of Greece
may be quoted:

> La vallée de Tempé, les bois de l'Olympe, les côtes de l'Attique
> et du Péloponèse étalent les ruines de la Grèce. Là commencent à
> paraître les mousses, les plantes grimpantes et les fleurs saxatiles. . . .
>
> .   .   .   .
>
> Les flots de l'Égée, qui viennent expirer sous de croulants portiques,
> Philomèle qui se plaint, Alcyon qui gémit, Cadmus qui roule ses an-
> neaux autour d'un autel, le cygne qui fait son nid dans le sein de quel-
> que Léda, mille accidents, produits comme par les Grâces, enchantent
> ces poétiques débris: on dirait qu'un souffle divin anime encore la
> poussière des temples d'Apollon et des Muses; et le paysage entier,
> baigné par la mer, ressemble à un tableau d'Apelles, consacré à Nep-
> tune et suspendu à ses rivages.—Vol. ii. 48.

Or, again, a picture of the north:

> Assis sur un autel brisé, dans les Orcades, le voyageur s'étonne de la
> tristesse de ces lieux; un océan sauvage, des syrtes embrumées, des
> vallées où s'élève la pierre d'un tombeau, des torrents qui coulent à
> travers la bruyère, quelques pins rougeâtres jetés sur la nudité d'un
> *morne* flanqué de couches de neige, c'est tout ce qui s'offre aux regards.
> Le vent circule dans les ruines, et leurs innombrables jours deviennent
> autant de tuyaux d'où s'échappent des plaintes; l'orgue avait jadis
> moins de soupirs sous ces voûtes religieuses. . . .

Quelquefois égaré dans sa route, un vaisseau caché sous ses toiles arrondies, comme un Esprit des eaux voilé de ses ailes, sillonne les vagues désertes; sous le souffle de l'aquilon, il semble se prosterner à chaque pas, et saluer les mers qui baignent les débris du temple de Dieu.—Vol. ii. 49–50.

Or, again, an eloquent peroration:

Sacrés débris des monuments chrétiens, vous ne rappelez point, comme tant d'autres ruines, du sang, des injustices et des violences! vous ne racontez qu'une histoire paisible, ou tout au plus que les souffrances mystérieuses du Fils de l'Homme! Et vous, saints ermites, qui, pour arriver à des retraites plus fortunées, vous étiez exilés sous les glaces du pôle, vous jouissez maintenant du fruit de vos sacrifices! S'il est parmi les anges, comme parmi les hommes, des campagnes habitées et des lieux déserts, de même que vous ensevelîtes vos vertus dans les solitudes de la terre, vous aurez sans doute choisi les solitudes célestes pour y cacher votre bonheur!—Vol. ii. 49–50.

He ends like a true artist on a quieter note and describes the simple piety of the peasant, his faith, his pilgrimages, his miraculous cures, and the comfort that religion can bring to the unfortunate. Religion, he claims, meets a great human need: it discourages exorcism and necromancy and even excess of superstition. Mankind needs the marvellous and hopes for the future just because he feels himself that he is made for immortality. Christianity keeps all this in check. To close the churches is to open the dens of the sorcerers. It is the supreme gift of the Faith that it can appeal at once to the heart and to the intelligence.

IV

The final Part deals with worship. It is concerned first of all with churches, their services and their ornaments. Chateaubriand recalls the terrors which the memory of the tocsin must evoke. 'Among the savages of America, when suppliants come to the door of a hut, it is the child of the place who leads them to his Father's fireside. If bells were denied us, we should have to choose a child to call us to the house of the Lord.' He dwells

on the beauty of the symbolism of the Church ritual, and he
asserts that the very fact that God is worshipped in a tongue we
do not habitually use satisfies the soul and increases the religious feeling of the people. Sunday is a day of pleasure as well
as of recreation, and he makes an attack on the 'décades' of the
Revolution. He quotes the saying of the peasants that even the
cattle know Sunday and are unwilling to work on that day, and
he remarks that after six thousand years of general consent,
after 'sixty centuries of hosannah, the wisdom of the Dantons
raised its head, and dared to judge as ill the work which the
Eternal had found good'. As he proceeds Chateaubriand shows
his hand more and more openly, and though much of what he
says is of little interest to-day, these chapters in which he turns
from defence to attack must have drawn to themselves more
notice than those which were purely literary or historical. He
proceeds to speak of the Mass, and many of those who may have
cordially appreciated the general purpose of his work must have
been surprised and scandalized at the line adopted by this strange
champion of orthodoxy. For the argument amounts to this:
every people in every age has endeavoured to appease the gods,
all have felt the need of a victim. He quotes the cases of
Iphigenia and Quintus Curtius as well as of Isaac and of Jeph-
thah's daughter. They began with human sacrifices, they proceeded to substitute beasts, but as time passed, mankind realized
that a material sacrifice was not enough. A victim worthier of
human nature was called for. God demanded rather the sacrifice
of a contrite heart, and Jesus Christ instituted the Eucharist in
which under the symbols of bread and wine 'he concealed the
invisible offering of his blood and of our hearts'. This is a prelude
to a short analysis of the Mass. The scientific study of comparative religion was, of course, unknown in Chateaubriand's day,
and it is remarkable that he should have followed so openly a line
of thought which can have been little acceptable in his time
and is by no means of universal acceptability even in our own.
He describes the Church festivals—Corpus Christi, Epiphany,
Christmas; the happy family reunions, the jolly meals, the simple
ceremonies in which each generation unites; the dancing in

which children and parents, masters and servants, all play their part, not forgetting the presence of the priest who sees to it that the needs of the poor are not overlooked. He reminds his readers that these scenes were familiar in the days before the statue of Marat had replaced that of St. Vincent de Paul. Funerals recall, as they were bound to do, the name of Bossuet, and Chateaubriand quotes with great effect as supporting his general argument passages from the sermon preached at the funeral of Queen Henrietta Maria. The Christian practice of praying for the dead brings something of dignity and beauty and honour to the end of the humblest of mankind. Again comparison is made with Latin rites and again there is a poem by Fontanes, relegated this time to a note at the end of the volume.

Chateaubriand turns to speak of tombs, and reviews the practices in dealing with the dead which are characteristic of Egypt, Greece, Rome, China, Turkey, ancient Scotland (with inevitable reference to Ossian), and the customs of Tahiti. When he speaks of Christian graves he works himself up in his character as a pamphleteer to remarks on the treatment by the Revolution of the royal vaults at St. Denis. 'It has been left to those of our own day to dishonour the dead.' How thoroughly this was done between October 14th and October 25th, 1793, is set out with much interesting and painful detail in another note. In Switzerland, he says, graves are perched on rocks with a wide prospect of lake and mountain, in Italy there are catacombs, while in England the dead are buried in woollen shrouds[1] and their graves sown with mignonette, and in France churches are beautified by tombs which recall the chivalry of the Middle Ages. The book ends with a quiet beauty which contrasts with the passionate and ironical invective which has immediately preceded.

Saint-Denis est désert; l'oiseau l'a pris pour passage, l'herbe croît sur ses autels brisés; et au lieu du cantique de la mort, qui retentissait sous ses dômes, on n'entend plus que les gouttes de pluie qui tombent par son toit découvert, la chute de quelque pierre qui se détache de ses murs en ruine, le son de son horloge, qui va roulant dans les tombeaux vides et les souterrains dévastés.—Vol. ii. 96.

[1] This enactment was in force from the reign of Charles II for 120 years.

From the Church as an institution and the tombs Chateaubriand turns to the Clergy, the Church as a living organism.
The chapter 'Of Jesus Christ and of His life' must have puzzled
devout Catholics no less than embittered Jacobins. Christ,
according to Chateaubriand, appeared on earth just at the right
moment when, in face of the universal corruption of religion and
social habit, mankind was ripe for a change, when the notions of
God and of immortality were beginning to grow, and when there
was in existence a universal language which could spread such
ideas. The simplicity of Christianity made a direct appeal to the
less civilized areas of the Empire. The moral virtues of Christ
attracted the centres of culture and refinement. A creed which
taught love and pity and sacrifice could not be of human origin.
'He who offered to suffering humanity persecuted virtue as the
object of worship of mankind, could only have been a God',
says Chateaubriand.

He draws the character of Christ. He finds him kind, open,
and tender, of boundless benevolence. He went about doing
good. He showed at all times resignation to the will of God.
He loved, he knew friendship, he was patriotic, full of pity and
of tolerance.

Ah! si la morale la plus pure et le cœur le plus tendre, si une vie
passée à combattre l'erreur et à soulager les maux des hommes, sont
les attributs de la divinité, qui peut nier celle de Jésus-Christ? Modèle
de toutes vertus, l'amitié le voit endormi dans le sein de saint Jean, ou
léguant sa mère à ce disciple; la charité l'admire dans le jugement de la
femme adultère: partout la pitié le trouve bénissant les pleurs de
l'infortuné; dans son amour pour les enfants, son innocence et sa can-
deur se décèlent; la force de son âme brille au milieu des tourments
de la croix, et son dernier soupir est un soupir de miséricorde.—
Vol. ii. 101.

It is writings like this which show how little Chateaubriand
cared for dogma and how much he cared for beauty. He next
reviews the organization of the Church from the Pope to the
parish priest, and his pages are here marked by many references
and notes. The country curé comes in for a just tribute to his
unselfish labour in spite of what is called his ignorance and

prejudice. Monasticism is once again treated as an essentially Christian institution, though, indeed, he quotes the case of Elijah fleeing from the corruptions of Israel and though he must have known of the monasticism which has always characterized the religions of the East. He suggests that Roman persecutions helped to populate the solitudes and that later, when the barbarians threw themselves upon the Empire and for a time destroyed the organization of society, men found their only hope in God and their refuge in the deserts. He describes various forms of monastic organization and gives vignettes of the lives of the anchorites of the Lebanon, and of the Hospice of the Great St. Bernard in winter, of the Trappists wandering silently among the forests, of the mendicant orders who face the rigours of every climate, equally at home in the castle and in the prison. These lead up to a peroration recalling the scene in the Place de la Révolution, seventeen years before.

Voici un des plus hauts spectacles de la terre: aux deux coins de cet échafaud, les deux justices sont en présence, la justice humaine et la justice divine; l'une, implacable et appuyée sur un glaive, est accompagnée du désespoir; l'autre, tenant un voile trempé de pleurs, se montre entre la pitié et l'espérance; l'une a pour ministre un homme de sang, l'autre un homme de paix; l'une condamne, l'autre absout; innocente ou coupable, la première dit à la victime: 'Meurs!' La seconde lui crie: 'Fils de l'innocence ou du repentir, *montez au ciel!*'—Vol. ii. 122.

After speaking of the clergy Chateaubriand turns to Missions, a very important and indeed essential element in the general scheme of the work. Again and again the reader of *Le Génie* may wonder what bearing can be attributed to his remarks on the case he is endeavouring to put forward for Christianity. No doubt he deliberately kept some of what he considered his strongest arguments to the last. In setting forth the spirit of Christianity, Chateaubriand was clearly entitled to lay considerable stress on the missionary enthusiasm which has always inspired it, and after many digressions he comes at last to deal with one of the really strong points in his case. Here he is less the poet than the advocate. He writes of the missions in the Levant, in India, in China, Paraguay, the Indies, Canada.

There are long and, it must be admitted, tedious quotations. He could certainly have developed his arguments with twice the effect in half the space he occupies. He praises the venturesome courage of the Jesuits:[1] his own enlightened attitude towards slavery, his broad humanitarianism, his admiration of the scientific work done by missionaries helped him to appreciate their efforts. He relates with some fullness stories of their sufferings at the hands of the Indians of Canada. Their simplicity, their learning, their lawgiving, their heroism all manifested in supreme degree what was the essential nature—*le génie*—of Christianity. Chateaubriand then turns to chivalry, another important factor in building up his case. But here Chateaubriand bases himself avowedly on his authorities. In this part of the book there is much more reference and direct quotation than in the earlier portions. This does not mean that authorities have not been freely used all the way through: the work is, indeed, full of references. It probably means no more than that in dealing with such matters as missions and chivalry, where he has no opportunity for dialectic and where he feels his case is strong, he is content not to be original, and keen to hurry on to that general view of the service of Christianity to mankind which supplies the finale to the whole work. Within a few pages Chateaubriand collects with great skill a formidable mass of information about medieval chivalry throughout the western world and emphasizes the service which it rendered to European civilization. He sketches the romantic story of an education which began at seven years of age—how the page became a squire and how only after long service the squire became a knight. He points out how effectively this wonderful organization protected commerce, and held up the advance of the Turks into Europe. It was chivalry that played its part in civilizing the barbarians when they poured into the Continent, and formed a sort of international militia. Not least (and this is a case which can justly be made), it gave everywhere

[1] A remark in connexion with China is worth quoting: 'If China is closed to us to-day, if we do not dispute with the English the Empire of India, it is not the fault of the Jesuits who were on the point of opening to us these rich areas.'

new standards of conduct to men under arms. English knight-hood he puts before French. Of Joan of Arc he says that she revived the spirit of chivalry in France. The cult of St. Joan which is so marked a feature of French Catholicism in our own day would have surprised nobody more than Chateaubriand. He refers to the knights of Malta and their services in the Mediterranean, to the Teutonic knights who held at bay the wandering hordes on the banks of the Baltic Sea, to the Spanish knights who held up the Moors. If fortune failed sometimes, courage was never lacking, and he quotes the saying of Francis, whom he calls the last of the French knights, at Pavia, 'All is lost, save honour.'

And so he comes to deal in his final book with 'Services rendered to society by the clergy and by the Christian religion in general'. Herein is the substantive case which Chateaubriand puts forward. Judged purely as an argument, *Le Génie du Christianisme* would lose little if Chateaubriand had confined himself to this section altogether with the two preceding sections on Missions and Chivalry and had dispensed with the greater part of what had preceded, even though it is the earlier portions which are the more interesting because the more original and arresting part of the work. He begins by dealing with the charitable activities which owe their inspiration to Christianity. Here he feels himself on strong ground. He is entitled to point out that no other religion had adopted a sounder attitude towards suffering, need, or helplessness. He claims that charity in the ordinary sense of the word was absolutely unknown to the ancients, and it is a claim which, broadly speaking, he can fairly put forward. He also calls it an 'absolutely Chris-tian virtue', in which he goes too far. His chief opponents were the eighteenth-century philosophers even more than the revolu-tionists, and those philosophers were all inspired in greater or less degree with human pity. It was Voltaire's *saeva indignatio* which lay behind the attraction which he had in the eyes of Chateaubriand. For all that, he is right in pointing out that the impulse of Christianity first set its face against slavery and infanticide. He goes on to refer to the religious orders of men and women who, in all parts of the world, have devoted themselves to medical and charitable work among lepers or foundlings or unmarried mothers. Where workers have been oppressed or prisoners maltreated they have not hesitated to oppose civil authority. Such examples have inspired numberless women of wealth and position in their turn to sacrifice everything in order to take vows and to devote their lives to service among the sick and the poor. Christianity and Christianity alone, he asserts triumphantly, could have inspired anything so wonderful and so unprecedented.

He then turns to education. His case here is that the Church which brings comfort brings also enlightenment. The world, he says, owes much of its education to the Benedictines, the Oratorians, the Jesuits. Universities in every country owe their foundation either to pious princes or to bishops. He considers the debt especially heavy in regard to the Jesuits, and he points out that Voltaire dedicated *Mérope* to a Jesuit father. Chateaubriand himself must have known that though all this may be true, it is yet not the whole truth. In his day, as in our own, those forces which are non-Christian or even anti-Christian have been among the most active and insistent in stressing the importance of education. From education he proceeds to speak of the services of the Papacy to science and art. Here Chateaubriand, often so prolix, dismisses in a single chapter an argument susceptible of development at considerable length. It is to fly in the face of history, he asserts, to suggest that Christianity has stood in the way of the advancement of culture. A long quotation from Barthélemy's *Voyages en Italie* provides the chief material for this chapter, a quotation mainly concerned with the Rome of Leo X. This quotation summarizes the situation in Italy during the age when Michelangelo was building the dome of St. Peter's, when Raphael was preparing his frescoes for the Vatican, when literature, the sciences, languages, the arts, philosophy, were eagerly studied in each great city, when once again public attention was drawn to the art and letters of ancient Greece and ancient Rome. Although our own age has resented that the Pantheon should have been turned into a church and that Trajan's column should be crowned with a statue of St. Peter, there is no doubt justice in Chateaubriand's remark that but for this policy of the popes the whole of the old monuments of Rome might well have become—as so much of the ancient city did in fact become—merely the raw material of the medieval city. 'A Carthusian monk', he says proudly, 'can show you the laurel which grows on Virgil's tomb, and a Pope crowned Tasso on the Capitol.' Gunpowder, the compass, eye-glasses, and the clock are all, so Chateaubriand claims, inventions of the Church, and Rome in modern times has linked the world together no less surely than did Rome of the Empire. It is strange that this cursory review contains no mention of Julius II, no mention of Dante or of Giotto or of the monastic artists of the thirteenth and fourteenth centuries. There has been, he proceeds to show, no aspect of the life of the community which is not deeply in debt to the Church. Throughout Europe the monasteries stimulated the development of arid tracts and set an example of careful and scientific cultivation. They built and they encouraged building. Where roads were bad or dangerous or non-existent they provided an indispensable convenience for travellers and pilgrims; and when they had led to the foundation of hostels and colleges and libraries they began to be the centres of the mechanical arts and of commerce. They made wine. The existence of the Church called for linen, wax, silk, marble, carpets, gold and silver work; and (an outstanding point) the Church supplied architects and artists with opportunities which they could have found in no other quarter. 'If their works [of the gothic age] seem to us uncouth', says Chateaubriand, 'the delicacy of our taste must not make us ungrateful.' This amusingly sententious remark should be borne in mind when *Le Génie* is represented, as is so often the case, as a precursor of the Gothic Revival. On the contrary, the remark shows that Chateaubriand was not merely of his time but even sometimes behind the times. The Gothic Revival had had its beginnings in England years before. Strawberry Hill and *The Castle of Otranto* were already forty years old.[1] It is strange, too, that the famous

[1] Rousseau in his Preface to *La Nouvelle Héloïse* speaks of its 'gothic tone'.

chapter on gothic architecture shows no appreciation of those Primitives who worked under the inspiration of its influence. While admiring the campanile of the Duomo at Florence, Chateaubriand would apparently have regarded with no more than good-natured tolerance the frescoes in the Capella Spagnuola at S. Maria Novella. And yet each is equally associated with the name of Giotto. Chateaubriand's remarks on the gothic blaze no new trail: perhaps he would even have been surprised at the notice given to that particular chapter. To him it was probably no more than just an element in the case he sought to build up. The symbolism of gothic appealed to the poet in him. It was enough that it was beautiful.

From the arts he turns to law, and stresses the undeniable influence of the canon law on the development of civilization. The canons of the Church have indeed a universality that no other law can rival. They cover, says Chateaubriand, the whole field of Christendom, and the spirit of the civil law is softened and humanized by their influence. The idea that civilization can be based on anything but religion was never contemplated by the ancients, and if it is suggested that that influence is on the whole, or in any degree, bad, the answer he gives is somewhat as follows. Chateaubriand sees in Nature a certain principle at work. He sees a mingling of force and gentleness, never a mingling of force and force or of weakness and weakness. Applied to politics this would mean that a timid and unwarlike people should have a rigid and bold constitution, an impetuous and changeable people should live under a gentle and moderate rule. Theocracy was therefore bad for the ancient Egyptians, who would have been better under a military rule rather than under priest-kings. In the early days of Rome, on the other hand, it was well that religion should have a leading place among a nation of warriors. He who does not fear man should fear God. This argument is more than a little obscure until he goes on to say that what was true of Rome is true of France. France has no need to fear the power of the priesthood, for never in history has priesthood led a militant people into servitude. This is his answer to those who might fear that Catholicism would mean loss of liberty: with a people like the French it never could do so. Chateaubriand lived to see his arguments under this head refuted by history, both under Louis XVIII and more markedly under Charles X. But he was writing in 1802, and to a generation who knew what crimes could be committed in the name of liberty; and it was a clever piece of dialectic to argue that Catholicism with such a people as the French could never mean reaction. Once again and for the last time Chateaubriand takes the offensive against Voltaire, Rousseau, the Encyclopédistes, and the eighteenth century, and claims that the attitude of the Church has all through the centuries been a moderating one. The Church, which possessed knowledge, experience, dignity, was always at hand to support the people against their oppressors and, if need be, to support the sovereign against a factious and disloyal nobility. The popes conducted themselves like great princes. It had been their initiative which had saved Europe from the Turks. The weapon of the interdict was used to bring to reason sovereigns who misgoverned, and he quotes with approval a dictum of Montesquieu to the effect that Christianity is opposed in its essential spirit to arbitrary power and that the principles of Christianity are able to effect more than rectitude in monarchies, force in republics, or fear in despotisms. The interest attaching to this remark is pointed out in a footnote to the edition of 1828. Chateaubriand had the weakness, common to all politicians in every age, of being anxious to justify his public record. In 1802 he was surrounded with friends of the First Consul and his book reinforced the First Consul's policy. In 1814 his pamphlet *De Buonaparte et des Bourbons* assisted the cause of the Restoration. In 1816 came *La Monarchie selon la Charte*, which was distinctly liberal in tone. No longer a supporter of absolutism, Chateaubriand lays down the principle that the king reigns but does not govern. In this note he points out that already, under the Consulate, he was saying what brought him into disfavour with Louis XVIII fourteen years later. The point is one which he was entitled to make. As a youth he had been repelled by the excesses of the Revolution and he had ceased to give it support. Later on he saw constitu-

tional government at work in England, and he remarks bitterly
that during the time of the Republic and the Empire the Bourbons had been almost forgotten, and it had been he who had
reminded France of her old Royal Family and he who had
brought to her recollection which of them were alive. This is
no doubt gross exaggeration, but Chateaubriand is justified in
pointing out that he went into opposition as an ultra-royalist
but emphatically not as an ultra-reactionary. Christianity, he
considers, gives a nobler meaning to citizenship than it ever
enjoyed under Greece and Rome, because it brought with it a
higher realization of the difference between right and wrong.
He approves a remark of Montesquieu that Christianity left to
the defeated their lives, for the first time in history, and not
merely their lives but their personal rights, their laws, their
private property, and, as a rule, their religion. To all this
Chateaubriand adds (writing exactly fifty years after the first
appearance of the *Esprit des Lois*, 1748) abolition of slavery.

The whole work concludes with a summary of its arguments.
He considers the question 'What would be the condition of
society to-day if Christianity had not appeared on the earth?'
He finds little to admire in the much-vaunted Roman virtues.
The spirit of Rome was fine, but in other things she was savage,
unjust, greedy, self-indulgent, and he quotes Sallust and Tacitus
and Suetonius in support of this view. Roman slavery he finds a
particularly execrable institution. His judgement on Athens is
less severe. The Athenians were cheerful under misfortune
and they loved knowledge and beauty. But morality must form
the foundation of the State, not mere political systems, and
because the Roman Empire had no foundation in public morality
it became the victim of the barbarian invasions. Of all the invaders the Goths, who accepted Christianity, were the least
destructive. Chateaubriand remarks that many of the invaders
showed some degree of respect for priests and monasteries:
but for this, the whole of western civilization might have been
utterly destroyed. In this very real sense, therefore, Christ
can be called the Saviour of the world. And to those who say
that good philosophers are better than bad Christians he replies

that in principle philosophy cannot do anything well which
religion cannot do better, and that religion does good in many
ways which are beyond the power of philosophy. Both the
question and the answer, it is interesting to note, are not
Chateaubriand's own but Rousseau's. On the last page of his
book he calls his great opponent as a witness in his own favour.

He ends confidently. Christianity will emerge triumphant
from the hideous ordeal which it has been called upon to
undergo. He quotes Pascal:

> A ceux qui ont de la répugnance pour la religion, il faut commencer
> par leur montrer qu'elle n'est point contraire à la raison ; ensuite
> qu'elle est vénérable et en donner respect; après, la rendre aimable
> et faire souhaiter qu'elle fût vraie ; et puis montrer par des preuves
> incontestables qu'elle est vraie; faire voir son antiquité et sa sainteté
> par sa grandeur et son élévation.

His own line of argument has been different but it leads to
the same conclusion, and that conclusion he sets out in logical
form. Christianity is perfect, men are imperfect. A perfect
consequence cannot result from an imperfect origin. Christianity
has not therefore come from man. If it has not come from man
it can only have come from God. If it has come from God, man
can only have obtained knowledge of it by revelation. Christianity is therefore a revealed religion.

So ends this strange work, which in its course has wandered
over the whole of French literature and history. Few books
indeed can ever have covered so wide a field. Its appeal was
irresistible to the old, to whom it brought memories of happier
days, and to the young, who believed that Napoleon and the
policy for which he stood would revive ancient glories and bring
freedom and peace, and if not peace then victory.

Chateaubriand is an outstanding example of the *homo unius
libri*; he could never get away from *Le Génie du Christianisme*.
The book once so famous is to-day neglected, almost forgotten. But Chateaubriand's literary posterity, according to
Victor Giraud and other equally competent authorities, make
up an extraordinary list. Victor Hugo, Lamartine, Leconte de
Lisle, de Vigny, and de Musset are among the poets. Béranger,

whom one would not expect to find on the list, nevertheless wrote to him: 'Do you know that I began by being your disciple. I was mad for *Le Génie du Christianisme.*' Philosophic historians like Thierry and de Barante, Quinet and in a measure Michelet, men of letters like Sainte-Beuve, Villemain, Ampère, orators like Montalembert and Père Lacordaire, all derive in greater or less degree from him. In George Sand, Mérimée, Balzac, Gautier, even in the gravity of Guizot and in the sombreness of Comte, is to be traced something of the spirit of Chateaubriand. He sent historians back to original authorities, and novelists to nature. To all who worked in any part of the literary field he taught that beauty was an end in itself. Émile Faguet has said of him that he is the greatest landmark in the history of French literature since La Pléiade. 'Il est l'homme qui a renouvelé l'imagination française.' The Concordat marked the end of a political chapter. *Le Génie du Christianisme* marked alike in politics and in literature the opening of a new volume.

THE ORATORY OF VICTOR HUGO

·⟨═══════⟩·

ANYBODY who turned to the article in the *Encyclopædia Britannica* on Victor Hugo used until lately to discover there perhaps the most whole-hearted tribute ever paid by one man of genius to another, even though Swinburne's Essay gave few facts about his life. The reader had to be content to know that the poems published before 1840 showed their author to have been one of the greatest elegiac and lyric poets born into the world. The *Châtiments* of 1853 recalled to the student, so we are told, the lyric inspiration of Coleridge and Shelley, the prophetic inspiration of Dante and Isaiah, the satiric inspiration of Juvenal and Dryden. *La Légende des Siècles* is the greatest book published in the nineteenth century. *Toute la Lyre* showed the author as one of the very greatest among poets and among men. As to the plays, *Hernani* showed him to be the greatest tragic and dramatic poet born since the age of Shakespeare. *Le Roi s'amuse* realized the ideal aim of tragic poetry among the countrymen of Aeschylus and Sophocles. *Lucrèce Borgia* was in prose, but the prose of Victor Hugo stands higher on the record of poetry than the efforts of any lesser dramatist or poet. And what is true of the poems and the plays is no less true of the prose fiction. *Notre Dame de Paris* is the greatest of all tragic or historic or romantic poems in the form of prose narrative, *Les Misérables* the greatest epic and dramatic work of fiction ever conceived. *Les Travailleurs de la mer* is unsurpassed even amongst the works of this author, and *L'Homme qui rit* shows no less magnificent mastery.

This article has now disappeared from the fourteenth edition and is replaced by a well-balanced estimate from the pen of Mr. Harold Nicolson, an estimate which reviews the work of Victor Hugo in relation to his life and reaches conclusions in regard to it which probably represent fairly enough the opinion which is generally held to-day both in France and in this country. Mr. Nicolson maintains that the dramas are dead; and though one may still see *Hernani* and *Ruy Blas* and *Le Roi s'amuse* performed in Paris from time to time, the statement is, broadly speaking, true. *Les Misérables*, in spite of its tedious *longueurs*, will, he tells us, probably always be read, and, perhaps, in spite of much that is fantastic and ridiculous, *Notre Dame de Paris*. *Les Travailleurs de la mer* is not the least valuable of the fruits of his long exile in Guernsey, and contains magnificent passages of description. To Mr. Nicolson, in the article above referred to, Victor Hugo is the greatest French poet of the nineteenth century. Professor Saintsbury, indeed, considers Hugo one of the greatest prose writers of France, and the greatest poet.

In all the books which have been written around Victor Hugo and his work, little attention has been paid to him as an orator. His poems, his plays, his public life, his private life, have all been examined, dissected, appraised, but his speeches have been for the most part ignored. This is the more surprising since they were carefully collected and edited by himself, and are available to anybody in five attractive volumes published by Messrs. Nelson.[1]

One of his biographers speaks roundly of his 'rhetorical inanities'. This is less than just, for the speeches of Victor Hugo deserve the attention of the student of his career partly because among much that is mere rodomontade there is also much resonant rhetoric, and also because a study of *Actes et Paroles* helps to demonstrate that extraordinary combination of greatness and littleness which marked the personality of the poet.

II

In dealing first with his parliamentary speeches we are met by a difficulty at the outset. In printing his speeches in his old age Victor Hugo, in order to heighten the effect to the reader, purports to give indications of how they were received. This certainly helps to make many of them interesting and sometimes exciting reading. Parliamentary speeches are, as a rule, tiresome to listen to, and those who attend the House of Commons

---

[1] Fuller extracts from the speeches of Victor Hugo are to be found in three volumes of the Collection Pallas (Éd. Delagrave) or in M. Maurice Levaillant's *L'Œuvre de Victor Hugo* (Éd. Delagrave).

must often be surprised to read in their newspapers the next morning of 'loud cheers' or 'loud and continued cheers' when they have merely recollection of an occasional 'Yah, yah, yah' rising and falling in intensity, but at its heartiest bearing but little relation to cheers. French parliamentary emotions are admittedly more easily aroused and more variously manifested, but for all that, it is impossible not to feel that in preparing his speeches for publication Victor Hugo has strained even the rich resources of the French language in his desire to impress upon his readers the reception which was accorded to his arguments. We read not merely of *applaudissements* and *acclamations*, of *mouvement* and *violentes dénégations*, of *bravos, murmures, clameurs,* and *rumeurs*. We have also *vive et profonde agitation, explosions de rire, rire universel, longue et vive sensation, profonde sensation, dénégations irritées, longue hilarité, hilarité bruyante*. There is even *vive et universelle émotion, immense acclamation*, and *tumulte inexprimable*. It is sad to learn that many of these represent no more than the recollection of Victor Hugo himself and that some of them are contradicted by the evidence of the official *Moniteur*.

Victor Hugo, who in his youth had been a legitimist and was the son of one of Napoleon's generals, had later become a Constitutional Royalist and had accepted a peerage from Louis-Philippe. 'Sire,' he had said to him in 1842, 'Dieu a besoin de vous.' In 1848 his paper *L'Évènement* uses exactly the same words about the Prince President. 'Prince, la Providence a besoin de vous.'—'A notre avis', said *L'Évènement*, 'quand Louis Bonaparte ne serait qu'un nom, la France ferait bien encore de se déclarer pour ce nom immense. Nous prouverons encore sans peine que sous ce nom de Napoléon il y a aujourd'hui un homme, que derrière l'idole il y a l'idée.'

In the election of December 10th, 1848, Victor Hugo supported Napoleon, and yet a few short months turned him into a violent enemy. Victor Hugo himself gives two reasons for this. The first was the Roman policy of the Government. General Oudinot had been sent to Rome by the Legislative Assembly in order to protect the city from invasion by Austrian troops. It was understood that this implied no intervention in the dispute between the Pope and his subjects; but Louis Napoleon had surrounded himself with Moderates, and in the Assembly elected in May the Moderates were strongly represented. When Oudinot found himself compelled to retire before the Garibaldians Montalembert and the Catholics were enthusiastic, and when, after his forces had been strengthened, he besieged Rome, took the city, and restored the Pope, the Radical parties and, not least, Victor Hugo were furious. The second reason arose out of the first. Little more than a week after the fall of Rome there was an insurrection in Paris following a protest in the Assembly by Ledru-Rollin, which the President and Changarnier, the Commander-in-Chief, put down with an iron hand.

Thereafter Victor Hugo was heart and soul with the Opposition. But these reasons do not in themselves entirely explain his attitude. He was a man of boundless self-confidence and ambition. Louis-Philippe had thought of him as a possible Prime Minister. After the Revolution of 1848 his aspirations soared even higher than that. At the moment when the popularity of Lamartine was obviously waning, Victor Hugo had said to a friend, 'I want to be President.' It is possible that Louis Napoleon, who had a certain easy and cynical good nature, might have been willing to include him among his Ministers. Even had he been acceptable to the Prince President, however, no Minister was willing to work with him as a colleague, and nothing remained for Victor Hugo but to constitute himself the bitter and life-long enemy of Louis Napoleon until the fall of the Empire in 1870.

When all this is taken into account the tortuous course of Victor Hugo's political pronouncements between 1848 and 1853 becomes more explicable. It is not difficult to appreciate what lay behind the fine rhetoric of his parliamentary speeches and why it was that, though they impressed by their eloquence, their influence upon the political situation was frequently so slight.

There is, for example, the peroration of the speech on the expedition to Rome of October 15th, 1849, delivered in the following May:

Ce qui n'est pas possible, c'est qu'une expédition entreprise, nous disait-on, dans un but d'humanité et de liberté, aboutisse au rétablissement du Saint-Office! Ce qui n'est pas possible, c'est que nous n'ayons pas même secoué sur Rome ces idées généreuses et libérales que la France porte partout avec elle dans les plis de son drapeau! Ce qui n'est pas possible, c'est qu'il ne sorte de notre sang versé ni un droit ni un pardon! c'est que la France soit allée à Rome, et qu'aux gibets près, ce soit comme si l'Autriche y avait passé! Ce qui n'est pas possible, c'est d'accepter le *Motu proprio* et l'amnistie du triumvirat des cardinaux! c'est de subir cette ingratitude, cet avortement, cet affront! C'est de laisser souffleter la France par la main qui devait la bénir! (Longs applaudissements.)

Ce qui n'est pas possible, c'est que cette France ait engagé une des choses les plus grandes et les plus sacrées qu'il y ait dans le monde, son drapeau; c'est qu'elle ait prodigué son argent, l'argent du peuple qui souffre; c'est qu'elle ait versé, je le répète, le glorieux sang de ses soldats; c'est qu'elle ait fait tout cela pour rien! . . . (Sensation inexprimable.) Je me trompe, pour de la honte!

Voilà ce qui n'est pas possible!

(Explosion de bravos et d'applaudissements. L'orateur descend de la tribune et reçoit les félicitations d'une foule de représentants, parmi lesquels on remarque MM. Dupin, Cavaignac et La Rochejaquelin. La séance est suspendue vingt minutes.)

The remark of Montalembert: 'The speech to which we have just listened has received the punishment it merits. I speak of the cheers which have accompanied it,' was deeply resented by Victor Hugo. Montalembert taunted him with his changes of opinion and commented on his absence from the Chamber while criticisms were being made. Victor Hugo was never a ready speaker, though in private he could amuse his friends by impersonations. He was no debater. His speeches needed careful preparation and were for the most part read. They were full of heightened colour and of words chosen carefully in order the more surely to annoy his opponents. In England a speech that is read is generally considered to lose much of its effectiveness.[1] A reader, as a rule, finds it difficult to hold his audience. Burke is the classic instance of this. But in France the written oration never lacks appreciation. The great preachers of the

[1] John Bright once remarked to the father of the present writer, who had said of a speech that it smelt of the lamp, 'I never heard a speech worth listening to that did not.'

seventeenth century, many of the greatest orators of the Revolution, did not speak extempore. The Frenchman has a pride in his language and an appreciation of the 'mot juste' which is lacking in England, and he has none of the Englishman's dislike of an address that is written and read. In addition, he has a natural aptitude for delivering his speeches, written or oral, which is rare in this country, and in France the art, for it is an art, of reading effectively from a written document is carefully developed. The reply to Montalembert is a good instance of this. The quotation which follows is from the latter part of the speech of the 23rd May, 1850:

L'honorable M. de Montalembert m'a reproché hier amèrement le crime d'absence. Je lui réponds:—Oui, quand je serai épuisé de fatigue par une heure et demie de luttes contre MM. les interrupteurs ordinaires de la majorité (cris à droite), qui recommencent, comme vous voyez! (Rires à gauche.)

Quand j'aurai la voix éteinte et brisée, quand je ne pourrai plus prononcer une parole, et vous voyez que c'est à peine si je puis parler aujourd'hui (la voix de l'orateur est, en effet, visiblement altérée); quand je jugerai que ma présence muette n'est pas nécessaire à l'assemblée; surtout quand il ne s'agira que de vous et de moi, oui, monsieur de Montalembert, je pourrai vous laisser la satisfaction de me foudroyer à votre aise, moi absent, et je me reposerai pendant ce temps-là. (Longs éclats de rire à gauche et applaudissements.) Oui, je pourrai n'être pas présent! Mais attaquez, par votre politique, vous et le parti clérical (mouvement), attaquez les nationalités opprimées, la Hongrie suppliciée, l'Italie garrottée, Rome crucifiée (profonde sensation); attaquez le génie de la France par votre loi d'enseignement; attaquez le progrès humain par votre loi de déportation; attaquez le suffrage universel par votre loi de mutilation; attaquez la souveraineté du peuple, attaquez la démocratie, attaquez la liberté, et vous verrez, ces jours-là, si je suis absent!

(Explosion de bravos.—L'orateur, en descendant de la tribune, est entouré d'une foule de membres qui le félicitent, et regagne sa place, suivi par les applaudissements de toute la gauche.—La séance est un moment suspendue.)

But unquestionably the greatest effort of Victor Hugo's career is his speech on the Constitution of July 1851. Whatever may be said against it, its violence, its inherent egotism, its mannerisms, it must be regarded as a fine effort. Its delivery took four and a half hours owing to the opposition it invited and received. As reported in *Actes et Paroles* it is even to-day intensely dramatic reading. This, of course, was the intention of the great artist who not merely wrote the speech but inspired the comments which accompanied it. It is full of Hugoesque eloquence and characteristic antitheses. Page after page of the report displays a triangular fight between the speaker, the President of the Chamber, and various interrupters, who are all three themselves constantly interrupted in a long, sustained scene of excitement, which must be rare in the records of any legislative Chamber. Victor Hugo is often charged with lack of courage, and there were occasions in his career when the charge appears not without substance. But as a parliamentarian he spoke out more than once like a brave man. He had been brave when he opposed the national workshops in June 1848 ('La Monarchie avait les oisifs, la République aura les fainéants'), and he was brave on this occasion too. He saw what was going to happen. He knew the Republic was doomed. He knew that many of those who interrupted him had been, or would shortly be, bribed with place or with money, and he said so. In reporting the interruptions he quotes in footnotes the positions and the salaries subsequently enjoyed by his interrupters under the Empire. The famous passage in which for the first time he made use of the nickname under which henceforward he so often referred to Louis Napoleon, runs as follows:

Quoi! parce que, il y a dix siècles de cela, Charlemagne, après quarante années de gloire, a laissé tomber sur la face du globe un sceptre et une épée tellement démesurés que personne ensuite n'a pu et n'a osé y toucher, — et pourtant il y a eu dans l'intervalle des hommes qui se sont appelés Philippe-Auguste, François Ier, Henri IV, Louis XIV! Quoi! parce que, mille ans après, car il ne faut pas moins d'une gestation de mille années à l'humanité pour reproduire de pareils hommes, parce que, mille ans après, un autre génie est venu, qui a ramassé ce glaive et ce sceptre, et qui s'est dressé debout sur le continent, qui a fait l'histoire gigantesque dont l'éblouissement dure

encore, qui a enchaîné la révolution en France et qui l'a déchaînée en
Europe, qui a donné à son nom, pour synonymes éclatants, Rivoli,
Iéna, Essling, Friedland, Montmirail! Quoi! parce que, après dix ans
d'une gloire immense, d'une gloire presque fabuleuse à force de grandeur, il a, à son tour, laissé tomber d'épuisement ce sceptre et ce glaive
qui avaient accompli tant de choses colossales, vous venez, vous, vous
voulez, vous, les ramasser après lui, comme il les a ramassés, lui,
Napoléon, après Charlemagne, et prendre dans vos petites mains ce
sceptre des titans, cette épée des géants! Pour quoi faire? (Longs applaudissements.) Quoi! après Auguste, Augustule! Quoi! parce que
nous avons eu Napoléon le Grand, il faut que nous ayons Napoléon le
Petit! (La gauche applaudit, la droite crie. La séance est interrompue
pendant plusieurs minutes. Tumulte inexprimable.)

III

His parliamentary speeches show Victor Hugo at his worst. His
addresses delivered before the Académie Française, three in
number, have been criticized with almost equal severity, but on
different grounds. The circumstances of their delivery precluded,
of course, any possibility of improvisation. They were prepared with the utmost care. Hugo's biographer, Biré, has little
good to say of any of them, but Biré's estimates are frequently
harsh, for, whilst appreciating Hugo's genius, he had a poor
opinion of his character and a keen resentment of his attitude
towards the Church. In regard to these Academic addresses
he is unfair to Hugo. The Reception Address of June 2nd,
1841, was a great occasion. Hugo, although only some thirty-
nine years of age, was already a figure outstanding among his
contemporaries. How great a figure he already had become is
shown by what the *Edinburgh Review* had written of him eight
years previously. It awarded to him without hesitation the
first place among French novelists.[1] This appreciation is almost
a foretaste of Swinburne.

[1] 'Though still young he has already distinguished himself in almost every
walk of imaginative literature: disputing the prize of lyric poetry with Lamartine,
in his *Odes*, his *Orientales*, and *Feuilles d'Automne*: occupying one of the most
eminent positions on the stage by his *Cromwell, Hernani, Marion Delorme, Le Roi
s'amuse*, and *Lucrèce Borgia*: and indisputably the head of Romance since his
publication of his *Notre-Dame de Paris*. Superior to his contemporaries in

During the years which followed, his reputation, already international in 1833, had been increased by *Les Chants du Crépuscule* of 1835, a social and an artistic success, by *Ruy Blas* and by *Les Rayons et les Ombres* of 1840. The years had also brought a subtle and not altogether happy change. The friends and comrades who had supported him in his early battles had drawn away. Grown more imperious, more self-centred, he was by 1841 surrounded by a younger generation of admirers, among whom Théophile Gautier was the outstanding figure. Already the engaging personality of the youthful Hugo was giving place to the more remote and austere figure of the Prophet. The Académie addresses must be appraised in the light of these facts. Successful at his third candidature, the distinguished and critical audience assembled for his formal Reception expected a literary masterpiece. What, in fact, they heard was a series of political reflections. This was resented, and there was general disappointment. Hugo's revolutionary ideas as a dramatist were distasteful to many and had been the cause of his previous unsuccessful attempts. As a poet, on the other hand, his eminence was universally conceded, and there was some resentment that on such an occasion he chose to talk history and politics. He did so, no doubt, partly and perhaps chiefly because he intended to be a politician, and sought to lay the foundations of a political career, but also because he thought that speaking in the Académie with its long and illustrious tradition he could, not unsuitably, point out that in spite of all the convulsions of the previous fifty or sixty years, what was really fundamental in the life of France had remained unaffected. The address therefore contained praise for Napoleon and praise also for those who had had the courage to oppose him, for Mme de Staël, Benjamin Constant, Chateaubriand. He worked in, as convention demanded that he should, praise of Lemercier, whose *fauteuil* he was occupying. Lemercier had not shared

creative imagination . . . superior to them even in that particular in which their strength lies, mere *power* of painting and description; he is yet more visibly elevated above their sphere of inspiration by the purer spirit with which his works as a whole have been animated, (and) the generous sympathy for goodness and devotion of every kind, which he evinces.' (*Edinburgh Review*, lvii, 1833, p. 346.)

Hugo's views and had little liking for him personally. But Hugo manages to speak at considerable length on the 'rare et beau talent' which characterized his historical plays, constructed though they were on very different lines from his own. The address, though packed with literary allusions, was certainly not a literary address. The idea underlying it is perhaps best shown in the words which he uses in regard to the Revolution of 1830.

La France fait partie intégrante de l'Europe. Elle ne peut pas plus briser avec le passé que rompre avec le sol. Aussi, à mon sens, c'est avec un admirable instinct que notre dernière révolution, si grave, si forte, si intelligente, a compris que, les familles couronnées étant faites pour les nations souveraines, à de certains âges des races royales, il fallait substituer à l'hérédité de prince à prince l'hérédité de branche à branche; c'est avec un profond bon sens qu'elle a choisi pour chef constitutionnel un ancien lieutenant de Dumouriez et de Kellermann qui était petit-fils de Henri IV et petit-neveu de Louis XIV; c'est avec une haute raison qu'elle a transformé en jeune dynastie une vieille famille, monarchique et populaire à la fois, pleine de passé par son histoire et pleine d'avenir par sa mission.

The second address was delivered some four years later when again a difficult task confronted him, and he was called upon as a Director of the Académie to reply to the speech of St. Marc-Girardin, a professor, a political journalist, and a severe critic of the modern drama. Hugo's speech lacked nothing in graciousness. He praised 'Vos lumières, votre érudition, votre esprit ingénieux, votre riche mémoire, votre langage élégant', and he then proceeded to speak of the aims of the literary calling: a trite subject, no doubt, but one which receives fine and characteristic treatment in the passage which follows:

Lettrés! vous êtes l'élite des générations, l'intelligence des multitudes résumée en quelques hommes, la tête même de la nation. Vous êtes les instruments vivants, les chefs visibles d'un pouvoir spirituel redoutable et libre. Pour n'oublier jamais quelle est votre responsabilité, n'oubliez jamais quelle est votre influence. Regardez vos aïeux, et ce qu'ils ont fait; car vous avez pour ancêtres tous les génies qui depuis trois mille ans ont guidé ou égaré, éclairé ou troublé le genre humain. Ce qui se dégage de tous leurs travaux, ce qui résulte de toutes leurs épreuves, ce qui sort de toutes leurs œuvres, c'est l'idée de leur puissance. Homère a fait plus qu'Achille, il a fait Alexandre; Virgile a calmé l'Italie après les guerres civiles; Dante l'a agitée; Lucain était l'insomnie de Néron; Tacite a fait de Caprée le pilori de Tibère. Au moyen-âge, qui était, après Jésus-Christ, la loi des intelligences? Aristote. Cervantès a détruit la chevalerie; Molière a corrigé la noblesse par la bourgeoisie, et la bourgeoisie par la noblesse; Corneille a versé de l'esprit romain dans l'esprit français; Racine, qui pourtant est mort d'un regard de Louis XIV, a fait descendre Louis XIV du théâtre; on demandait au grand Frédéric quel roi il craignait en Europe, il répondit: Le roi Voltaire. Les lettrés du XVIIIe siècle, Voltaire en tête, ont battu en brèche et jeté bas la société ancienne; les lettrés du XIXe peuvent consolider ou ébranler la nouvelle. Que vous dirai-je enfin? le premier de tous les livres et de tous les codes, la Bible, est un poème. Partout et toujours ces grands rêveurs qu'on nomme les penseurs et les poètes se mêlent à la vie universelle, et, pour ainsi parler, à la respiration même de l'humanité. La pensée n'est qu'un souffle, mais ce souffle remue le monde.

Finally, there is the address delivered a month later in February 1845 at the Reception of Sainte-Beuve. This must have been one of the most difficult tasks that a public man has ever been called upon to undertake, and Hugo's success has never received the recognition it merits. Sainte-Beuve had been in love with Madame Hugo already for about fifteen years. Hugo for some time had not taken the matter seriously, and it is to-day generally believed that at no period was there any real reason for Hugo to mistrust his wife. Sainte-Beuve, on the other hand, comes badly out of the story. He made trouble between the Hugos. He who signed himself 'your devoted friend' in August 1833 wrote of Hugo three years later that he was 'not of the race of men but born of dragon's teeth', and by 1844 he says: 'My relation with Hugo is very simple: enemies, .mortal enemies, are we at bottom.' Nor was Sainte-Beuve at any pains to disguise his personal hostility. Charles Eliot Norton quotes a remark made by him when comparing Hugo with Lamartine: 'Charlatan pour charlatan, je préfère Lamartine.' At the date of his Académie Reception Hugo had become the 'jeune et illustre Caliban'. The situation was complicated by Hugo's own liaison with Juliette Drouet which began about the same time, 1830, as Sainte-Beuve's attraction to Madame Hugo. Of this, no doubt, Sainte-Beuve made what use he could in pressing his attentions. His privately printed *Livre d'Amour* of 1833 was intended to convey the impression that he was Madame Hugo's lover, a fact which did not prevent him from calling on Victor Hugo to support his candidature for the Académie, which he did in 1844. There was much drama, therefore, behind the Address in Reply. It is said, and often with truth, that Hugo was no gentleman, but on this occasion, at least, he behaved with faultless taste. Sainte-Beuve was occupying the *fauteuil* of Delavigne, who had stood as a drama-tist for the classical tradition, and had had no dealings with Hugo and his school. The position was, therefore, doubly deli-cate, and the reader is tempted to wonder whether in any other language it would be possible to say so much with such graceful and harmonious felicity without the appearance of crude in-sincerity.

When Hugo, having spoken of Delavigne, turns to deal with Sainte-Beuve, he says that in choosing him the Académie has done well.

Poète, dans ce siècle où la poésie est si haute, si puissante et si féconde, entre la messénienne épique et l'élégie lyrique, entre Casimir Delavigne qui est si noble et Lamartine qui est si grand, vous avez su dans le demi-jour découvrir un sentier qui est le vôtre et créer une élégie qui est vous-même. Vous avez donné à certains épanchements de l'âme un accent nouveau. Votre vers, presque toujours douloureux, souvent profond, va chercher tous ceux qui souffrent, quels qu'ils soient, honorés ou déchus, bons ou méchants.

Comme romancier, vous avez sondé des côtés inconnus de la vie possible, et dans vos analyses patientes et neuves on sent toujours cette force secrète qui se cache dans la grâce de votre talent. Comme philosophe, vous avez confronté tous les systèmes; comme critique, vous avez étudié toutes les littératures.

Par vos recherches sur la langue, par la souplesse et la variété de votre esprit, par la vivacité de vos idées toujours fines, souvent fécondes, par ce mélange d'érudition et d'imagination qui fait qu'en vous le poète ne disparaît jamais tout à fait sous le critique, et le critique ne dépouille jamais entièrement le poète, vous rappelez à l'Académie un de ses membres les plus chers et les plus regrettés, ce bon et charmant Nodier, qui était si supérieur et si doux.

Then by easy transition from La Fontaine and Nodier he proceeds to speak of the Hotel de Rambouillet and Port-Royal, and concludes with some further gracious words on Delavigne. These three Académie addresses, indeed, though dismissed in comparatively few words by Biré and by Hugo's English biographer, Davidson,[1] seem, on the contrary, to merit careful attention from any student of his life and character, quite apart from their perfection of form.

IV

When one turns from his parliamentary and academic speeches to the general *corpus* of his public addresses as collected in *Actes et Paroles*, the first impression is as to the wide field they cover. Political education, child welfare, freedom of the Press, the death penalty, the rights of women, trade marks, national defence, the franchise, international peace, by no means complete the list. From time to time in his speeches and his public letters he expresses his sympathy with, or his disapproval of, the Italians, Germans, Serbs, Poles, Russians, Americans, Mexicans, Ireland, Crete, Spain, Cuba, and Portugal.

On many of these matters, it is true, he has little of value to say, though it is, as a rule, said effectively enough. Those who claim that Victor Hugo was a first-class genius with a second-rate mind can no doubt turn to many of these speeches to vindicate that view, but those who have regarded him as insincere, as a poseur, an 'arriviste', a sophisticated rhetorician, in the Disraelian phrase, inebriated with the exuberance of his own verbosity, will find little justification for that view in these speeches. The opinions of Victor Hugo develop no more and no less than is usual in a man who during many years plays a prominent part in public life; and, in his case, behind the development

---

[1] *Victor Hugo*, by A. F. Davidson. Eveleigh Nash, 1912.

of opinion we may yet find fundamental consistency of stand-point. In religion Hugo started as a Catholic, and by the time he died he had become a Deist. It is a gradual evolution due largely to his disgust with Papal policy, his personal dislike of Catholic leaders in France, his contempt for their views, and his mistrust of their influence on the foreign policy of the Empire. But as his belief in the Church failed his belief in God grew greater, and in later years he lost no opportunity of pro-claiming it.

And side by side with his Deism he shows himself consis-tently humanitarian. He is often enough unpractical and has no sense of proportion, but he did not vary, he developed. From first to last he was a consistent opponent of the death penalty. Pity for the poor, which underlies so much of his writing, mani-fests itself in the burning indignation aroused in him by harsh or oppressive government. Not least we may remark that he was all his life a believer in the brotherhood of nations, though he remained very much a Frenchman. Of all the strange docu-ments which came from his pen, perhaps the strangest was the address to the Germans, which he issued during the early days of September 1870 when they were advancing on Paris. It is a caricature of his own style.

Allemands, celui qui vous parle est un ami.

Il y a trois ans, à l'époque de l'Exposition de 1867, du fond l'exil, je vous souhaitais la bienvenue dans votre ville.

Quelle ville?

Paris.

Car Paris ne nous appartient pas à nous seuls. Paris est à vous autant qu'à nous. Berlin, Vienne, Dresde, Munich, Stuttgart, sont vos capitales; Paris est votre centre. C'est à Paris que l'on sent vivre l'Europe. Paris est la ville des hommes. Il y a eu Athènes, il y a eu Rome, et il y a Paris.

Paris n'est autre chose qu'une immense hospitalité.

Aujourd'hui vous y revenez.

Comment?

En frères, comme il y a trois ans?

Non, en ennemis.

Pourquoi?

And so on. It concludes:

Maintenant, j'ai dit. Allemands, si vous persistez, soit, vous êtes avertis. Faites, allez, attaquez la muraille de Paris. Sous vos bombes et vos mitrailles, elle se défendra. Quant à moi, vieillard, j'y serai, sans armes. Il me convient d'être avec les peuples qui meurent, je vous plains d'être avec les rois qui tuent.

This only repeats what he had said much more effectively in his Proclamation to the Army at the time of the *Coup d'état*.

Soldats! c'est un faux Napoléon.

Tournez vos yeux sur la vraie fonction de l'armée française. Protéger la patrie, propager la révolution, délivrer les peuples, soutenir les nationalités, affranchir le continent, briser les chaînes partout, défendre partout le droit, voilà votre rôle parmi les armées d'Europe; vous êtes dignes des grands champs de bataille.

Soldats! l'armée française est l'avant-garde de l'humanité.

Tennyson rightly called him in his sonnet 'French of the French'. For him humanity often meant France and France meant Paris. His attitude towards Goethe is significant and characteristic. He was not merely jealous of a reputation as world-wide as his own. It was rather that he could not understand Goethe's attitude towards politics. He was 'not a good German'. 'Je regarde Goethe comme Jeanne d'Arc aurait regardé Messaline'—a judgement delivered, so we are told, in authoritative and serenely unchallengeable tone.[1]

His speech of August 21st, 1849, at the opening of the Peace Conference, of which he was President and Mr. Cobden Vice-President, contains much that has been said again and again during the last eighty years by earnest men. The two final paragraphs may be quoted. The last but one might well have provided a peroration for any statesman in any country at any time since 1918; only the last paragraph of all proclaims the speaker beyond a doubt.

Désormais, le but de la politique grande, de la politique vraie, le voici: faire reconnaître toutes les nationalités, restaurer l'unité historique des peuples et rallier cette unité à la civilisation par la paix, élargir

---

[1] *Memoirs and Notes.* Colvin, Arnold, 1911.

sans cesse le groupe civilisé, donner le bon exemple aux peuples encore barbares, substituer les arbitrages aux batailles; enfin, et ceci résume tout, faire prononcer par la justice le dernier mot que l'ancien monde faisait prononcer par la force. (Profonde sensation.)

Messieurs, je le dis en terminant, et que cette pensée nous encourage, ce n'est pas d'aujourd'hui que le genre humain est en marche dans cette voie providentielle. Dans notre vieille Europe, l'Angleterre a fait le premier pas, et par son exemple séculaire elle a dit aux peuples: Vous êtes libres. La France a fait le second pas, et elle a dit aux peuples: Vous êtes souverains. Maintenant faisons le troisième pas, et tous ensemble, France, Angleterre, Belgique, Allemagne, Italie, Europe, Amérique, disons aux peuples: Vous êtes frères! (Immense acclamation.—L'orateur se rassied au milieu des applaudissements.)

Another piece of Hugoesque eloquence is the speech of November 20th 1853 at the dinner to celebrate the anniversary of the Polish Revolution.

Ô Polonais, je vous le dis du fond de l'âme, je vous admire. Vous êtes les aînés de la persécution. Cette coupe d'amertume où nous buvons aujourd'hui nous y trouvons la trace de vos lèvres. Vous portez les chevrons de l'exil. Vos frères sont en Sibérie comme les nôtres sont en Afrique. Bannis de Pologne, les proscrits de France vous saluent.

Nous saluons ton histoire, peuple polonais, bon peuple! Lève la tête dans ton accablement. Tu es grand, gisant sur le fumier russe. Ô Job des nations, tes plaies sont des gloires.

Nous saluons ton histoire et l'histoire de tous les peuples qui ont souffert et qui ont lutté.

Quand les tyrans ont scellé sur un peuple la pierre du tombeau, qu'est-ce qu'ils ont fait? Ils croient avoir enfermé une nation dans la tombe, ils y ont enfermé une idée. Or, la tombe ne fait rien à qui ne meurt pas, et l'idée est immortelle. Citoyens, un peuple n'est pas une chair; un peuple est une pensée! Qu'est-ce que la Pologne? c'est l'indépendance. Qu'est-ce que l'Allemagne? c'est la vertu. Qu'est-ce que la Hongrie? c'est l'héroïsme. Qu'est-ce que l'Italie? c'est la gloire. Qu'est-ce que la France? c'est la liberté. Citoyens, le jour où l'indépendance, la vertu, l'héroïsme, la gloire et la liberté mourront, ce jour-là, ce jour-là seulement, la Pologne, l'Allemagne, la Hongrie, l'Italie et la France seront mortes.

Ce jour-là, citoyens, l'âme du monde aurait disparu.

Or, l'âme du monde, c'est Dieu.

Citoyens, buvons a l'idée qui ne meurt pas! buvons aux peuples qui ressuscitent!

To Englishmen, whose capacities and temperaments would never allow them to attempt such exercises in rhetoric, it appears a matter of wonder that speeches like these are acceptable at any time to their audience. It is to be remembered, however, that Hugo's powers of speech were aided by his personality and his fine voice. 'A golden voice', as described by de Banville, 'which charmed all ears.' Sir Sidney Colvin, who knew him in his old age, received a similar impression. His voice was mellow, but subdued rather than loud, and even when declamatory its delivery was serene.

V

But it was probably in his funeral addresses that Victor Hugo appeared at his best, and there are many reasons which account for the fact. Graveside speeches are a special form of oratory greatly appreciated in France. They call for just those qualities in the speaker which Hugo possessed in a remarkable degree. He was a poor debater, ill equipped for the give and take, the thrust and parry, inherent in parliamentary discussions. He had little power of repartee. He resented the interference of the President of the Chamber when that official felt called upon to interrupt his remarks, and he combined great powers of invective with a thin-skinned sensitiveness when his opponents, as they were entitled to do, retaliated upon him. In delivering an obituary address, on the other hand, all the circumstances favoured his particular qualities as a speaker. He could say what he liked, and Hugo was happier in the pulpit than in the rostrum. He was sure, too, of his audience. There were no interruptions to be faced, and he found stimulation in knowing that he could count on approval, which frequently broke into applause. Then again, the nature of the occasion made it proper that he should read his speech, and he found pleasure, as an artist, in polishing his phrases. The just criticism that much of Hugo's speaking combined eloquence of form with tenuity of thought applies only too often to his funeral addresses, but as exercises in oratory they show Hugo always at his most characteristic, and sometimes at his best.

It is, perhaps, only to be expected of him that his appreciations of many of his contemporaries—George Sand, Balzac, Edgar Quinet, Alexandre Dumas—are often little more than mere formal exercises in Hugoesque prose. George Sand had always been a generous admirer of his genius, and wrote to him in Guernsey with cordial and affectionate regard. Hugo had met her only once, and confessed later to having no more than a slight acquaintance with her work. In speaking of her he uses very generous terms, but there is no warmth of feeling. The address on Balzac is again not one of his most successful efforts in this line. Balzac's correspondence with Madame Hanska shows clearly enough the terms on which he stood with Victor Hugo. Like so many others, he regarded the first address at the Académie as a failure, and he was hurt that Hugo did not more actively promote his own candidature. He mocked at the viscountcy conferred by Louis-Philippe. But Balzac never disguised his admiration for Hugo's poems, and Hugo recognized him as a 'grand esprit'. Edgar Quinet had shared many of Hugo's ideas and had been content like him to suffer exile. The address does not lack eloquence, but the appreciation of the man is strangely impersonal. It needed a Hugo to be able to say so much, to say it so well, and yet to leave the impression that the praise came from the lips and not from the heart. With Dumas relations had often been difficult. They had been young together and there had been periods of estrangement. Dumas had never been chary of adopting and using other people's ideas in his work, and Hugo had suffered from this. But we may believe that Hugo was genuinely sorry that Dumas died at the moment when he himself returned from exile, and that there was truth in his statement, 'We loved one another.'

All through his life, from the time when, as a young man, he had resented buying chocolate from Madame de Chateaubriand for the benefit of her orphanage, Hugo was never easy in his relations with the greatest of his contemporaries, however much he might honour them with his posthumous eulogies.

Another feature of Hugo's character that is brought out by a study of his speeches is his lack of humour and his lack of taste. Bad taste, indeed, often mars the effect of his finest efforts. He can, at times, be terribly malapropos and disfigure a fine address with an almost incredible bathos. A good example of this is to be found in his speech at the funeral of Frédérick Le Maître, to whom he was greatly indebted as the creator of the part of Ruy Blas. At the cemetery he delivered a short speech on the merits of Le Maître which was both graceful and grateful. Unable to stop there, however, and no doubt inspired by the huge crowd assembled, he proceeded to indulge in one of his favourite themes—praise of Paris and the Parisians. Le Maître is forgotten in the torrent of political rhetoric. The speech ends with these words:

Ah! peuple! te voilà acculé dans l'antre. Déploie ta stature inattendue. Montre au monde le formidable prodige de ton réveil. Que le lion de '92 se dresse et se hérisse, et qu'on voie l'immense volée noire des vautours à deux têtes s'enfuir à la secousse de cette crinière!

Faisons la guerre de jour et de nuit, la guerre des montagnes, la guerre des plaines, la guerre des bois. Levez-vous! levez-vous! Pas de trêve, pas de repos, pas de sommeil. Le despotisme attaque la liberté, l'Allemagne attente à la France. Qu'à la sombre chaleur de notre sol cette colossale armée fonde comme la neige. Que pas un point du territoire ne se dérobe au devoir. Organisons l'effrayante bataille de la patrie. Ô francs-tireurs, allez, traversez les halliers, passez les torrents, profitez de l'ombre et du crépuscule, serpentez dans les ravins, glissez-vous, rampez, ajustez, tirez, exterminez l'invasion. Défendez la France avec héroïsme, avec désespoir, avec tendresse. Soyez terribles, ô patriotes! Arrêtez-vous seulement, quand vous passerez devant une chaumière, pour baiser au front un petit enfant endormi.

Car l'enfant c'est l'avenir. Car l'avenir c'est la république.

An example of bathos is to be found in the speech dealing with the Philadelphia Exhibition, an impassioned plea for peace and international understanding. He calls the men and women of Paris the ambassadors of fraternity, and continues:

Vous êtes les représentants de Gutenberg chez Franklin et de Papin chez Fulton; vous êtes les députés de Voltaire dans le pays de Washing-

ton. Dans cette illustre Amérique vous arriverez de l'orient; vous
aurez pour étendard l'aurore; vous serez des hommes éclairants;
les porte-drapeau d'aujourd'hui sont porte-lumière. Soyez suivis et
bénis par l'acclamation humaine, vous qui après tant de désastres et
tant de violences, le flambeau de la civilisation à la main, allez de la
terre où naquit Jésus-Christ à la terre où naquit John Brown!

On the other hand, the peroration of the address on Frédéric
Soulié, the dramatist, is striking:

Oh! les nobles âmes de nos morts regrettés, ces âmes qui, comme
celle dont nous pleurons en ce moment le départ, n'ont cherché dans ce
monde qu'un but, n'ont eu qu'une aspiration, n'ont voulu qu'une récompense à leurs travaux, la lumière et la liberté, non! elles ne tombent
pas ici dans un piège! Non! la mort n'est pas un mensonge! Non! elles
ne rencontrent pas dans ces ténèbres cette captivité effroyable, cette
affreuse chaîne qu'on appelle le néant! Elles y continuent, dans un
rayonnement plus magnifique, leur vol sublime et leur destinée immortelle. Elles étaient libres dans la poésie, dans l'art, dans l'intelligence, dans la pensée; elles sont libres dans le tombeau!

There is also the climax of the speech delivered in 1878 at the
inauguration of the tomb of Ledru-Rollin, who had been a member of Lamartine's Government, a consistent republican of the
left. This address is once again a plea for national and international peace, and might have been made by Hugo at any time
during the previous half-century.

Ici la majesté des morts nous environne, et j'ai, quant à moi, le
respect profond de cet horizon sombre et sublime. Les paroles qui
constatent le progrès humain ne troublent pas ce lieu auguste et
sont à leur place parmi les tombeaux. Ô vivants, mes frères, que la
tombe soit pour nous calmante et lumineuse! Qu'elle nous donne de
bons conseils! Qu'elle éteigne les haines, les guerres et les colères!
Certes, c'est en présence du tombeau qu'il convient de dire aux hommes:
Aimez-vous les uns les autres, et ayez foi dans l'avenir! Car il est simple
et juste d'invoquer la paix là où elle est infinie. (Acclamation immense.
Cris de: Vive l'amnistie! vive Victor Hugo! vive la république!)

VI

The speeches delivered during exile strike, as was inevitable, a
sterner and more militant note. Hugo appears to reach his

highest eloquence on occasions when his pity is touched, at the same time that his imagination against the Second Empire is fired. There are addresses delivered over the graves of three young exiles, Bosquet 1853, Louise Julien 1853, and Félix Bony 1854, which are fine examples of Hugo's power of dramatic vituperation. Of Bosquet he says:

Il pouvait revoir la France, il n'avait qu'un mot à dire: cette humiliation exécrable que M. Bonaparte appelle amnistie ou grâce s'offrait à lui, il l'a chastement repoussée, et il est mort. Il avait trente-quatre ans. Maintenant le voilà! (L'orateur montre la fosse.)

Citoyens! aujourd'hui, en France, les apostasies sont en joie. La vieille terre du 14 juillet et du 10 août assiste à l'épanouissement hideux des turpitudes et à la marche triomphale des traîtres. Pas une indignité qui ne reçoive immédiatement une récompense. Ce maire a violé la loi, on le fait préfet; ce soldat a déshonoré le drapeau, on le fait général; ce prêtre a vendu la religion, on le fait évêque; ce juge a prostitué la justice, on le fait sénateur; cet aventurier, ce prince a commis tous les crimes, depuis les vilenies devant lesquelles reculerait un filou jusqu'aux horreurs devant lesquelles reculerait un assassin, il passe empereur. Autour de ces hommes, tout est fanfares, banquets, danses, harangues, applaudissements, génuflexions.

Amis, nos souffrances engagent Dieu. Il nous en doit le prix. Il est débiteur fidèle, il s'acquittera. Ayons donc une foi virile, et faisons avec transport notre sacrifice. Opprimés de toutes les nations, offrez vos plaies; Polonais, offrez vos misères; Hongrois, offrez votre gibet; Italiens, offrez votre croix; héroïques déportés de Cayenne et d'Afrique, nos frères, offrez votre chaîne; proscrits, offrez votre proscription; et toi, martyr, offre ta mort à la liberté du genre humain.

The case of Louise Julien aroused Hugo's bitterest feelings. A woman 35 years of age, and lame, she had played her part in the disturbances in Paris at the time of the *Coup d'état*. She stimulated the insurgents by her poems, and tended the wounded in the street fighting. In fact, she played a very much more active part during the days of December than Victor Hugo himself, whose account of his activities during that period is regarded by many as one of the finest examples of the exercise of his imaginative powers. The facts, which appear to be beyond dispute, are that Hugo was seen cheering the mob from the top of an omnibus; that on another occasion he called out rude remarks to passing soldiers, again from an omnibus. On another occasion he appears to have shouted something to a general when he was in a cab. When finally he escaped to Brussels it was with the knowledge and connivance of the police. Louise Julien, on the other hand, was arrested, shut up for three weeks in a cell, and finally joined her exiled compatriots in Jersey, where she died of consumption. Hugo's address concludes as follows:

Ô morts qui m'entourez et qui m'écoutez, malédiction à Louis Bonaparte! Ô morts, exécration à cet homme! Pas d'échafauds quand viendra la victoire, mais une longue et infamante expiation à ce misérable! Malédiction sous tous les cieux, sous tous les climats, en France, en Autriche, en Lombardie, en Sicile, à Rome, en Pologne, en Hongrie, malédiction aux violateurs du droit humain et de la loi divine! Malédiction aux pourvoyeurs des pontons, aux dresseurs des gibets, aux destructeurs des familles, aux tourmenteurs des peuples! Malédiction aux proscripteurs des pères, des mères et des enfants! Malédiction aux fouetteurs de femmes! Proscrits! soyons implacables dans ces solennelles et religieuses revendications du droit et de l'humanité. Le genre humain a besoin de ces saintes indignations de la pitié. Exécrer les bourreaux, c'est consoler les victimes. Maudire les tyrans, c'est bénir les nations.

Félix Bony, a man 29 years of age, out of work at the time of the disturbances, had joined the malcontents in Paris and was exiled. Hugo's speech on this occasion was very long and discursive. He seized the opportunity to make an attack, not merely upon Napoleon III, but upon tyranny and the war spirit wherever it might be, and he concludes on a lofty note. One who knew him during his years of exile describes the impression he made at the time: 'The voice of the poet, more and more inspired, continued to be heard above the great silence of the land and the wild and terrible music of the waves.'

Oui, les despotes triomphent; oui, les despotes rayonnent; oui, eux et leurs sbires, eux et leurs complices, eux et leurs courtisans, eux et leurs courtisanes, ils sont fiers, heureux, contents, gorgés, repus, glorieux; mais qu'est-ce que cela fait à la justice éternelle? Nations opprimées, l'heure approche. Regardez bien cette fête; les lampions et les lustres sont allumés, l'orchestre ne s'interrompt pas; les panaches et l'or et les diamants brillent; la valetaille en uniforme, en soutane ou en simarre se prosterne; les princes vêtus de pourpre rient et se félicitent; mais l'heure va sonner, vous dis-je; le fond de la salle est plein d'ombre; et, voyez, dans cette ombre, dans cette ombre formidable, la Révolution, couverte de plaies, mais vivante, baillonnée, mais terrible, se dresse derrière eux, l'œil fixé sur vous, peuples, et agite dans ses deux mains sanglantes au-dessus de leurs têtes des poignées de haillons arrachées aux linceuls des morts!

There are several addresses, pitched in a lower tone, which are no less effective. There is the speech delivered in 1874 at the funeral of Madame Paul Meurice. Paul Meurice was a writer who shared in large measure the political views of Victor Hugo, and behind the fine phrases of this oration we may perhaps see some genuine feeling for the lady and for the old friend who had given him hospitality during the siege of Paris.

Que la belle âme, envolée, mais présente, qui m'écoute en ce moment, soit fière; toutes les vénérations entourent son cercueil. Du haut de la sérénité inconnue, elle peut voir autour d'elle tous ces cœurs pleins d'elle, ces amis respectueux qui la glorifient, cet admirable mari qui la pleure. Son souvenir, à la fois douloureux et charmant, ne s'effacera pas. Il éclairera notre crépuscule. Une mémoire est un rayonnement.

Que l'âme éternelle accueille dans la haute demeure cette âme immortelle! La vie, c'est le problème; la mort, c'est la solution. Je le répète, et c'est par là que je veux terminer cet adieu plein d'espérance, le tombeau n'est ni ténébreux, ni vide. C'est là qu'est la grande lueur. Qu'il soit permis à l'homme qui parle en ce moment de se tourner vers cette clarté. Celui qui n'existe plus pour ainsi dire ici-bas, celui dont toutes les ambitions sont dans la mort, a le droit de saluer au fond de l'infini, dans le sinistre et sublime éblouissement du sépulcre, l'astre immense, Dieu.

Louis Blanc had shared many of Victor Hugo's political efforts, and the funeral of his wife, an Englishwoman, must have been a remarkable occasion. Immense crowds thronged the streets, and their admirers seized the opportunity to demonstrate their affection both for Louis Blanc and for Victor Hugo.

For once he devoted the greater part of his speech to the memory of the dead. He then continued:

Vous voilà seul, ô Louis Blanc.

Ô cher proscrit, c'est maintenant que l'exil commence.

Mais j'ai foi dans votre indomptable courage. J'ai foi dans votre âme illustre. Vous vaincrez. Vous vaincrez même la douleur.

Oh! tous, qui que nous soyons, ô peuple, ô citoyens, oublions nos douleurs, et ne songeons qu'à la patrie. Elle aussi, cette auguste France, elle est bien lugubrement accablée. Soyons-lui cléments. Elle a des ennemis, hélas! jusque parmi ses enfants! Les uns la couvrent de ténèbres, les autres l'emplissent d'une implacable et sourde guerre. Elle a besoin de clarté, c'est-à-dire d'enseignement; elle a besoin d'union, c'est-à-dire d'apaisement; apportons-lui ce qu'elle demande. Éclairons-la, pacifions-la. Prenons conseil du grand lieu où nous sommes; une fécondation profonde est dans tout, même dans la mort, la mort étant une autre naissance. Oui, demandons aux choses sublimes qui nous entourent de nous donner pour la patrie ce que la patrie réclame; demandons-le aussi bien à ce tombeau qui est sous nos pieds, qu'à ce soleil qui est sur nos têtes; car ce qui sort du soleil, c'est la lumière, et ce qui sort du tombeau, c'est la paix.

Paix et lumière, c'est la vie. (Profonde sensation. Vive Victor Hugo! Vive Louis Blanc!)

VII

The question may be raised whether the passages quoted above deserve to be called oratory at all. It may be asserted that there is little thought behind them, that they frequently amount to no more than turgid antitheses covering certain vaguely humanitarian ideas. Jules Simon said wittily that all Victor Hugo's parliamentary speeches might have been put into verse. Biré denies that he was an orator at all. He grounds his opinion, first of all, on the fact that Hugo did not improvise. But in France oratory is as it was in Greece and in Rome—an art—and therefore it demands preparation. It was a saying of Lord Brougham: 'The highest reaches of the art are only to be attained by him who well considers and maturely prepares and oftentimes studiously corrects and defines his oration.' The greatest extempore orators in all ages have not disdained to write out their finest passages beforehand. The greatest classical orators, who always prepared their speeches, did so not because they could not speak well extempore but because in the serious practice of an art they desired to follow the rules laid down for it. Demosthenes, who could always improvise well, nevertheless, for this reason, wrote out his speeches. Long passages of the speeches of John Bright, which he called 'islands', were written out beforehand. Even the famous Gettysburg speech of Lincoln was, it is said, written out in the train.

The suggestion that a man is not an orator because he is not an improviser is untrue of any nation, and absurdly untrue of the French. Lamartine knew better. He says of Victor Hugo: 'Une telle éloquence était une grande force que Dieu nous prêtait pour imposer à la multitude.'

The other reason alleged is that Victor Hugo was too self-centred to be an orator. This criticism was well expressed by Alphonse Daudet in a conversation with his son, M. Léon Daudet, not long before his death. He calls Hugo 'le plus grand lyrique, c'est-à-dire, le plus gros *moi*, la personnalité la plus envahissante du siècle'. But this surely does not justify the denial that he was an orator. His parliamentary speeches failed, it is true. They were thought to lack sincerity. His Académie addresses failed also; they, too, were deemed insincere. Nor could it be denied that mannerisms grew upon him and that he found it hard as the years passed to forget that he was the Master. But we may detect real feeling in many of the speeches made to humble people or delivered in support of humane causes. Untranslatable as they are into English, his speeches touched and stimulated the public audiences to which they were addressed. Lord Curzon, in his Rede lecture, quotes a saying of Machiavelli in regard to Savonarola: 'The secret of oratory lies not in saying new things but in saying things with a certain power that moves the hearers.' Judged by this standard, it may fairly be claimed for the speeches of Victor Hugo that they are oratory of a high order.

A further reflection suggests itself. Consideration of these addresses leads the reader to wonder whether after all Victor

Hugo had not more sincerity than is usually credited to him, whether, in fact, he was not more sincere than he himself realized. There has, indeed, lately been a reaction against the harsh view of Hugo which was the outcome of Biré's long and well-documented biography. There were some things in which Hugo consistently believed and there were others to which he was with equal consistency opposed. When he said to those who during the last months of his life endeavoured to stimulate his failing spirits, 'It is time that I ceased to fill the world with my glory', he was quite serious. According to his lights he had sought to serve the interests of mankind. His last message to the world sums up what he really stood for, and it is possible to read into it much of his character. 'I give 50,000 francs to the poor. I wish to be carried to the cemetery in their hearse. I refuse the prayers of all the churches. I ask a prayer from all souls. I believe in God. Victor Hugo.'

In his later days, when, as so often, he was called upon to listen to addresses or poems or messages of reverent eulogy, he used merely to reply with a gentle inclination of the head, 'C'est bien!' France has hitherto reserved the supreme honour of a lying in state under the Arc de Triomphe to three individuals—Napoleon, the Unknown Warrior, and Victor Hugo. Could he have known of it, this would have afforded him great gratification, but no surprise. He would merely have smiled quietly and have remarked, 'C'est bien!'

JOHNSON AND SIR JOHN HAWKINS

FATE has treated Sir John Hawkins harshly. Here is a man who cuts a prominent, if not an important, figure in the life of his time, a man of solid qualities and solid achievements, for whom nobody seems to have a good word. The distinguished personalities with whom he was brought into contact agree in referring to him with dislike and contempt. Johnson himself called him unclubbable, and, according to Madame D'Arblay, while admitting that he was an honest man at bottom, went on to say that he was penurious and mean, and had a degree of brutality and a tendency to savageness that could not easily be defended. It is this remark, thrown out no doubt in a mood of humorous exaggeration, that is remembered whenever the name of Hawkins is mentioned. All the Johnsonian circle follow their leader; and it would be easy to compile from the memoirs of the period a selection of remarks about Hawkins from which it could only be inferred that he was a man with hardly a redeeming quality.

The mutual jealousies among Johnson's friends would provide a subject for an amusing essay; and it is abundantly clear that jealousy lay behind much of the criticism that fell upon Hawkins. Boswell, who attacks him with persistent malevolence, says that he only saw him twice in Johnson's society, and it must indeed have been annoying for one who came to regard Johnson almost as his own property to remember that while he had himself known Johnson during the last twenty-one years of his life, Hawkins's acquaintance with him covered almost exactly double that period. As with Boswell, so with all the others. Walpole laughs at him; Mason considers him petulant and impertinent; Dr. Percy and Malone call him a detestable fellow; Burke would have nothing to do with him; and Reynolds, a man by no means prone to harsh judgements, describes him as mean, grovelling, and absolutely dishonest. The consensus of opinion about Hawkins is too general to allow of any doubt that it was substantially, though perhaps not entirely, justified.

It may be claimed for Hawkins that he was a many-sided man. Born in 1719, the son of an architect, he was originally intended for that profession, and retained through life a keen interest in architectural questions. He was, however, brought up to the law, in which he appears to have attained no great measure of success. When he was thirty-four he married a woman with means, and when later she inherited a fortune from her brother he retired from practice. He sat for many years as a magistrate and chairman of quarter sessions, and was knighted in 1772 for his services in this connexion. But his real interests were literature and music. When twenty years of age he was already contributing to the *Gentleman's Magazine*, and while still a young man his compositions were played and applauded at Vauxhall and Ranelagh. A keen fisherman, he brought out an edition of the *Compleat Angler* in 1760, and in 1776 there appeared his *General History of the Science and Practice of Music* in five volumes. It was an unfortunate coincidence that the first volume of Dr. Burney's *General History of Music*, completed in four volumes in 1789, was published in the same year. The latter work was much the more popular of the two, as is shown by the once famous catch:

> Have you Sir John Hawkins' History?
> Some folks think it quite a mystery
> Musick fill'd his wondrous brain.
> How d'ye like him? Is it plain?
> Both I've read and must agree
> That Burney's History pleases me.

As performed it sounded like—

> Sir John Hawkins!
> Burn his History!
> How d'ye like him?
> Burn his History!
> Burney's History pleases me.[1]

[1] *Grove's Dictionary of Music*, i. 346, edition of 1919.

Comparisons in this case were, in fact, ridiculous. Dr. Burney's was a careful, scholarly treatise on music generally, beginning with that of the Egyptians, the Hebrews, and the Greeks, and going on to the great names of succeeding centuries. As is to be expected, there are many valuations which our own day would not accept, many composers now almost entirely forgotten who receive praise, while such names as Bach and Handel are barely noticed. It was a time when Reynolds himself was valuing the Caracci and Guido Reni far above the earlier masters whom later generations have learnt to appreciate. Hawkins's work was something entirely different, a collection of rare pieces of music with a continuous commentary; and, as Sir W. H. Hadow has pointed out, posterity has reversed the verdict of his contemporaries. Burney's work has only lately been reprinted, while Novello issued a second edition of Hawkins's in 1852, and the one hundred and fifty items he prints are of permanent interest and value. The means brought him by his wife enabled him to purchase the rare works which had been collected by Dr. Pepusch, organist of the Charterhouse, and these no doubt formed the basis of his *History*.[1] He subsequently gave them to the British Museum. Hawkins was Horace Walpole's neighbour at Twickenham, and Walpole had all along encouraged the undertaking. There is a touch of contempt in his attitude: but the work appealed to him as an antiquarian, and his tone is not unfriendly. '[Hawkins] is so exceedingly religious and grave', he writes to Sir Horace Mann, 'as to abhor mirth except it is printed in the old Black Letter, and then he calls the most vulgar ballad pleasant and full of humour.'

Hawkins met Johnson through Cave, and when in 1749 Johnson founded the Ivy Lane Club, he was one of the original members, together with Salter, Bathurst, Hawksworth, Ryland, Payne, Dyer, McGhie, and Barker. Johnson was then forty, Hawkins was thirty. Boswell, born in 1740, did not make Johnson's acquaintance until fourteen years later. The account

---

[1] When Hawkins presented a copy of the book to the king, 'our amiable Monarch' said that he should not like to meet in the dark a man who had no love of music.

he gives of the Ivy Lane Club is therefore inevitably slight, and he mentions but two names besides Hawkins—Dr. Richard Bathurst and Dr. Hawksworth. For information about this club, founded by Johnson, we are told, with a view to enjoying literary discussion and amusing his evening hours, we must look not to Boswell but to Hawkins, who gives some account of most of the members, and incidentally throws light on his own personality. There was, first of all, Dr. Salter, Archdeacon of Norfolk, a man of about seventy when the club was founded. Of him Hawkins says no more than that he was a deep scholar. Next comes Dr. Hawksworth, who had succeeded Johnson as reporter of the Parliamentary Debates in the *Gentleman's Magazine* while still in his twenties; and in his earlier years their relations were close. Boswell conjectures that it was because he resided at Bromley that Mrs. Johnson was buried there in 1752. Literary success may have turned his head; at any rate, it is significant that his name does not appear in Boswell's record of the last eight years of Johnson's life, and when Boswell praised his imitation of Johnson's style, 'he had the provoking effrontery to say he was not sensible of it'. Hawkins, quoting the *Gentleman's Magazine*, records of Hawksworth's narrative of discoveries in the South Seas that he was not a proper person to write it, and that the performance did not meet expectation. He died in 1773, 'some say of high living, others of chagrin from the ill reception of his narrative'. It was also broadly hinted that he owed his directorship of the East India Company to feminine influence. To this report he merely adds that Dr. Hawksworth 'had been taught no art but that of writing, and was a hired clerk to one Harwood'. John Ryland, though mentioned but casually by Boswell, was a lifelong friend of Johnson, who was with him during his last days. When, within a few months of his death, Johnson placed a stone on his wife's grave, he wrote to Ryland: 'Shall I ever be able to bear the sight of this stone? In your company I hope I shall.' John Payne had published the *Rambler*, and was one of the survivors of the Ivy Lane Club who dined with Johnson during the last year of his life. 'Dear Payne' became Accountant-General at the Bank of England. Of Ryland

and Payne, Hawkins says nothing: but the rest of his fellow members were less fortunate. Samuel Dyer was a young man of twenty-four when the club was founded. Johnson thought highly of his understanding and attainments, and he won the friendship of Burke. He was something of a dilettante, who, attaining a small fortune in middle life, promptly lost it. Hawkins devotes ten pages to a vicious attack on his memory, and states that, growing indifferent to the strict practice of religion, he showed 'easy compliance with invitations to Sunday evening parties in which mere conversation was not the chief amusement'. But this was not the worst. 'He had improved his relish for meats and drinks to such a degree of refinement that I once found him in a fit of melancholy, occasioned by a discovery that he had lost his taste for olives.' He refused, when pressed by Hawkins, to write a life of Erasmus; he became a theist, he 'entered into engagements for the sale and purchase of stock, and by violating them made shipwreck of his honour'. It is fair to add that according to Malone and Dr. Percy the picture drawn by Hawkins is greatly overcharged and discoloured by his own malignant prejudices. McGhie was a doctor who came south after the '45, and though a physician at Guy's appears to have met with little professional success. He gets off comparatively lightly as 'one of those few of his countrymen whom Johnson could endure', a phrase which Boswell no doubt duly noted. Even Hawkins realized the pathos of his end: he 'died of a broken heart, and was buried by a contribution of his friends'. Dr. Bathurst was another physician who failed to attain success in spite of considerable attainments, and died an army physician twenty years before Johnson. 'He never opened his hand to more than a guinea', says Hawkins. 'Dear Bathurst', says Johnson to Mrs. Piozzi, 'was a man to my heart's content: he hated a fool and he hated a rogue and he hated a Whig: he was a very good hater.' The last of the company, Edmond Barker, another doctor, was a Unitarian and of the philosophical school of Lord Shaftesbury. The meetings must have been enlivened with many a battle, and so considerable were his attainments as a scholar and a metaphysician that the victory need not always

have rested with Johnson, so long as he was content to use the
rapier and not the bludgeon. But, perhaps because he found the
contests too unequal or too exhausting, Barker's attendances
became less frequent, and though in later life he was Librarian
to the College of Physicians, his association was not renewed
with Johnson. Hawkins, while admitting his intellectual capacity, calls him a thoughtless young man of slovenly appearance,
and when fully dressed a caricature. These, then, were the men
with whom Johnson and Hawkins were associated when the
former was still struggling into fame, and the latter, ten years
his junior, was already fairly well known in musical and literary
circles. It is in reading his remarks on his fellow members that
we are able to understand the dislike which Hawkins succeeded
in evoking. If Johnson called Hawkins unclubbable it can hardly
be doubted that the epithet was deserved. The Ivy Lane Club
came to an end in 1763, and some seven years afterwards, on the
proposition of Sir Joshua Reynolds, there was founded the more
famous 'Literary Club', generally known as 'The Club'. The
original members of this, in addition to Reynolds and Hawkins,
were Burke, Nugent, Beauclerk, Langton, Goldsmith, and
Chamier. These seven years had seen a substantial change in
Johnson's fortunes. The Dictionary, which had appeared shortly
before the Ivy Lane Club broke up, had established his reputation. The *Idler* and *Rasselas* had increased it. He had obtained
a pension from the Government. The members of this club were
not, as were for the most part the members of the Ivy Lane
Club, seekers after fame. On the contrary, they were men of
established reputation or of high social standing, whereas
Hawkins, still unknighted, was known, so far as he was known
at all, merely as a man interested in music, an active magistrate,
and a contributor to various magazines. It is therefore a safe
conjecture that he owed his place in the club to Dr. Johnson,
whose loyalty to old friends and to old associations was already
a marked characteristic. Had the members of the new club been
acquainted with the members of the old, it is doubtful, to say the
least, whether they would have accepted Hawkins: and, as it was,
they soon found him out. Hawkins gives two reasons for his

withdrawal from it: first, that the meetings continued too late
in the evening, and next that he 'foresaw the impossibility of
preventing the subversion of our society by the admission of
exceptionable persons', yet another phrase which Boswell, who
joined in 1773, must have noticed. The real reason, however,
was almost certainly that given by Reynolds: Hawkins was on
one occasion so rude to Burke that he was made to feel at the
next meeting that his company was no longer desired. Rude-
ness to Burke was an unforgivable sin. 'Burke', said Johnson, 'is
the only man whose common conversation corresponds with the
general fame he has in the world.' If Johnson was the outstanding personality of the club, Burke was indubitably the second.
Johnson did not grudge Burke his pre-eminence in Parliament,
for he said Burke was always the first man everywhere, while
Burke on his side was content to allow Johnson more than his
share of the conversation: 'It is enough for me to have rung the
bell for him.' This relation between the two was something
that Hawkins's small-mindedness could not understand, and
more than his jealousy could bear. The incident recorded by
Burney, that he refused to pay his portion of the reckoning for
supper because he rarely ate his supper at home, can hardly
have conduced to his popularity.

He makes, however, an interesting remark about these
meetings of the Literary Club. Though Johnson led the conversation, 'yet was he far from arrogating to himself that
superiority which, some years before, he was disposed to con-
tend for'. The very vivacity of Boswell's narrative, it may be
suggested, tends frequently to give a false impression. The
most extended accounts of conversations which he supplies are
no more than severely condensed reports of symposia which
lasted during several hours. His purpose is to record the outstanding remarks of Johnson, and to quote others only to the
extent that they led up to, or induced him to expand, his table
talk. Hawkins's remark quoted above reminds us that a mental
picture of Reynolds listening patiently, trumpet to ear, Goldsmith scowling in a corner, Burke placidly silent, Beauclerk and
Langton and the rest admiringly attentive while the stream of

monologue flows on, broken only by occasional interjections crushingly silenced, is incorrect. On the contrary, everybody took their turn, though no doubt it was Johnson who gave the conversation its direction; and if in the warfare of words somebody sometimes got unhorsed, or even suffered momentary injury, it was no more than an incident, and the game went merrily on.

Hawkins was not a member of the club founded by Johnson in the last year of his life, the Essex Street Club. He speaks of it as a sorry 'expedient to kill time', and says that it was a mortification to his friends to associate in idea the clink of the tankard with moral disquisition and literary investigation. This is supercilious nonsense on his part. Johnson was old, he was lonely, he was ill. The new club was intended to assure him company on three evenings a week; and the names of the members which Boswell supplies sufficiently show that those he collected around him were thoroughly qualified to enjoy his society. Miss Hawkins said later in her *Memoirs*: 'Boswell was well justified in his resentment of my Father's designation of this club as a Sixpenny Club, meeting at an Alehouse. Honestly speaking, I dare say my Father did not like being passed over.'

Boswell's last meeting with Johnson was on June 30, 1784, at dinner with Sir Joshua Reynolds, and two days later he left for Scotland. It was Hawkins who was with Johnson during his last days, Hawkins who induced him to make his will, Hawkins who was his executor, and Hawkins who arranged his funeral. The friendship between Boswell and Johnson was, it is clear, subject from time to time to interruptions, partly owing to Johnson's lethargy, but even more to Boswell's peculiar temperament. He was ready to sustain with perfect good humour, and subsequently to record, treatment which few other men would willingly suffer, and yet during his absences in Scotland he would write letters which show him to be petulant and exacting. He becomes silent, and a kindly and soothing letter from London is necessary in order to evoke a cheerful reply from Edinburgh or Auchinleck. In July 1779, for instance, Johnson writes to him: 'What can possibly have happened that keeps us

two such strangers to each other? . . . Is it a fit of humour that
has disposed you to try who can hold out longest without
writing?' And again in the following month: 'Are you playing
the same trick again and trying who can keep silence longest? . . .
What can be the cause of this second fit of silence, I cannot conjecture; but after one trick, I will not be cheated by another, nor
will harass my thoughts with conjecture about the motives of
a man who, probably, only acts by caprice' (September 9th).
Johnson's diagnosis was perfectly correct, for in the letter to
him of July 17th Boswell says: 'In a livelier state I had often
suffered severely from long intervals of silence on your part: and
I had even been chid by you for expressing my uneasiness. I was
willing to take advantage of my insensibility, and while I could
bear the experiment, to try whether your affection for me would,
after an unusual silence on my part, make you write first. . . .
I shall never again put you to any test.' During the summer and
autumn of 1784 Johnson was failing: at any rate, he was not well
enough for any more tests. It is noteworthy that Boswell, once
he had left London, can quote no more of his own letters to Johnson, and only one from Johnson to himself. Boswell himself
frankly admits that owing to ill-health he wrote but rarely.
'Having conjured him not to do me the injustice of charging me
with affectation I was with much regret long silent.' In his final
letter to Boswell (November 5th) Johnson writes: 'Are you sick
or are you sullen? Whatever be the reason, if it be less than
necessity drive it away: and of the short life that we have, make
the best use for yourself and your friends.' Boswell comments on
this: 'Yet it was not a little painful to me to find that in a paragraph of this letter, which I have omitted, he still persevered in
arraigning me as before, which was strange in him who had so
much experience of what I suffered. I, however, wrote to him
two as kind letters as I could: the last of which came too late to
be read by him, for his illness increased more rapidly upon him
than I had apprehended; but I had the consolation of being informed that he spoke of me on his deathbed with affection, and
I look forward with humble hope of renewing our friendship
in another world.' Though there is something very touching in

the phrasing of these sentences, it is significant that with the
alarming details contained in Johnson's letter of November 5th
before him Boswell yet made no attempt to undertake the four
days' journey to London. Mr. Percy Fitzgerald conjectures that
though Johnson had been ailing so long, Boswell failed to realize
that the end was indeed at hand, or that, being in one of his
frequent moods of depression, he could not face the death-bed
of his friend. But he also points out that during his last visit to
London Boswell was less frequently than hitherto in Johnson's
society, and that he had ceased to keep the same detailed reports
of his friend's conversation. However this may be, in the codicil
to his will Johnson made bequests of books to certain of his
friends, and Hawkins's name stands first on the list. He received
the *Annales Ecclesiastici* of Baronius, Holinshed's and Stowe's
Chronicles, and an octavo Prayer Book. The names of Dr.
Burney, Dr. Taylor, Dr. Adams, and Boswell himself are all
omitted, but this is no doubt due to the fact that the codicil was
signed only five days before death. Boswell remarks that 'by
assiduous attendance upon Johnson in his last illness [Hawkins]
obtained the office of one of his executors, in consequence of
which the booksellers of London employed him to publish an
edition of Dr. Johnson's works and to write his life'. The implication here is clearly that Hawkins forced himself upon Johnson when he was dying in order to serve his own ends, to obtain
the office of executor and to write his life. Hawkins was one of
those unfortunate people who, even when they do the right
thing, do it in the wrong way. But he was a lawyer, and felt
himself justified in urging Johnson to make his will. He was a
man of standing and repute well fitted to be an executor; he was
an author and an editor who had known Johnson well during
thirty-five years. It is, therefore, not strange that the booksellers should invite him to write a life and to edit the works,
galling though it might be to Boswell away in Scotland, sulking
or indifferent. One might indeed have thought that Hawkins was
treated by his contemporaries with gross unfairness were it not
that he is one of that great company who have committed the
fatal error of writing a book. It is sufficient to read his *Life of*

Johnson for any one to be able to judge with a considerable measure of accuracy how much truth there was in the charges so freely brought against him. The answer can only be that there was a great deal.

It is perhaps curious that Hawkins's *Life*, which appeared in 1787, three years after Johnson's death, has never been reprinted *in extenso*. Dr. Birkbeck Hill gives about fifty-four pages to it in his *Johnsonian Miscellanies*, a substantial portion of which is taken up by his own excellent, if somewhat discursive, notes. With all its serious faults the book throws light on many things besides the opinions of Hawkins. Its very discursiveness, naturally irritating to those contemporaries eager to read about Johnson, gives it an interest of its own for readers of to-day. Discursive it undeniably is. There is an account of a Portuguese mission to Abyssinia, and a dissertation on the decline of British watchmaking. Long quotations are given from Urquhart's *Life of the Admirable Crichton*, and a statement as to the respective rights of debtor and creditor. We are given the author's views as to the proportions of columns, and as to the respective merits and defects of Fielding, Smollet, and Richardson. Among other things dealt with—sometimes in considerable detail—are the humanity of the law and its tenderness to felons, life in St. Kilda, the weakness and difficulties of the medical profession, the first Prayer Book of Edward VI, the gradual improvement in public morals, the failings of authors, Jonas Hanway's *Essay on Tea* (in which he asserts 'that the practice of drinking tea is productive of harm among the lower classes of people'), the genius of Sterne, and a perambulation of London. The mention of Johnson's lack of appreciation of Milton in his *Lives of the Poets* is made the excuse for eight pages regarding an attack on Milton's memory and reputation in another quarter. As instances of the Parliamentary Reports contributed by Johnson to *Cave's Magazine*, he occupies no less than twelve pages in giving Lord Hardwicke's speech on Carteret's Address to the Crown praying for the removal of Walpole, and about nine in setting out Chesterfield's speech in regard to the retailing of liquor. No book was ever so outrageously padded. Out of its 600 pages, not more than half can truthfully be described as having any direct bearing on the life of Johnson.[1]

Hawkins's *Life* has been blamed for exhibiting Johnson in an unfavourable light, for emphasizing his weaknesses and peculiarities and inconsistencies; but in fact the picture drawn by Hawkins does not differ materially from the more famous work of Boswell. The qualities and weaknesses of the author are equally apparent in each book: and though the work of Hawkins is no more than a sketch, it supplies something that is lacking in the more finished portrait, and in no particular contradicts it. Whether either author, or all the contemporary writers put together, have given posterity a correct impression of Johnson raises an interesting question. It was Hawkins himself who described him as 'the most humorous man I ever knew', and Jowett used always to maintain that he was much more what he called 'a rollicking King of Society' than is generally realized.

Within two years of the appearance of his book, Hawkins was dead. In the spring of 1789 he went to drink the waters of Islington Spa, in May he had a paralytic seizure, and on the 21st of that month he died. He lies buried in the cloisters of Westminster Abbey under a stone bearing, in accordance with his wish, merely the initials J. H.[2] In 1791 Boswell's work appeared and the references to Hawkins in the text and in the notes make piquant reading. Hawkins has made a selection from material afterwards used by Johnson in the *Rambler*. 'But he has not been able to read the manuscript distinctly. . . . It would have been better to have left blanks than to write nonsense.' Hawkins compares the methods of Johnson in preparing his *Rambler* papers with Addison's rough notes for his *Spectator* articles. Boswell remarks that Hawkins was 'unlucky upon all occasions', and that in fact there is no comparison possible between them. Hawkins's *Life* gives, among many other things, an account of the controversy as to whether the arches of the new Blackfriars

[1] It is worth mentioning in extenuation that within three months of beginning the work, Hawkins lost his library by fire.

[2] The Wits wrote an epitaph mocking his pompous and affected drawl:
'Here lies Sir John Hawkins,
In his shoes and stawkings.'

Bridge should be semicircular or elliptical. On this Boswell remarks: 'Sir John Hawkins has given a long detail of it in that manner vulgarly but significantly called *rigmarole*. . . . To follow the knight through all this would be a useless fatigue to myself, and not a little disgusting to my readers.' He considers that Hawkins regarded Johnson's character and conduct 'with an unhappy prejudice'. This criticism arose from the statement made by Hawkins that those who lent books to Johnson seldom saw them again. This, after all, was no very serious charge. Johnson kept a record of books borrowed and books lent, and the record was no doubt imperfect, as such records are liable to be. Those who lend books must face risks. Boswell even states that Hawkins's account of Johnson's last days is such as to 'suggest a charge against Johnson of intentionally hastening his end'. This is grossly unfair to Hawkins. What happened was, according to Frank Barber's[1] story, that Johnson on the day before his death, when he was suffering terrible pains as a result of dropsical symptoms, plunged scissors into the calf of each leg. Hawkins states: 'That this act was not done to hasten the end but to discharge the water that he conceived to be in him, I have not the least doubt.'

Two further matters may be mentioned as throwing light on Hawkins's character. There were apparently two volumes in manuscript, in one of which Johnson had written with considerable detail an account of his earlier years; the other contained meditations and reflections, also in manuscript. Boswell had seen the autobiographical volume, and had even asked Johnson what he would have felt had he stolen it and disappeared, to which Johnson replied: 'Sir, I believe I should have gone mad.' Eight days before Johnson's death, when looking for a paper containing instructions to his executors, Hawkins, according to his own story, came across these volumes and put them in his pocket, at the same time informing Langton and Strahan. He did this because he was informed by Frank Barber that 'a joint proprietor of a newspaper, well known among the booksellers', was anxious to obtain access to Johnson, and might misuse

[1] Johnson's negro servant.

documents he found lying about. Hawkins admitted to Johnson
that he had taken the books, and gave his reasons. He even
wrote an apology the next day, to which Johnson replied, 'If I
was not satisfied with this, I must be a savage.' Boswell's
account makes Hawkins look like a thief detected in his larceny;
and even Dr. Birkbeck Hill speaks of him as being 'detected' in
pocketing the volumes. But Johnson's subsequent conduct towards him was entirely cordial, and it may be no undue excess of
charity to suggest that this was no more than another instance
of the officiousness and tactlessness which were so characteristic
of him. The other incident, about which Porson makes great
play in a satirical article in the *Gentleman's Magazine*, concerned
Frank Barber, the residuary legatee under the will. Hawkins
resented this, and in the postcript to his *Life* suggested that pro-
vision instead should have been made for a certain Humphrey
Heely, whom he calls a 'relation' of Johnson, though in fact he
was no more than the husband of a deceased cousin who had re-
married. Mention of the fact, he says, 'may serve as a caveat
against ostentatious bounty, *favour to negroes*, and testamentary
dispositions *in extremis*'. It is Reynolds who explains this
venomous attack. Barber, apparently, did not choose to do
anything for Heely: but apart from that, Reynolds, together
with their co-executor, Sir William Scott, had insisted that
Hawkins should return to Barber Johnson's gold watch, which,
together with other articles, he had taken for himself. Though
there was no specific gift of the watch to Barber either in the will
or in the codicil, the other executors felt it was fitting that Barber should have this memento of his master. Hawkins certainly
behaved in a petty way, charging his coach hire against the
estate every time the executors met; but executors before and
since Hawkins have charged travelling expenses, and there is no
evidence to show that, except purely as an act of grace, Barber
had any specific title to the watch. It was his meanness combined
with his sanctimoniousness that exasperated his contemporaries
and induced them to put the most unfavourable construction on
his actions.

An obituary notice at the time of Hawkins's death speaks of

his high reputation for abilities and integrity, combined with the well-earned character of an active and resolute magistrate, an affectionate husband and father, a firm and zealous friend, a loyal subject, and a sincere Christian. Sir John could be (or appear to be) all this, and nevertheless a thoroughly unpleasant person. The type is indeed not unknown even to-day. Hawkins was pompous and a prig, and utterly lacked any sense of humour. A man may have fine qualities of intellect and character, but with these defects he is damned. Humble to his superiors, Hawkins's attitude to his inferiors and equals was apt to be truculent. A religious man, he lacked some of the essential Christian virtues. A man of literary taste, he could yet write a thoroughly bad book. We may liberally discount much of the censure and unpopularity which he had to face as being harsh and unjust, but his virtues made him only less intolerable than his defects. Sir Leslie Stephen has summed him up with his usual judicial fairness as 'a man of coarse fibre, not without solid good qualities'. This is more than most of his contemporaries would have said for him, even if it is far below the estimate which Hawkins no doubt formed of himself. But the judgement stands.

PASQUALE PAOLI

I

PASQUALE PAOLI was a great man who played his part on a small stage. That he was *magnanimus* in the Latin sense, that he possessed what are called the Roman virtues, that he showed a *mens aequa* during the extraordinary vicissitudes of his long life—all this was widely recognized by his contemporaries, and has been freely conceded by posterity.

The period during which he was a prominent member of the Johnsonian circle—i.e. between 1769 and 1790—is in fact an interlude between two periods, one long and one short, of political activity in his own island: and it is not necessary to say more of Corsica than will explain how it was that from the moment he arrived in London he found so high a place in the political and literary society of the day.

The troubled record of invasion and occupation which makes up the history of Corsica can have few parallels elsewhere, and at the end of it all the Corsicans remain to-day what they have always been, a spiritually independent race. The Greeks came there from Ionia in 500 B.C. The Greeks were followed by the Etruscans, and the Etruscans by the Carthaginians. Here is at least a partial answer to the question, so much debated, what became of the Carthaginians: for their settlements in Corsica were considerable. Then came the Romans, and Mariana—the site of which lies near the route followed by Boswell—was a settlement named after Marius. The Vandals followed, and then the Eastern Empire. To the Eastern Empire succeeded the Moors, and to the Moors, in the ninth century, the Marquisate of Tuscany, and to the Marquisate of Tuscany the Holy See, represented by the Bishop of Pisa. Then during a hundred years the island was contested between the Pisans and their inveterate enemies, the Genoese. At the end of the thirteenth century the Pope conferred the sovereignty over Corsica upon King James of Aragon, and the Corsicans, after

much fighting, offered their allegiance to Genoa. In all the long
history of their relations with Corsica, the Genoese never did
more than occupy the chief towns and build those towers the
ruined remains of which are so familiar a feature of the landscape. The Corsicans at all times hated them, and found them,
in Horace Walpole's words, 'the most detestable of all tyran-
nies'. The fifteenth century is a record of contests between
the Aragonese and the Genoese for Corsica. The Milanese
then took a hand, not very successfully, and finally French intervention, in co-operation with the Turks, defeated Genoa in
1553. Here, it might have been hoped, was a final solution,
but the Genoese were back again in 1559. The leader of the
movement against Genoa was Sampiero of Bastelica, the William
Wallace of Corsica, who endeavoured to induce the Turks to
interest themselves in the island. For 150 years there continued
bitter discontent on the part of the Corsicans and systematic
exploitation on the part of the Genoese. In 1729 two men—
Giafferi and Ceccaldi—led a revolt, and two years later there
was a second revolt led by Giafferi in association with a certain
Giacinto Paoli and Count Rivarola. By the Corsicans, indeed,
the name of Rivarola is only less honoured than Paoli. Sprung
from the family of Rossi, a name conspicuous among the Italian
nobility, the Rivarolas sought refuge in Genoa from the constant
political turmoil during the fifteenth century. They prospered,
and spread into Spain, Sicily, and the Sardinian dominions, as
well as into Corsica. Count Domenico Rivarola had properties
near Bastia as well as within the territory of the Republic, and,
as was only natural in his situation, he did his best to promote
understanding between the Corsicans and the Genoese. Failing
in this, he unselfishly and courageously espoused the Corsican
cause. His lands were confiscated, and he fled to Leghorn.

In common with Giafferi and Giacinto Paoli, he was responsible for the strange chapter in Corsican history which is
concerned with King Theodore. Theodor von Neuhof was a
Westphalian baron who had served in the armies of France,
of Sweden, and of Spain. In his wanderings he came across
Corsicans in Genoa and no doubt dazzled them with his tales

about his financial association with John Law and his political influence with Cardinal Alberoni. When, therefore, he held out hope that he could obtain assistance for them, they expressed themselves ready to acknowledge him as king. He came and conducted himself with regal dignity, accompanied by German mercenaries. When after some eight months Theodore left the island, ostensibly to obtain ammunition, the Genoese threw themselves into the arms of the French and the French supported them for fear the island would fall into the hands of the British. But again, as later in the eighteenth century, they retired, after two years. In 1743 Theodore suddenly returned under protection of the British flag, but in no quarter did he get the slightest support. He therefore sailed away, to die penniless many years later in the Fleet Prison. His tombstone is to be found, with an epitaph by Walpole, against the wall of St. Anne's Church in Wardour Street. The whole episode is often regarded as little more than a prank on the part of a plausible adventurer, but Paoli asserted to the last that in keeping alive the spirit of liberty he had done Corsica real service. After Theodore's departure there was yet another occupation by the French, and again the island was handed over to Genoa. The Corsicans still showed themselves united only in their hostility to the Genoese, but at last the power of Genoa was waning. At this stage the Corsicans elected two men as their leaders—*protettori della patria*. One was Giampietro Gaffori, son of the leader of an earlier movement, and the other was Alerio Matra. Matra was succeeded by his son Emmanuele, and when Gaffori was assassinated, with Genoese connivance, he was succeeded by Clemente Paoli, son of Giacinto Paoli. Clemente was conscious, however, that he had no powers of leadership, and so voluntarily handed over his position as Matra's colleague to his younger brother, Pasquale Paoli.

Pasquale Paoli was born in 1725 and was therefore sixteen years younger than Johnson and fifteen years older than Boswell. He was born at Morosaglia in the north centre of the island, then, as now, a collection of small hamlets. At fourteen years of age he had accompanied his father into exile after the Genoese, with French help, had re-established their supremacy. In

Naples he was trained in philosophy and economics and obtained
a commission in the regiment, consisting mainly of Corsican
exiles, of which his father was colonel. With them he saw service
in Calabria. The Corsicans at this time turned to one of the few
Mediterranean Powers which had not hitherto interested themselves for good or ill in the island, the Knights of Malta. Against
this the youthful Paoli protested and at the same time sent a
plan of government to the Corsican leaders which impressed
them favourably. It was becoming increasingly clear even to the
Corsicans that unity was the essential condition precedent to
success, when in 1755, aged twenty-nine, Paoli returned to the
island. Thanks to the efforts of his brother Clemente, he was
elected generalissimo. Paoli was justly dissatisfied when he
found that only half the cantons had voted, since he realized that
faction fighting would begin again; and, indeed, only twenty-five
days after his own election, Mario Matra was elected general
by the maritime cantons and turned for support to the Genoese.
Matra then insulted and opposed Paoli with all the vehemence
that Corsicans can display to one another, and it was fortunate
for the cause that he was killed early in 1756 when, with his
adherents, he was making an attack on the Paolists. During the
nine years that followed hostilities continued against the Genoese.
One after another the coastal towns fell into Paoli's hands; and
it was during these years that he was able to put into operation
the constructive ideas in regard to government which he had
so much at heart. As early as 1755 Paoli had drafted a scheme
and had sent it to Rousseau, who expressed his cordial admiration of it; but the ideas were Paoli's and not Rousseau's.
Under Paoli's constitution every citizen of twenty-five was to
have a vote, and every thousand of the population was to send
one representative to the National Council. He tried to eliminate
the vendetta. He humanized the penal laws and he evolved a
code well suited to the social and economic conditions of the
island. He succeeded in reducing crime and disorder and he
kept taxation low. Paoli, in short, gave Corsica a constitutional
government under a president with moderate powers, a constitution which the more advanced political thinkers in many

countries admired as an achievement and welcomed as an omen
for the future. He founded the port of Îles Rousses, to-day one
of the most prosperous in Corsica. But Paoli probably regarded
as his outstanding achievement the University of Corte.
There were four faculties—theology, morals, mathematics, and
rhetoric—and he often presided at the examinations in person.
The university is described as a 'tolerable building with a pretty
large collection of books'. Corte, which was then the capital,
is situated in the centre of Corsica, and is built on a rock where
several deep valleys meet. To this day it is a grim, gaunt town
of steep, narrow streets, inhabited by frugal and hardy people.
A university in such a place is even now difficult to imagine,
and in fact since 1790 the building has been used as a secondary
school.

Many sayings of Paoli have been piously collected. For the
most part they are rather sententious and not very original, but
they show the seriousness with which he exercised his powers
and the high sense he had of his duty to the community. 'I
should not care', he said, 'to live my life over again if I could
not be sure of avoiding those faults which in my previous
existence I had committed.' 'An open heart and a straight road'
is another saying ('*Cuore in fronte e strada dritta*'). And again,
'It is not glory which counts, but goodness.'

The fame of his achievements spread abroad, and his work
was widely acclaimed. Pitt said of him what Cardinal de Retz
said of the great Marquess of Montrose: 'C'est un de ces hommes
qu'on ne trouve plus que dans les Vies de Plutarque.' Alfieri
dedicated his *Timoleone* to 'the noble Paoli' as one who 'having
a very correct idea of other times, would have been worthy to
have been born and to have acted in an age somewhat less
effeminate than our own'. Frederick the Great presented him
with a sword and named him the first captain in Europe. The
poet Gray called him a man born 2,000 years after his time and
remarked of the *Tour in Corsica* that it was a 'dialogue between
a green goose and a hero'. Napoleon—his opponent—said of
him: 'He was a great man; he loved his country.' Cities in
Pennsylvania, Oklahoma, Indiana, and Colorado, named after

him, attest his fame in America. Even Horace Walpole calls him 'poor, brave Paoli', and informs Sir Horace Mann that 'he is much approved in London'. Only after twenty-three years does his tone change. Paoli then becomes 'that dirty fellow', and Walpole remarks: 'I would not send a man to him unless it were his panegyrist, Boswell, whose pygmies are always giants, as the geese of others are swans.' This was in 1793 and is probably due to fundamental misconception as to Paoli's attitude towards the Revolutionary Government of France. Boswell's father's description of him as 'a land-louping scoundrel of a Corsican' may be dismissed as Pickwickian.

But the very success of Paoli's régime was its undoing. Once again Genoa was in despair and once again she turned to France. In 1764 strong French forces landed and occupied the chief coastal towns. Paoli's endeavours to rouse the interest of other nations were in vain. For some time there was a lull in the military operations, and there were relations of formal courtesy between the French commander, the Comte de Marbœuf, stationed at Bastia, and the Paolists. It was during this truce, which lasted for some four years, that about the middle of October 1765 James Boswell landed in Corsica.

II

At the date of his arrival Boswell was twenty-five years of age, and nearly two years and six months had passed since that famous meeting with Johnson in Mr. Davies's back parlour. Lord Auchinleck, exasperated by what appeared to him, rightly enough, to be his son's long delay in making up his mind whether to be a soldier or a lawyer, had instructed him to proceed to Utrecht, there to study law as he himself and (for a time) Lord Chatham had done. In August 1763, accordingly, Boswell left Johnson 'rolling his majestic frame' at Harwich. At the beginning he took his studies seriously, but the romance with Zélide (Mademoiselle de Zuylen) shows that he did not take them too seriously. He visited Leyden and Berlin, Hanover and Brunswick. Returning to Berlin he formed the project of a tour in Italy; but his father, who desired him to return to his studies, would listen to no more than a short tour in France. And then a fortunate thing happened. George Keith, Earl Marischal of Scotland, exiled after the '15, had lately been pardoned and had become acquainted with Lord Auchinleck. The trusted adviser of Frederick the Great, the friend of Voltaire and of Rousseau, Boswell joined him when he returned from Scotland in 1764. With him he travelled to Berlin again and through him it was easy to get an introduction to Rousseau, who was living at Motiers in the Principality of Neuchâtel, of which Keith was Governor. 'Open your door', wrote Boswell to Rousseau on December 3rd, 'to a man who dares to say that he deserves to enter there. Trust a solitary foreigner. You will never repent it.' The visit to Rousseau inspired the hope that it might be possible to visit Corsica, but Boswell got no more from him than a promise of a letter of introduction. He thereafter proceeded to Italy, meeting Wilkes (already known to him) in Turin, and again in Rome. As late as June 1765 he wrote from Terni that he intended travelling with Lord Mountstuart, son of Lord Bute, and Lord Mountstuart endeavoured in vain to secure Lord Auchinleck's consent to the arrangement. But quite suddenly he changed his plans. A letter dated May 30th arrived from Rousseau in reply to an appeal from Boswell. This letter gave him a recommendation to M. Buttafoco of Bastia, who had corresponded with Rousseau about a constitution for Corsica. It adds a curious touch to the story that M. Buttafoco was in fact in league with the French. He was the agent of Choiseul, and in later years, as deputy to the Constituent Assembly, he showed himself a bitter opponent of Paoli and his party. Nor did Boswell get any further introduction to Paoli than the right to show him this letter. But for Boswell it was enough. Corsica was little known, Paoli was a hero of international repute fighting for freedom. To go to Corsica would bring him fame: it was an expedition like visiting Formosa or the Great Wall of China. He therefore gave up the Grand Tour as he had cast aside his legal studies. He threw over Lord Mountstuart and he plunged into the adventure, arriving at Centuri from Leghorn after two days' sailing.

III

Centuri remains to-day the tiny fishing-port it was then. The greater part of the shipping between Corsica and Leghorn passes through Bastia, the largest town on the island; but in 1765 Bastia was one of the ports occupied by the French, and Boswell naturally feared that the Comte de Marbœuf might not give him a passport even though no hostilities were in progress. He therefore worked his way down to Corte, staying *en route* in convents and private houses. Paoli happened to be absent, holding a court in Sollacaro,[1] a small village farther south, and here at last Boswell met him. Boswell showed him the letter from Rousseau and a letter given him by Count Rivarola, the Sardinian consul in Leghorn. Paoli, who, with good reason, feared treachery, was at first polite and reserved, and looked at Boswell with a 'steadfast, keen, and penetrating eye'. He had probably already heard that somebody whom the simple Corsicans regarded as an 'English ambassador' was on his way. Boswell, we may be sure, had done nothing to discourage the interest and excitement that the sudden arrival of this stranger had aroused in the island, and the feeling persisted that the visit was at least semi-official. Even to this day the Corsicans are not quite sure about it, for a book on Paoli published at Bastia in 1921 refers to 'Boswel' as 'an English traveller considered to be a secret envoy of the British Government. In all probability [*selon toute probabilité*] he had no official mission in Corsica.' Paoli's own account of the meeting given to Miss Burney in 1782 is amusing enough and shows that thirteen years after he arrived in England his command of the language remained imperfect.

[Boswell] came to my country and he fetched me some letter of recommending him: but I was of the belief that he might be an imposter and I supposed in my mente he was an espy: for I look away from him and in a moment I look to him again and I behold his tablets. Oh, he was to the work of writing down all I say. But soon I discover he was no imposter and no espy, and I only find I was myself the monster he had come to discern. Oh, is a very good man: I love him

[1] Scene of Dumas's story *Les Frères corses.*

indeed, so cheerful so gay so pleasant: but at the first, oh, I was indeed
angry.[1]

In Sollacaro the conversation certainly covered a wide field.
They discussed history, especially English history, and Boswell
noted among Paoli's books some volumes of the *Spectator*,
Pope's *Essay on Man*, and Barclay's *Apology for the Quakers*.
They argued as to the Being and the attributes of God. They
spoke of marriage and of music and of the intelligence of beasts.
Paoli justified his preference for the Stoic in comparison with
the Epicurean philosophy, and he praised Livy and Plutarch.
The politics of Corsica were not, indeed, overlooked, but it was
probably Boswell who pressed for information on these matters.
Paoli in power in his island is just what he showed himself to
be in exile: the philosopher, the scholar, the reformer, as well
as the soldier and the patriot. In reading of Boswell's visit to
Sollacaro one is tempted to forget that the conversations took
place in a little house with few comforts, in a mountain village
with wild and ignorant peasants in attendance. It is exactly
the same type of conversation which was to be heard a few
years later in South Audley Street or in Leicester Square
when Paoli, in company with many of the greatest figures of
the day, was happy to enjoy the society and the friendship of
Johnson.

Those days, indeed, were not far ahead. On leaving Paoli,
Boswell's health became bad: otherwise he might have pro-
longed his stay. He returned northward by a somewhat different route and sailed from Bastia, after much polite treatment
from M. de Marbœuf. 'Corsica Boswell' reached England in
February 1766.

We are dealing here with the *Tour to Corsica* only so far as it
concerns Paoli personally. It must be remembered that the
tour made by Boswell in Corsica was not a comprehensive tour
like the tour to the Hebrides. If one thinks of Corsica as a
clenched fist with the index finger extended, Boswell saw most
of the area represented by the finger and travelled southwards
to a point somewhere below the centre of the palm. He saw

[1] Quoted in her letter of Oct. 13, 1782, to Mr. Crisp.

nothing of the south or south-east of Corsica or of the wonderful scenery of the west. He never visited Bonifacio. He obtained only a distant view of Ajaccïo, he never saw Calvi. The *Tour to Corsica* was published in 1768 as a sort of supplement to the three chapters of the *Account of Corsica*. About half of the *Account* deals with Paoli and the events immediately preceding his assumption of leadership, and in Mr. S. C. Roberts's edition of the *Tour*, fifty-two pages out of 110 are concerned with Paoli exclusively. There is no doubt good reason why the *Account* has never been reprinted, for it is quite obviously put together out of other books, and the handsomely engraved map, adorned with Boswell's family arms, is in many respects—more particularly from the orographical point of view—full of inaccuracies. But the *Account* at the moment of its appearance had considerable political importance and did much to secure for Paoli a good reception in this country. Burke spoke for the Corsicans. The Duke of Devonshire raised money for them. Shelburne shared the idea widely held in the navy that Corsica in French hands would damage British interests. The Chatham Papers bear evidence how pertinaciously Boswell plied Pitt with his letters about Paoli. Indeed, they must be a delight to all Boswellians. He obtains Pitt's ear for Paoli by quoting his remark, 'La publica fama esalta fino alle stelle i talenti del signor Pitt', and he calls him a 'Pericles'. He informs Pitt that to correspond with a Paoli and with a Chatham is enough to keep a young man ever ardent in the pursuit of virtuous fame, and he remarks, 'with the confidence of one who does not fear to be thought a flatterer that your character has filled many of my best hours with that noble admiration which a disinterested soul can enjoy in the bower of philosophy'.

After Boswell had left Corsica, matters soon came to a head. Paoli had always been content that the island should be under the 'high patronage' of France provided she retained her nationality, just as to-day in the case of Italy and Albania. But Choiseul wanted more. He wanted Cap Corse, including Bastia and St. Florent, the ports on either side of it, as well as Ajaccio and Bonifacio: and when in the spring of 1768 Genoa definitely ceded the island to France the truce was at an end. Paoli won a great victory against the French at Borgo, but in May 1769 he and his levies were defeated at Ponte Nuovo. This disaster has been the theme of much ballad poetry in the island. It means to the Corsicans what Kossovo has always meant to the Serb, and there is something engaging about a people which can make songs about its defeats. After Ponte Nuovo further resistance was useless. Paoli left the country, visited his friends and supporters in Leghorn, and travelled to London. Corsica became a French province.

IV

Paoli was forty-four when he arrived in England in September 1769. Dr. Burney describes him as tall and genteel in his person and remarkably attentive, obliging and polite, and soft and mild in his speech. The earlier portraits of Paoli show him as rather full-faced, but as time passed portraits, drawings, and busts all agree in representing him with a broad, straight brow, high cheek-bones, rather thin, compressed lips, and a long, straight nose: a personality of considerable dignity, with a certain grave charm. He made the most favourable impression on all sides. The King and Queen took much notice of him when he attended their Court. Mr. Tinker quotes a letter from Boswell to Sir Alexander Dick relating to Paoli's reception by King George. 'I have read Boswell's book', said the King, 'which is well written [*scritto con spirito*]. May I depend upon it as an authentic record?' To which the general replied: 'Your Majesty may be assured that everything in that book is true, except the compliments which Boswell has been pleased to pay his friend.' He was received with distinction in Oxford and in Bath. Miss Burney relates how on the occasion of his being introduced he called her—artfully, we may believe—Miss Evelina. When his mistake was pointed out, he replied 'O charming book! it is my favourite studioso for apprehending the English language.' Shortly after his arrival Paoli was granted a pension of £1,200 a year by the Government of Pitt, at the instance not of Pitt himself but of the Duke of Grafton, and on October 10th he was introduced by Boswell to Johnson. Few things gave Boswell more pleasure than to introduce people to one another, especially distinguished people, and nothing could have been more entirely satisfactory than this first meeting. The general began by telling Johnson that he had long held him in veneration, and when the conversation turned to languages (arising from the fact that they conversed, Johnson in English and Paoli in Italian) Johnson remarked, 'Sir, you talk of languages as if you had never done anything else but study them instead of governing a nation.' When Paoli deprecated what, he said, was too great a compliment, Johnson replied, 'I should have thought so, Sir, if I had not heard you talk.' The reader who expects to find much material about Paoli in Boswell's *Johnson*—even with Dr. Hill's notes—is liable to be disappointed. References to him are numerous, both in the *Life* and in Johnson's correspondence, but for the most part they merely record that he was host or that he was one of the company. On only two occasions does Boswell summarize at any length conversations in which he took an active share. One was in 1773 when they were discussing the *History of England* by Vincenzio Martinelli. The remark made by the general that Martinelli was a Whig in his attitude raised a debate as to how far an historical writer, dealing with a foreign country, was entitled to show partiality. The second was the famous and rather terrible occasion, when, as also in the previous instance, Paoli was host, in which the subject of wine-drinking was introduced and Johnson, most inexcusably, said to Reynolds: 'I won't argue any more with you, Sir, you are too far gone.' Paoli appears to have kept the little misunderstanding from developing, for the evening ended with his repeating at Johnson's request a stanza of the *Gerusalemme Liberata*, and the general bade them all farewell after having introduced as a final topic the question of the date of the Homeric poems. Paoli loved to entertain. Boswell mentions nine separate occasions when he was host in South Audley Street, where he lived in dignity with several servants, and where he kept a private coach. To Boswell his attitude was almost paternal. Paoli visited Boswell at Auchinleck in 1771 and they went

together to Edinburgh. On another occasion they had a trip
into Wales, where they met the Thrales and Johnson. Mrs.
Delany gives a delightfully vivacious account of how Boswell,
Paoli, and some others turned up suddenly for lunch at the
Duchess of Portland's, how the duchess was in bed, and how she
herself, then in her eightieth year, gave them their meal and
entertained them in the garden. There is a welcome suggestion
here that the ordinarily rather grave Paoli could unbend on
occasion and, in Johnson's phrase, enjoy a frisk like other dogs.
Boswell, whom he endeavoured to keep away from drink, was
frequently his guest in London. 'Paoli's attitude to me', he says,
'is beautiful', and, indeed, he seems to have understood Boswell
well. He teased him about his journal and about fine writing.
'Je ne puis souffrir longtemps les diseurs de bons mots', he said.
Boswell appears to have venerated Paoli only less than Johnson.
'I ventured', he says, 'to reason like a libertine that I might be
confirmed in virtuous principles by so illustrious a preceptor',
and there is a fine remark in his commonplace-book: 'I had
got upon a rock in Corsica and jumped into the middle of life.'
In his devotion to Johnson, Paoli was surpassed by nobody. It
was in his home that the project of the tour to Italy and how it
was to be financed was discussed, only a day or two before he
entertained Johnson for the last time. Paoli foresaw that the
end was near, and was content that he should eat what he liked
and as much as he liked: 'See how very ill he looks; he can live
but a very short time.' Paoli attended Johnson's funeral, and
is one of the rather long list of those who might have expected
to receive bequests and did not do so, such as Dr. Burney, Dr.
Taylor, Dr. Adams, and Boswell himself. This was probably
due to the fact that the will was made only a few days before
Johnson's death by Hawkins (whose own name comes first),
who no doubt had a large share in compiling the list. Like
many other people Johnson delayed making his will too long.
Paoli, it is clear, impressed his friends in this country by the
dignity and charm of his personality and by the philosophical
bent of his mind. But just as, in Sollacaro, Boswell found him
ready to discuss questions of scholarship, law, history, and

literature while in the midst of grave political anxieties and in the full plenitude of his authority as the leader of his people, so, in the period of his dignified ease in this country, the condition of Corsica and the possibilities of a return there were never out of his mind. There is not a trace of this to be found in the English memoirs of the period: the matter is never mentioned. The occasion on which he visited Langton and his militia on Warley Common and commended the soldiers is the only occasion on which he showed openly the slightest interest in military matters. And yet it is perfectly clear from the French and Italian authorities that all through the period of his exile Paoli was in constant touch with his friends in Corsica, Pisa, Leghorn, Naples, Prato, and elsewhere. When they exhausted their slender resources it was Paoli who gave them financial help month by month. The gifts were graded sometimes as small as 15 francs: one letter mentioned £50 to be divided among three. In all cases he demanded statements of how the money was spent. Some of the authorities speak of his allowance as £2,000 and not £1,200. Considering the way in which he lived in London, it seems hard to believe that he was in a position to supply his friends out of the smaller sum; and it is at least possible that Government or individual sympathizers made him a special and private allowance out of which he was able to assist his supporters. This may explain why it was that he was careful that no hint of his very active correspondence with the Corsicans ever reached his friends in England. Paoli had no private resources other than his modest house and property, which, of course, brought him in nothing during his exile; and though it is only conjecture, the theory of a private and special allowance from the Government explains the discrepancy between the figures quoted in the English and in the French and Italian authorities, and how it was that he could afford to live so comfortably and yet—in complete secrecy—give his friends substantial help. So matters continued until 1789, when the Constituent Assembly declared Corsica to be an integral part of France and invited all exiles to return. Paoli was ready: for he believed that for Corsica, too, the day of glory had come.

V

The years that followed brought only disappointments to Paoli, with France and with England alike, but at the beginning all went well. As he passed through Paris he was fêted as a hero and received by Louis XVI. He attended the Assembly in person and was welcomed as the Father of Freedom. At Lyons, Orleans, Marseilles, and Toulon he was enthusiastically greeted, and landing on Cap Corse he reached Bastia on July 17th, 1790. Among those who welcomed him were Lucien and Napoleon Bonaparte, whose father, years before, had acted as Paoli's secretary. Paoli himself had been godfather to Joseph Bonaparte. Another who welcomed him was one destined to play a sinister role towards both Paoli and the Bonapartes—Pozzo di Borgo. After twenty years of exile Paoli returned, a white-haired man of sixty-five, to be reunited with his brother Clemente and his old comrades. He endeavoured to retire, but his friends elected him Commander of the National Guard of the Department by 387 votes out of 388. His instinct had been sound, for trouble began almost at once. The Corsicans, always devout Catholics, resented the civil constitution of the clergy. Paoli was called upon to put down rioting in Bastia, and his soldiers quartered themselves on the town. Giafferi, whom years before he had supplanted, declared himself his enemy. Buttafoco, to whom Rousseau had given Boswell his letter of introduction, openly opposed the Corsican national spirit and sided with the Government of Paris, as extreme men and extreme courses superseded the idealism of 1789. An expedition against Cagliari failed, the raw Corsican levies mutinied, and though Paoli was not present he was blamed. His enemies got the ear of the Convention. Lucien Bonaparte, then only eighteen, bitterly assailed him, as did the other Corsican deputies—Saliceti, Casabianca, Multedo, Chiappe, Bozio, and Andrei, most of them former friends, alienated in some cases by his moderation and in others by fear that he wanted to become king of the island. The young Napoleon, it is said, pleaded with him that he should support the Jacobins, that the revolutionary fury would pass, and that nature demanded that

France and Corsica should stand together: all in vain. Cambon
in his report of July 11th, 1793, told the Convention frankly
that they might lose Corsica. St. Just accused Paoli of con-
spiracy against the Republic. Barrère attacked him with vehement
rhetoric. 'Pascal Paoli', he said, 'anglais par reconnaissance,
dissimulé par habitude, faible par son âge, italien par principe,
sacerdotal par besoin, se sert puissamment de la langue italienne
pour pervertir l'esprit public.' The suggestion that Paoli
always had at the back of his mind the idea of placing the island
under British rule is without foundation; indeed Lucien Bonaparte, who made it, withdrew it in later life. What the Corsicans
wanted was their independence. Like Paoli, those of them who
were not blinded by jealousy or inheritors of a feud against him
or in some personal way placated by Paris shared his hatred
of the Convention and feared the social, religious, and economic
implications of its policy. Paoli like Voltaire had lived in England and like him had learnt to respect British institutions; and
when in despair he threw himself into the arms of the British
and surrendered the island to Lord Hood, the people for the
most part supported him eagerly. Except for the ports of
Bastia, St. Florent, and Calvi, Paoli and his supporters held the
whole island. History repeated itself, and France, as so often
in the case of Genoa, held effectively no more than the coast
towns. These the Corsicans besieged with the help of the
British fleet, the garrisons surrendered—for the forces of the
Republic were sufficiently occupied elsewhere—and Corsica was
free.[1] The British remained in Corsica just over two years,
and but for their mistakes they might, many Corsicans assert
to-day, have held the island indefinitely. It was not, of course,
a possible solution, but there is much justification for thinking
that the self-government which the Corsicans would have enjoyed under the Crown of Britain would have suited them better
than being saddled with non-Corsican officials from the continent and pressed into the strait jacket of the French administrative system. Paoli certainly expected that he would have
been appointed Governor. It had been at his invitation that the

---

[1] It was at the siege of Calvi that Nelson lost his eye.

British had come, he knew and understood his people, and he already had successful experience in governing them. But his age and his health and the jealousies he would have aroused made his appointment impossible. On the other hand, it is clear that the British Government, busy no doubt with more important matters, dealt clumsily with the Corsican situation. Nor was Paoli's appointment the only possibility. In earlier days Boswell had toyed with the idea that the sovereignty of the island might be offered to the Old Pretender, and now in March 1794 he pointed out to Henry Dundas that he himself had been the first to make Corsica known, and that he was the friend of Paoli. He told the Minister, with considerable frankness, that he considered his own claim 'to have such weight as almost to preclude competition'. In spite of this, however, Sir Gilbert Elliot, afterwards Lord Minto and Viceroy of India, was sent out instead, a man whom Sir Walter Scott calls 'a man among a thousand'. Elliot's relations with Paoli were difficult from the first, though letters in the British Museum show many endeavours to conciliate him. Hood, Nelson, and Elliot are most warm in their expressions—indeed Elliot signs himself 'Unalterably with the most profound veneration and the most unfeigned affection'. Paoli was hurt that he received no thanks from London. He would, no doubt, have welcomed an opportunity of making a gesture of renunciation, but the opportunity never came. Even the portrait surrounded by brilliants, sent him by King George, never reached him, and the Corsicans believed that Elliot had stolen it. Elliot on his side was never easy in his position; he never understood the mentality of the Corsican or the true character of Paoli. His correspondence shows him not merely suspicious of Paoli, but obsessed by the idea that he was not supported at home and that he might be superseded. He tried, as many had tried before, to govern with the consent of a section only of the population. When it was proposed that Paoli should be President of the Corsican Parliament, Elliot wrote: 'I shall regard this election as a virtual deposition of the King . . . it would be as if the Crown were taken from His Majesty's head and placed on Paoli's. If this happens

I shall retire from Corsica at once.' Pozzo di Borgo became President of the Council of State and this aroused the resentment of the Paolists. 'Pozzo di Borgo is an excellent razor', said Paoli: 'it works splendidly in capable hands, but in the contrary case, it cuts the throat.' The *Dictionary of National Biography* states that Paoli conspired for the expulsion of the British from the island, a statement for which no justification can be found in the Wyndham papers or in any books on Paoli or Elliot or in the British Museum. On the contrary, Paoli believed to the last in the British connexion, and his subsequent treatment by the British Government and people are the best evidence of his sincerity. The French authorities speak of 'Sir Elliot' as jealous of Paoli, but it would be more correct to say that he regarded him as played out. On arriving in Corsica Elliot had described him as 'extremely infirm, harassed and fatigued beyond his strength and impatient to return from the scene of labour, perplexities and danger'. On his side Paoli remained mortified, ready to strike a Roman attitude, the victim of suspicion and, as it seemed to him, of base ingratitude. At last King George wrote to him: 'Your presence in Corsica excites your enemies and renders your partisans hard to manage. Come to London where we will repay your fidelity and give you a place of your own in our family.' Paoli accepted the invitation and Elliot courteously bade him farewell at St. Florent on October 14th, 1795. Exactly a year later, in October 1796, Elliot himself left Corsica. It had been nothing but a source of expense and anxiety, and the people as a whole had never willingly acquiesced in British rule. Corsica was reunited to France and became what she remains to-day, a French department, at the moment when the names of the Bridge of Lodi and Castiglione and Roveredo were resounding throughout the world.

VI

As for Paoli, he returned to London, where he lived out the last twelve years of his long life. He was received by the king, his pension (increased from £1,200 to £2,000) was at once

restored to him, and he settled down at No. 200 Edgware Road.
He was a man of 70, prematurely aged. Of his friends, many
of the dearest were already dead: Johnson and Reynolds, Garrick
and Goldsmith and Warton. Boswell had died in the preceding
May. Burney, though still an indefatigable worker, was a
chronic invalid, and in poor spirits, which his wife's death in
1796 greatly intensified. Burke was within two years of his end,
giving the last of his fading strength to his attacks on Revolutionary France, finding solace for the most part among his trees
at Beaconsfield. Paoli still loved to entertain and remained in
active correspondence with his Corsican supporters. His purse
was still open to them and he was somehow able to leave a
substantial sum to his relatives on his death. Although he was
in many respects a Benthamite utilitarian in advance of his time,
in himself he remained to the last a man of his century, and the
century to which he belonged had come to its end in 1789. He
fell ill in February 1807 and died after five days' illness. He was
buried in St. Pancras Old Catholic Cemetery, and his monument,
which stood at the end of an avenue known as 'Paoli Avenue',
bore a long Latin inscription. In the following April his Corsican
friends Giacomorsi and Pietri and his doctor, Barneby, obtained
permission to erect the tablet, surmounted by a bust by Flaxman,
which stands in the south choir aisle of Westminster Abbey.

The story of Paoli has an epilogue. In response to a strong
movement in Corsica, his body was transferred there in 1889.
A deputation came to this country headed by Franceschini
Pietri, one of his descendants. The British Government was
represented at the cemetery when the coffin, with its inscription
'Corsorum olim Dux et Moderator', was handed over. A drawing
in the *Graphic* shows a small congregation in the rather bare
church of St. Louis de Gonzague in Somers Town. The body
of Paoli was received on arrival at Îles Rousses, and from Ponte
Leccia it was accompanied in the noisy and excited disorder
characteristic of Corsican crowds up and along the mountain
highway to the modest whitewashed house—now become a
national monument—standing beside the road at Morosaglia.
Here below the floor of the little room on the left of the entrance

the coffin was deposited. Few visitors call, for Morosaglia is on no main route nor is there much to see, except a room containing a number of brittle and rather dusty wreaths, including one from Queen Victoria, and at the end facing the road a marble bust of the patriot. On the stone which covers the vault in which he lies and on the door of the house itself is inscribed 'Padre della Patria'. And the words used of him with characteristic Corsican exuberance on the day of his final return are still true. His memory is *amata, benedetta, glorificata*.

BYRON, THE LAST JOURNEY OF ALL

HOBHOUSE was at home in the Albany on the morning of May 14th, 1824, when an express dispatch from Corfu announced to him the death of Byron. The news became generally known almost immediately afterwards, and there was a deep and spontaneous outburst of sorrow in the press which can hardly have had its parallel. What is most striking in the newspaper tributes paid to his memory is not so much their generosity as their justice. In recent times it has become customary that obituary notices, following the old maxim, should say nothing but what is good. The notices evoked by Byron's death, while extolling his genius, made no attempt to disguise his frailties, and deplored the melancholy and inconclusive end of his amazing career, while recognizing the gallant spirit which underlay his last enterprise.

Hobhouse has not escaped the gently ironical criticism which is nowadays so often meted out by the younger school of biographical writers. It may well be that he was something of a busybody who liked to manage people. He always wanted to be in the centre of the picture, and he could no doubt be fussy and sententious. It is true, too, that as years went by his progressive and reforming energy cooled. This after all is no rare phenomenon. At any rate he was a man so congenial to Byron that the poet said of him pathetically that he would rather he had never come than that he should have to go, and in his old age Hobhouse wrote of his 'strong affection' for Byron, 'an affection not weakened by the forty years of a busy and chequered life that have passed over me since I saw him laid in his grave'. We can safely accept the estimate published within two years of his death, which speaks of his chivalrous sense of honour, his unflinching courage in action, his genuine love of freedom, and we can forgive, as Byron forgave, his foibles.

It was on July 1st that Hobhouse heard that the *Florida* with Byron's body had arrived in the Downs. It was indeed a mixed company that Captain Blaquière had on board. There was first of all Colonel Leicester Stanhope. Colonel Stanhope, who later became fifth Earl of Harrington, had arrived at Missolonghi in the autumn of 1823 as representative of the Greek Committee. The tragi-comedy of his relations with Byron is amusingly described by Mr. Nicolson.[1] He supported the republican idea for Greece which Byron opposed. Byron was a partisan of Mavrocordato, Stanhope's sympathies lay rather with Odysseus. He was something of a theorist and pedant. A follower of Bentham, he had that great man's lack of humour. His schemes, inspired though they were by an earnest desire for the greatest good of the greatest number, did not as a rule work out very successfully. At the time of Byron's death he had been ordered home by the War Office owing to complaints made by the Turkish Government. It was under these circumstances that he sailed in charge of Byron's body on the *Florida*. Then there was Tita Falcieri, who had been Byron's gondolier in 1820 and thereafter never left him. Byron greatly admired his strength, loyalty, and courage. He was one of the chief figures in the affair at Pisa in which the dragoon who had attacked and unhorsed Shelley was wounded, and for this Tita was banished from Tuscany. The fame of his beard and moustache had preceded him to England and he was a noticeable figure in the ceremonies in London and at Hucknall. More fortunate than Fletcher, he ended his days as chief messenger at the India Office. There was also Dr. Bruno, who had joined Byron at Genoa in 1823, having just left the university with a considerable reputation. Writing from Cephalonia in October, Byron describes him as an 'excellent little fellow', though when the ship was driven on the rocks shortly before reaching Missolonghi, he speaks of him as 'running about like a rat'. But Bruno attended Byron devotedly in his epileptic attack in February 1824 and also during his last illness in the following April. Both he and Milligan, who was in charge of a dispensary at Missolonghi, were young men ('novices' Trelawney calls them, only too truly) who, in the

---

[1] *Byron, The Last Journey*, by Harold Nicolson, Constable, 1924. It is superfluous to praise Mr. Nicolson's remarkably vivid and detailed narrative.

terrible and sudden crisis with which they found themselves faced, lost their heads, as Parry justly remarks in his *Last Days of Lord Byron*. Each in after years told his story, and each story had to face criticism and contradiction. Bruno's account has the merit that it was written at the time; and whatever may be said of his skill, his honesty and credibility are unimpeachable. The fourth of this strangely assorted party was Lega Zambelli, who had been Byron's secretary since 1820, when we first hear of him at Ravenna. It was through Lega that Byron at Pisa made application to be allowed the use of fire-arms, and after the affray Lega accompanied the party to Leghorn. Byron's references to him are scanty and impersonal, but he was evidently a trusted and devoted servant. Finally there was Fletcher. Fletcher had been originally a farm-hand at Newstead and was Byron's personal attendant from 1808 with a few intervals until his death. Byron calls him 'a poor creature' and sent him home after the first journey to Greece as being an encumbrance 'like all English servants'. But in April 1816 when Byron left England for the last time Fletcher accompanied him again. He was frequently a target for Byron's bitter wit, and he was no doubt ignorant, superstitious, and not very brave. But his fidelity was beyond question, and at the final scenes at Hucknall his grief was uncontrollable. Byron was certainly a hero to his valet. Fletcher's subsequent career was chequered, and we finally hear of him in the seventies of the last century as the beadle who patrolled Gordon Square.

On the same evening that Hobhouse received the news, he went to Rochester and the next day proceeded on board, where he found Colonel Leicester Stanhope, Dr. Bruno, Fletcher, and three other servants. The *Florida* sailed up river to Gravesend, and later anchored at London Docks Buoy where he rejoined it on Monday the 5th, having in the meantime, with Hanson, his fellow executor, proved Byron's will. On arriving on board the *Florida* he found Woodeson the undertaker emptying the spirit from the large barrel which contained the box in which Byron's body had been placed. Whether this Woodeson was the undertaker in whose hands the subsequent long and elaborate funeral arrangements were left is not clear, but his competent and business-like conduct on the ship justify one in assuming that this was in fact the case. He had brought with him a leaden coffin to which Byron's body was transferred, and Hobhouse then accompanied it together with the undertaker to Palace Yard Stairs. Many boats surrounded the ship and spectators crowded the shore. From there it was but a few minutes to Number 25 Great George Street (on which site now stands the Institute of Civil Engineers), where in the house of Sir Edward Knatchbull preparations had been made for reception of the body.

Meanwhile the question of burial in the Abbey had arisen. One of the most delicate responsibilities which falls from time to time to a Dean of Westminster must be to decide in what cases burial in the Abbey should be offered or accorded, and perhaps no more difficult case has arisen than that which faced Dean Ireland in 1824. There are occasions when a Dean of Westminster must be conscious that in offering a grave in the Abbey he is merely the representative of the national sentiment. This was certainly the case with Dean Stanley when Palmerston died in 1865 and with Dean Bradley when Gladstone died in 1898. On the other hand Stanley himself had to withdraw the proposal to bury the Prince Imperial in the Abbey in deference to public opposition, and the burial of Darwin in 1882, though generally, was not unanimously approved. In our own day the same remark would apply to the case of an eminent statesman, while it is known that a widely signed request that the honour of Abbey burial should be accorded to Herbert Spencer was not entertained favourably. Dean Stanley himself points out[1] what is often forgotten, that in the earlier part of the century interment in the Abbey had not the same importance in the public eye that it has since acquired. And it is a remarkable coincidence that at a period when the country was richer than it has ever been in poetic genius, one only of the company has found a grave at Westminster, Thomas Campbell, who is remembered to-day for little more than a few ballads. Burns and Scott are buried respectively at Dumfries and Dry-

[1] *Memorials of Westminster Abbey*, p. 299.

burgh, Wordsworth at Grasmere, Southey at Crosthwaite, Coleridge at Highgate, Keats and Shelley at Rome, Rogers at Hornsey.

The case of Byron appears to have been badly handled by his friends. There seems to be no doubt that they wished Abbey burial for him. Hobhouse had understood that, as is usually done in such cases, the Dean of Westminster would be sounded before a definite request was put forward. But according to his own account Murray, quite without his knowledge and without any preliminary approaches, made a request to the Dean of Westminster in Hobhouse's name as executor, which request the Dean 'politely' refused. This not unnaturally distressed him, and he pressed upon Murray to let the Dean understand that the request had never been put forward officially. These interviews took place on Tuesday, July 6th, and although for a day or two longer London newspapers continued to canvass the possibility of Abbey burial, it was certain within twenty-four hours of the arrival of the body at Great George Street that the funeral would be at Hucknall Torkard, which indeed had all along been the desire of Mrs. Leigh. Hobhouse had consulted Lady Byron about the funeral arrangements, but she merely replied that, 'if the deceased has left no special instructions', the best course would be for Hobhouse himself to make the plans.

On Friday the 9th the lying in state began. At no period in recent times have funeral arrangements been more elaborate or lugubrious than during the twenties of the last century, and Hobhouse, Hanson, and Mrs. Leigh between them saw to it that nothing was lacking in this respect. Sir Edward Knatchbull's front parlour, a small room entered only by one door, was hung throughout with black cloth, and lit with wax tapers placed in gilt girandole lamps. The coffin was covered with crimson velvet and is described as having at the head and foot coronets entwined in a wreath composed of brass furniture, while the edges of the case were adorned by three rows of brass-headed nails. On each side were three handles with cherubim between. At the head of the coffin stood four Greek urns containing the heart, brains, liver, spleen, stomach, and kidneys of Byron. The lungs, in accordance with the request of the citizens, had been buried at Missolonghi (see report of the Municipal Authorities quoted by Mr. Nicolson). A contemporary writer who describes the spectacle as 'very sombre' was no doubt correct. Admission was by ticket only, but crowds day after day continued to collect in the street outside. This went on until the following Monday, July 12th, when the final journey to Hucknall Torkard began. The direct route from London to Nottingham lies through St. Albans, Newport Pagnell, Northampton, Leicester, and Loughborough, but the route taken on this occasion, at Hanson's suggestion, though rather longer was no doubt more suitable, since it avoided any considerable towns except Bedford and Kettering, and yet provided inns large enough to house the cavalcade at night.

The fate that has befallen the fine word 'undertaker' is a sad one.[1] But the man who organized the pageant which thrilled Westminster on that Monday morning, who led the procession half across England, who arranged for its accommodation in successive towns, and who carried everything through, so far as can be discovered, without a hitch, was a master of his craft and well deserves the name. From an early hour the streets were blocked with crowds and carriages, the Abbey bell tolled, and at 10.30 the procession set forth. First came mutes on horseback, then pages and six attendants on horseback. Then followed the state horse led by two pages, caparisoned in black velvet trimmed with gold; the rider, who was probably the undertaker himself, bare-headed, carried a coronet on a velvet cushion. Then followed the hearse with six horses and the mourning coach with six horses carrying the urn which enclosed the heart, and a further mourning coach in which were the chief mourners, Captain Byron, Colonel Leigh, Trevannion, and the executors Hobhouse and Hanson. Behind them followed thirty or forty carriages containing private friends. It is noticeable and perhaps not surprising that the attendance, large as it was, was confined

[1] It was used in 1614 to designate a group of men who undertook to secure the return to the English Parliament of members favourable to King James I.

almost entirely to those who shared Byron's political sympathies.
Sir Francis Burdett was there, Joseph Hume, 'Bear' Ellice, Lord
Lansdowne, together with Lord Grey, Lord Aberdeen, and Lord
Holland.   Moore, Campbell, and Rogers rode together in a
coach with Colonel Leicester Stanhope and Orlando, the Greek
Deputy. Rogers, who liked comfort, had been persuaded by
Moore to return to London for the funeral, and it was with some
hesitation that he made the long, rackety journey across the City.
Lord Carlisle, Lord Morpeth, and Lord Melbourne rode together
in the carriage of the Byron family. They alone of the company
did not belong to the Whig Opposition, but their presence had
no political significance. Carlisle had been Byron's guardian
when he was a ward in Chancery. *Hours of Idleness* (second
edition) is dedicated to him by 'his obliged ward and affectionate
kinsman'. Later on in *English Bards and Scotch Reviewers* the
reference is:

> No muse will cheer with renovating smile
> The paralytic pulings of Carlisle.

Finally there is the apology in *Childe Harold*, canto III. 29, when
he refers to Carlisle's son Frederick who was among the killed
at Waterloo;

> Yet one I would select from that proud throng
> Partly because they blend me with his line
> And partly that I did his sire some wrong.

Melbourne, too, an indolent and pleasure-loving man, attended
as a family connexion, for his mother had been a Milbanke, and
must always bear a heavy responsibility in regard to the tragedy
of Byron's marriage.

The strange procession passed into Whitehall and proceeded
by the Haymarket to the Tottenham Court Road.

We cannot (says Macaulay) even now retrace the close of the
brilliant and miserable career of the most celebrated Englishman of the
nineteenth century without feeling something of what was felt by those
who saw the hearse with its long train of coaches turn slowly north-
wards, leaving behind it that cemetery which had been consecrated by
the dust of so many great poets, but of which the doors were closed
against all that remained of Byron.

Moore's diary of July 12th strikes a note of more genuine feeling.

> Was with Rogers at half past eight; set out for George Street, Westminster at half past nine. When I approached the house and saw the crowd assembled, felt a nervous trembling come over me which lasted till the whole ceremony was over. The riotous curiosity of the mob, the bustle of the undertakers &c., and all the other vulgar accompaniments of the ceremony mixing with my recollections of him who was gone, produced a combination of disgust and sadness that was deeply painful to me. Saw a lady crying in a barouche as we turned out of George Street, and said to myself, 'Bless her heart, whoever she is'. Left the hearse as soon as it was off the stones, and returned home to get out of my black clothes and try to forget as much as possible the wretched feelings I had experienced in them.

Among the spectators, from the window of a small house at the bottom of Highgate Hill, were Mary Shelley and Jane Williams, whose husband had been drowned with the poet. Byron had very generously renounced his prospective right to a legacy under Shelley's will, but after a time his relations with his widow had perceptibly cooled. Attached as she was to Leigh Hunt personally, Mrs. Shelley had found his family at Genoa almost as great a trial as did Byron himself. This no doubt lay at the back of difficulties which subsequently developed with Leigh Hunt. Whatever the cause Mrs. Shelley was glad to leave Genoa in June 1823, eleven months after Shelley's death. Many bitter-sweet memories must have surged up in her mind as the procession went by. Mr. Wilfred Whitten quotes a conversation at the bottom of Tottenham Court Road in which one of the parties was George Borrow. 'Whose body is in that hearse?' 'The mortal relics of Lord Byron, great poet, Sir, but unhappy.'

All along the road great crowds collected and frequently interrupted progress. Short of calling out the soldiers there was little idea of street management or traffic regulation in the London of 1824.[1] It was midday when the turnpike near St.

---

[1] Only four years previously the determination of the populace had diverted the funeral of Queen Caroline from the bottom of Edgware Road along Oxford Street.

James's Church was reached. The procession halted, all the mourners left it, the undertaker's party occupied the mourning coaches and, still accompanied by pedestrians, proceeded along the North Road where the first night was spent at Welwyn.

It was on this day also that, when travelling near Brocket, which lies to the left of the road just south of Welwyn, there occurred the final adventure, the meeting with Lady Caroline Lamb. There exist many accounts of this incident. Sometimes it is placed in the neighbourhood of Nottingham where the Melbournes had a property, Lambclose House, Eastwood, near Greasley. Lady Caroline is represented as riding with her husband in one version and as driving by herself in another, and of going into convulsions on recognizing the Byron coat of arms. Prothero,[1] however, prints a long statement addressed to Medwin in or about November 1824 which gives her own account of what happened.

Judge what my horror was, as well as grief, when long after the news came of his [Byron's] death, it was conveyed to me in two or three words, 'Caroline, behave properly, I know it will shock you— Lord Byron is dead!' This letter I received when laughing at Brocket Hall. Its effect or some other cause produced a fever from which I never yet have recovered. It was also singular that the first day I could go out in an open carriage as I was slowly driving up the hill here—Lord Byron's hearse was at that moment passing under these very walls, and rested at Welwyn. William Lamb who was riding on before me, met the procession at the Turnpike, and asked whose funeral it was. He was very much affected and shocked. I of course was not told: but as I kept continually asking where and when he was to be buried, and had read in the papers it was to be at Westminster Abbey, I heard it too soon, and it made me very ill again.

On Tuesday they reached Higham Ferrers and on Wednesday Oakham. Apparently the undertaker rode on ahead each day and made the final arrangements for the reception of the procession. The London papers of the Friday (the actual date of the burial) contain a report sent by him from Kettering on the Wednesday, describing the interest aroused in the various towns

[1] Vol. ii. 454.

through which they passed, and the growing excitement as they neared the end of the journey. Kettering is about seventy-four miles from London, and this affords a good instance of how slowly news travelled even in 1824. It was 5 o'clock on Thursday evening when they got to Nottingham, and Colonel Leigh, the chief mourner, and the executors arrived direct from London. Great crowds thronged the streets, so that when the hearse and carriages entered the yard of the Blackmoor Head Inn the gates were instantly shut.[1] Once again the indefatigable undertaker organized a lying in state. The coffin and the urns were placed in a room no doubt suitably decorated, and the public were allowed to enter twenty at a time.

It seems clear that the feeling in and around Nottingham was one of genuine sorrow and pride. The attitude of the London crowd was largely, though by no means entirely, a matter of curiosity. To them Byron was a famous Englishman. They knew something of the scandals and sorrows of his private life, they knew he was a lover of liberty, and (but quite vaguely) that he had lost his life in Greece in the cause of Freedom. His funeral was almost a political demonstration. It was an occasion for wonder and pity. But at Nottingham it was very different. Byron, they felt, belonged to them in spite of the shortness of his connexion with Newstead: and he was coming home. Nothing that could be done to do him honour was left undone. The Corporation desired to meet the procession at the town limits and to escort it to the inn. This, however, the undertaker refused on the ground that the hearse and carriages would be in a bad condition after four days' travelling. His desire was evidently to get them into the inn as soon as possible so as to be able to put them into proper order for the ceremonies of the following day. This affords yet another instance of the seriousness with which he took his responsibilities. The Municipal Council therefore had to be content to send resolutions to Hobhouse and Hanson through their Town Clerk that same evening,

[1] The hotel stands just off the north side of the market-place and is now known as the Black Boy Hotel. It has been entirely rebuilt since Byron's time, but the spacious yard still exists and the tradition of that great day in its history is not forgotten.

stating that a deputation would attend the funeral officially. Black-edged notices were placarded all through the city, setting out the arrangements. The public were invited to join the procession and were told that room would be found for all who wished to attend, and that mourning dress was not necessary.

On the following day, Friday, July 16th, crowds filled the streets from an early hour. Bells tolled and evidences of mourning were general. The carriages of the nobility and gentry of the county began to arrive in the market-place, a large rectangular area in the centre of the town. Lord Rancliffe, a connexion of the Byron family, rode in, accompanied by his tenantry, and, what would have pleased Byron more than anything else (perhaps the only thing that would have pleased him at all in these elaborate arrangements), the owner of Newstead, Colonel Wildman, attended in a similar way with all his tenantry on horseback. Colonel Wildman had purchased Newstead some seven years previously for £94,500. He had been Byron's schoolfellow at Harrow, and writing to Hanson on December 11th, 1817, Byron says, 'I recollect him as a man of honour and would rather, as far as my personal feelings are concerned, that he should be the purchaser than another.' A letter to Wildman[1] dated November 18th, 1818, shows Byron at his best.

I should regret to trouble you with any requests of mine in regard to the preservation of any signs of my family which may still exist at Newstead, and leave everything of that kind to your own feelings, present or future, upon the subject. . . . I trust that Newstead will, being yours, remain so, and that it may see you as happy as I am very sure you will make your dependants. With regard to myself, you may be sure that, whether in the Fourth, Fifth or Sixth Form at Harrow, or in the fluctuations of after-life, I shall always remember, with regard, my old school-fellow, fellow-monitor, and friend: and recognize, with respect, the gallant soldier, who, with all the advantages of fortune and allurements of youth to a life of pleasure, devoted himself to duties of a nobler order, and will receive his reward in the esteem and admiration of his country.

Ever yours, most truly and affectionately.

[1] *Prothero*, iv. 270.

This must have been a bitter letter to write, for it is in effect the last farewell to Newstead. But Wildman appears to have been a man of great delicacy of feeling: certainly he spared no pains to show honour to Byron's memory at the funeral, and it was at Newstead that the mourners were entertained after the final ceremonies.

Hucknall Torkard—now known as Hucknall—stands some three miles to the north of Nottingham, and Newstead is farther on, about two miles to the north-west. Whatever picturesqueness it may have possessed a hundred years ago as a village has to a considerable extent been lost, now that it has become a town of small houses on the edge of a mining district with a population approaching 20,000. Hucknall indeed, to be frank, is rather a depressing place. But the church stands well, overlooking the market square, and is a good example of Early English architecture, though no doubt little of what is beautiful in its dark interior to-day was in existence in 1824. It is approached from Nottingham by a road passing through Basford and Bulwell. Bulwell, like Hucknall, has become a fair-sized town of ugly, red-brick houses such as is to be found by the hundred all through the Midlands. Basford has become a suburb of Nottingham, and large double-decked trams clank up and down its characterless streets of small homes. Along this road numbers of people assembled to see the procession pass. But they were disappointed. It was determined, whether by Hobhouse or the undertaker or perhaps at the suggestion of Colonel Wildman, to take a much longer and more circuitous route along the Mansfield road through Papplewick passing close to Newstead, and so, turning to the left, back to Hucknall. Thus it happened that though the procession left the inn at 10.45 it was 3.30 before the church was reached. The spectacle must indeed have been remarkable as, with bells tolling and accompanied, and no doubt impeded, by huge crowds, the procession, extending for about a quarter of a mile, passed through the market square, the hearse with twelve large plumes and the six horses equally plumed, the state horse, the mourning carriages, the Corporation, private carriages, some fifty horsemen, and an immense concourse on foot. When at last they arrived at Hucknall the whole church was found to be decorated with black cloth, this work having been carried out by an advance party of the under-taker's men during the morning. Even here one is struck, in reading the contemporary accounts, by the absence of order. In the opened vault a number of lead coffins were visible, and the floor was littered with wood and brass furniture from the coffin of Byron's mother, who had died on August 1st, 1811. These fragments the crowd in the church were able to seize on and to carry away as mementoes. The service was read by the vicar, Mr. Nixon. All was over at 4.20. Colonel Wildman took Hobhouse and others back with him to Newstead, and Rogers relates how he walked in the park with Moore and talked about the projected 'Life'. Rogers had a bitter tongue ('A very devilish old man' Mrs. Carlyle called him) but he was a good friend to Moore, who said of him, 'I always feel that the fear of losing his good opinion almost embitters the possession of it.' Rogers, and indeed most of Moore's friends, regarded it as quixotic that he should have repaid to Murray, with interest, the 2,000 guineas advanced for the manuscripts of Byron's *Memoirs* and have refused to accept any compensation. In Rogers's opinion this was almost too romantic a sacrifice, and in his benevolent way he sought on this occasion to develop a plan for settling the money on Moore's son Tom. It was this son who was the great anxiety of Moore's life and finally broke his heart.

That same evening the undertaker, the hearse, the mourning coaches, and the state horse returned to Nottingham.

What Byron himself would have thought of it all, it is hardly worth while to inquire. If he was not to be buried in Greece or at Westminster, perhaps it was the next best thing to bury him, with the ceremonial befitting his rank of which he was always so conscious, at Hucknall with his mother.

Byron's cynicism about women will always remain one of the charges his reputation has to meet. But did ever man have his lot cast more unfortunately in this respect than the essentially warm-hearted Byron, when one thinks of his mother, of Lady Caroline, and of his wife? Yet a real tenderness underlay his strange and tempestuous relationship with Mrs. Byron; and it was highly creditable to Hobhouse's insight that when the ceremonies at the church were at last over he should have gone down into the vault and satisfied himself that mother and son had been laid side by side.[1]

. . . .

The words of Goethe (quoted in the Conversations with Eckermann) are surely the most generous tribute ever paid by genius to genius.

Goethe earnestly advised me to [learn English] particularly on account of Lord Byron: saying, that a character of such eminence had never existed before, and probably would never come again.

[1] The grave is marked by a brass plate let into the chancel floor, close to the lectern, bearing the inscription 'Byron'. The well-known mural tablet erected by Mrs. Leigh is near the Communion rails on the same side of the church.

SAMUEL ROGERS, THE BANKER POET

SAMUEL ROGERS will always have a place of his own in the history of English Letters, and he will owe it not to what he wrote or to what he did, but to what he was, the friend and companion of three generations of men. During his early years his family associations and his political partialities brought him into touch with the Whig leaders and the progressive thinkers of the time. The shock of the French Revolution and all that it brought in its train, his own love of art in any of its manifestations, his leisurely existence, his delicate health, all combined, as time passed, to lessen his political enthusiasm, though he never ceased to be, in the widest sense of the term, a liberal. In his middle years he was pre-eminently the man of letters, and in his final phase the Oracle portrayed for us in *Table Talk*. As a youth he shook hands with Wilkes and assured him of his father's support, and in his old age he was in friendly relations with Mr. and Mrs. Gladstone. He visited Paris before Napoleon was ever heard of, and lived to see Napoleon's nephew our ally in the Crimea. He knew Boswell, and he lent Tennyson his suit in which to go to Court. He read Goldsmith's *Traveller* on its first appearance, and he died in the year in which Browning showed the full flower of his genius in *Men and Women*. His own writings are to-day almost forgotten. The generations that read and enjoyed *The Pleasures of Memory* and *Italy* have long since passed away, and the handsomely produced volumes owe the place they still retain in many a library to the delicate work of Turner and Stothard, with which they are adorned, more than to their intrinsic qualities.

There is a passage in Byron's *Journal* for November 24, 1813, where he draws a triangular *Gradus ad Parnassum*. Nearly forty years later the Queen, through the Prince Consort, offered to him, 'who would so much adorn it', the Laureateship on the death of Wordsworth; and nothing is more remarkable than the unanimity of praise and appreciation with which Rogers was regarded by the most critical minds among his contemporaries. The one exception was Hazlitt, who never knew him personally.

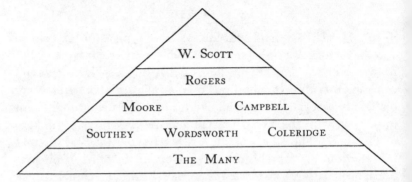

To Hazlitt he was 'a very ladylike poet', 'an elegant but feeble writer', almost to be classed with Mrs. Barbauld and Joanna Baillie and Hannah More. But even Hazlitt came into line later on with the rest, for years afterwards we find him speaking of Rogers as 'an elegant and polished writer with an admiration of the Muse and with an interest in humanity'. This is discriminating praise, and most people will agree even to-day that it was not undeserved.

The life of Rogers was singularly free from incident. He was born at Stoke Newington on July 30th, 1763. His father, Thomas Rogers, originally the manager of a warehouse business, became later a partner in a City bank, and in this bank the poet spent many years of active work. Rogers was carefully educated at various Nonconformist schools, and a Nonconformist he remained throughout his life. At 25 his responsibilities and his profits at the bank were alike augmented by the death of his elder brother, some two years after the appearance of his first book, *An Ode to Superstition, with some other poems* (1786). *The Pleasures of Memory* came nine years later, and meanwhile he had visited Scotland and France. In Scotland he was able to make the acquaintance of most of those who rendered the Edinburgh society of that day illustrious. The Piozzis, together with the youngest Miss Thrale, were for some time Rogers's travelling companions, and left on Rogers the impression that

they were a very happy couple. The *Journal* notes an amusing
and characteristic touch: '[Mrs. Piozzi] said, "You know why
the Scotch wished to send me to the Highlands?" Piozzi hinted it
afterwards and said they wanted her to contradict Dr. Johnson.'
In 1791 there followed a visit to France. It was an interesting
moment, eighteen months after the fall of the Bastille, when
Mirabeau was in his prime and President of the National
Assembly. Lafayette gave Rogers and his party a general invitation to dine with him every day, and it was at Lafayette's
table that they met Condorcet, de la Rochefoucauld, and many
others, most of whom afterwards came to an untimely end. It
was the general view among those with whom Rogers consorted
that the heat of the Revolution was over. They talked of what
they would do when they had finished the Revolution. The
influence of the *Encyclopédie* or of the philosophy of Rousseau
interested them little. Their talk was of Pitt and Franklin and
Thomson and Gray. One man, and one man only, of all those
whom Rogers got to know in Paris, seems to have had some
prevision of what the immediate future had in store, a Mr. Keay.
Mr. Keay said quite frankly that the people were 'the most
barbarous in the world', and quoted what Diderot said to him
on his deathbed, 'Never let a Frenchman come nearer to you
than this', and stretched out his arm. Rogers next visited Paris,
as did so many other Englishmen, in 1802, just after the Peace
of Amiens. The diary of his earlier visit shows that his artistic
interests were already keen. On this second occasion they may
be said to have been the chief purpose of the journey. At the
moment Paris was crammed with works of art—the spoil of the
victories in Italy—and Rogers was then on the eve of the great
event of his life, his move to 22 St. James's Place. The letters
from Paris speak of Canova and David, of Madame Récamier,
the Louvre, the Gobelins, and though he saw his old acquaintance Lafayette, 'silent, thoughtful and melancholy', it is evident
that his main interest was no longer in politics.

It was in 1803, when 40 years of age, that Rogers moved
from the Temple to the house that will always be associated
with his name. 22 St. James's Place was not large. There were

only two sitting-rooms, the dining-room and the drawing-room, the bow windows of which overlooked the Green Park. The dining-room decorations and furniture were based on Greek models. The ornaments on the mahogany sideboard were carved by Chantrey. There was a mask of his master, Pope, taken after death by Roubillac. Etruscan vases stood along the walls. The lighting was subdued. Round the staircase ran a frieze copied from the Elgin Marbles; and on the staircase nightingales were kept in cages covered up from the light in order that they might be ready to sing to him when required. The drawing-room on the first floor occupied practically the whole area of the house. The mantelpiece was executed by Flaxman, whom Rogers rated much above Chantrey, and on the mantelpiece was a glass case full of wedding-cards. There was a cabinet designed and ornamented by Stothard with groups from Shakespeare, Chaucer, and Boccaccio, and a choice library, according to Dr. Burney, of 'the best editions of the best authors in all languages'. There were portfolios of drawings, miniatures, antiques, autographs, curios. A woman's hand in marble stood on one of the tables, and the door-stop was a woman's foot. The walls and the furniture were covered in red silk in order the better to show off the great glory of the house, the pictures. Hayward, a man who reproduced in himself Rogers's combination of a kind heart and a bitter tongue, has described the beauty of the Raphael Madonna which hung on the left-hand wall as you entered. Rogers also possessed two Titians, a small but indisputably genuine Giorgione, 'St. George', a Bassano, two Reynoldses ('The Strawberry Girl' and a 'View from Richmond Hill'), and a Rubens based on one of the Hampton Court Mantegnas. The pictures did not number more than thirty in all, but they were chosen with wise discrimination. Nevertheless Rogers had his weaknesses like other men. Although, we are told, he 'delighted in sweet sounds, in soft-flowing harmonies, he had slight relish for the acknowledged masterpieces of Handel, Beethoven, or Mozart'. When he dined at home and alone, it was his custom to have an Italian organ-grinder playing in the hall, the organ being set to the *Sicilian Mariners'* air and other popular tunes of the south. In this house, except for rare visits to his friends, particularly in the Lake District, and a journey to Italy, Rogers spent the last fifty-two years of his life.

Even in the first volume of the books on Rogers, which the skill and industry of the late Mr. P. W. Clayden[1] put together, based on innumerable memoirs, letters, and diaries covering some sixty years, great figures already crowd the canvas. Erskine was a travelling companion and Dr. Priestley a frequent guest, who admitted to Rogers that he had published more books than he would like to read. Reynolds appears, with his waistcoat all powdered with snuff; and we have a first-hand account of the famous scene after his final lecture to the students of the Royal Academy, when, descending from the rostrum with the name of Michelangelo on his lips, Burke came forward and, taking his hand, quoted the lines of Milton:

> The Angel ended, and in Adam's ear
> So charming left his voice that he awhile
> Thought him still speaking, still stood fix'd to hear.

Mackintosh talked metaphysics with Rogers and toured in Scotland with him; and an epilogue written for Mrs. Siddons cemented their friendship and aided his own public reputation. With Horne Tooke Rogers was intimate during the latter part of his life, though it was a sorrow to the poet that the famous Westminster Election and the litigation which arose out of it should have involved enmity between that strange genius and Fox. There is a quaint passage in a short *Public Life of John Horne Tooke, Esq.*, published in 1812, which goes far to explain the pleasure that a man like Rogers found in his society:

Mr. Tooke had long left off powder, but was still remarkably clean and neat in everything respecting his person. It has also been said that with all those various powers of conversation which rendered his company so delightful to the studious and the 'inquirer' he was capable of all the little attentions that captivate the female world; and that in the company of the ladies, in his respectful

---

[1] *The Early Life of Samuel Rogers*, 1887, and *Rogers and his Contemporaries*, 2 vols., 1889, by P. W. Clayden.

conduct to the sex, he still kept up all that was amiable in the *old*, while he avoided everything disgusting in the *new* school.

Rogers's relations with Sheridan show him at his best. The friendship covered many years. It was to Rogers that the dying Sheridan wrote the pathetic little note which concludes: 'They are going to put the carpets out of the window and break into Mrs. S.'s room and *take me*. For God's sake let me see you!' Rogers's *Table Talk* is full of anecdotes of Sheridan, but there is no suggestion that Sheridan was ever in Rogers's debt, and it is only comparatively lately that the researches of Mr. Clayden have disclosed the fact that he possessed freehold and copyhold properties, in his dealings with which he could always count on the poet's advice.

But of all the personalities who play a part during his earlier years, incomparably the greatest, the most honoured, and the most loved was, of course, Fox. He was no longer the wild liver of his younger days, but had settled down to quiet domestic life and to agricultural and literary occupations at St. Anne's Hill. Eighteenth- and early nineteenth-century memoirs tend to give the reader of to-day an exaggerated idea of the conversations which made so many of the breakfast-tables of the period famous. Lady Holland, according to a well-known anecdote, used on occasion to tell Macaulay to be quiet; but Macaulay was exceptional, and so indeed was Lady Holland.[1] Even at Rogers's table conversation often flagged; and it was only in his own house and among his own friends that Fox, during his later years, would talk with perfect freedom and ease. To Rogers, who was only just over forty when Fox died, he remained his idol. 'Pray come over,' wrote Mrs. Fox when her husband was on his deathbed, 'as I know he will enjoy seeing you.' It is that something in Rogers that made so wide an appeal for so long a period to all sorts and conditions of men that keeps his memory alive.

---

[1] Rogers relates that she announced the death of Fox in her own odd manner to those relatives and intimate friends of his who were sitting in a room near his bed-chamber, and waiting to hear that he had breathed his last: she walked through the room with her apron thrown over her head.

After the move to St. James's Place, Rogers reached the full meridian of his career. With the death of Fox and the reopening of the European war, liberal ideas ceased for some thirty years to exercise any but a fugitive influence on public affairs. He was now in early middle life, well-to-do without being rich, hospitable and well-housed, with a wide circle of personal friends and an established reputation with the public. In 1810 appeared *Columbus, A Fragment,* in 1819 *Human Life,* and in 1822 *Italy,* the work by which, perhaps, he is best remembered and the last he ever wrote. For this period of his life the chief authority is the *Memoirs* of Thomas Moore, in eight volumes, edited by Lord John Russell. As a monument erected by a distinguished statesman to the memory of his friend, it must always command our respect. As a quarry, students of the period will no doubt continue to hack out of it what they want. It must be remembered that the price paid for it, on condition that the work was edited by the Prime Minister, enabled Mrs. Moore in her widowhood to enjoy an annuity equal to the pension on which they had lived during her husband's last years. To Moore as to so many others Rogers was an ever-willing adviser, and if he did not assist him with loans on more than two occasions during a life marked by many a financial crisis, it was only because there was a strain of independence and personal pride in Moore which revolted against such services from anybody but his publisher. It was characteristic of Moore that his two most violent quarrels laid the foundations of two of his chief friendships, and it was characteristic of Rogers that in each instance he played a helpful part. Jeffrey had criticized Moore in the *Edinburgh* in terms which the poet justifiably resented. The police arrested the combatants on the field of battle, but Rogers was soon at hand, and not merely arranged the bail, but, after an amicable meeting at his house, played an important part in the negotiations which resulted in Moore's becoming one of Jeffrey's contributors. The other quarrel arose out of Byron's criticism of Moore's work in *English Bards and Scotch Reviewers.* Moore talked almost in the same breath of accepting compromise and demanding satisfaction, and the correspondence shows Byron to great advantage. Here is the description of the reconciliation dinner:

Neither Moore nor myself had ever seen Byron when it was settled that he should dine at my house to meet Moore; nor was he known by sight to Campbell, who, happening to call on me that morning, consented to join the party. I thought it best that I alone should be in the drawing-room when Byron entered it, and Moore and Campbell accordingly withdrew. Soon after his arrival they returned, and I introduced them to him severally, naming them as Adam named the beasts. When we sat down to dinner I asked Byron if he would take soup? 'No, he never took soup.' 'Would he take some fish?' 'No, he never took fish.' Presently I asked if he would eat some mutton? 'No, he never ate mutton.' I then asked if he would take a glass of wine? 'No, he never tasted wine.' It was now necessary to inquire what he *did* eat and drink, and the answer was, 'Nothing but hard biscuits and soda-water.' Unfortunately neither hard biscuits nor soda-water were at hand, and he dined upon potatoes bruised down on his plate and drenched with vinegar. My guests stayed very late discussing the merits of Walter Scott and Joanna Baillie. Some days after, meeting Hobhouse, I said to him: 'How long will Byron persevere in his present diet?' He replied: 'Just as long as you continue to notice it.' I did not then know what I now know to be a fact, that Byron after leaving my house had gone to a club in St. James's Street and eaten a hearty meat supper.

Byron's relations with Rogers, as with most people, had their ups and downs. It was Rogers who introduced him to Lord Holland, which was a service, and to Miss Milbanke, which was a disaster. *The Giaour* is dedicated to Rogers, and Lady Blessington relates that Byron compared his poems to a flower-garden. 'The Tithonus of poetry—immortal already', he says elsewhere. Within a year, however, there is a change, and in a letter to Murray, Byron says that he continued Rogers's friend 'until the black drop of his liver oozed too palpably to be overlooked'. The visit paid to Byron and Shelley at Pisa does not appear to have improved matters, and indeed it is clear that Byron never really wanted him to come. 'I shall not assail Rogers if he lets me alone; but it is a sad old fellow', wrote Byron shortly after the visit was over. And yet but a few months before he had exclaimed with generous impulsiveness: 'We are all wrong except Rogers, Crabbe, and Campbell.'

With the Lake Poets, on the other hand, Rogers's relations were uniformly happy. He recognized from the beginning the genius of Wordsworth and Coleridge and Southey, and he remained their constant friend, supporter, and business adviser. Southey's recantation of his earlier political opinions involved some coolness between him and Rogers later on, but with Wordsworth, and especially with his sister Dorothy, the friendship became increasingly intimate, though, as Crabb Robinson's diary shows, Rogers characteristically became more critical as Wordsworth's eminence became more widely recognized. Fanny Kemble amusingly describes her experience of 'listening to Rogers and hearing Wordsworth—the gentle rill of the one speech broken into by sudden loud splashes of the other', and Rogers's pathetic complaint, 'He won't let me tell my story.' An account of a visit with Wordsworth to Coleridge when he was living with Gillman at Highgate is worth repeating:

We sat with him two hours, he talking the whole time without intermission. When we left the house we walked for some time without speaking. 'What a wonderful man he is!' exclaimed Wordsworth. 'Wonderful, indeed,' said I. 'What depth of thought, what richness of expression!' continued Wordsworth. 'There's nothing like him that I ever heard,' replied I. Another pause. 'Pray,' inquired Wordsworth, 'did you precisely understand what he said about the Kantian philosophy?' R. 'Not precisely.' W. 'Or about the plurality of worlds?' R. 'I can't say I did. In fact, if the truth must out, I did not understand a syllable from one end of his monologue to the other.' W. 'No more did I.'

Rogers was a naturally benevolent man who found pleasure in being helpful. The passport to his goodwill was to be in trouble; prosperity and public repute not infrequently aroused those acrid comments which lost nothing by the small, gentle voice in which they were uttered. 'I could never *lash* myself into a feeling of affection and admiration for him', says Lady Dufferin. 'He never seemed to me to be thoroughly in earnest, save in expressing contempt and dislike. . . . He gave what he valued least, money; he never gave what he valued most, admiration.' This is certainly unjust to Rogers. That he took pleasure in saying wittily malicious things is true, but it is equally true that he gave lavishly of his admiration to those— like the unfortunate Haydon, for instance—who appeared in need of its stimulus. When he is criticized for often saying neat things but for seldom saying kind things, one may quote in his defence such a letter as the following, addressed to Lady John Russell on the death of her mother: 'May He who has made us and alone knows what is best for us support you under your great affliction. Again and again have I taken up my poor pen, but in vain, and I have only to pray that God may bless you and yours wherever you go.' The man who could write that in his ninety-first year was no cynic at heart.

The last phase of Rogers's life brought him into touch with a new generation—the generation which gave distinction to the later Victorian Age. All the men he had known in his prime predeceased him. *Italy* had been republished in handsomer form in 1830, and a reissue of his poems in 1834 had been final. Thenceforward he was, as described by Mrs. Norton, 'a watch-tower, showing for ever what a quiet port literature and the fine arts might offer in an age of "progress"'. Already, before Rogers died, the public estimate of his poetry was very much what it is to-day. It was, in a sentence, damned by Byron's praise of the *Pleasures of Memory*: 'There is not a vulgar line in the poem.' Poetry cannot live by elegance alone. It is unfair, and indeed, except as regards metre, incorrect, to represent Rogers as of the school of Dryden and Pope. His impeccable taste and what Mr. Roberts[1] has rightly called his 'laborious artistry' were, on the contrary, essentially of his time. During Rogers's later years the wind was blowing in another direction, and it shows the soundness of his judgement that he made no attempt to catch the breeze.

Tennyson found him a kindly old man 'except when he was bilious', and discovered not a trace of venom in his conversation. Gladstone in his diary notes his agreeably discursive talk about

---

[1]   *Samuel Rogers and his Circle*, 1910.

Monckton Milnes's verses, Swift's views on women, Peel's manners, Brougham's eloquence. Ruskin writes to him in the overflowing eloquence of his early style. Only in the diaries of Monckton Milnes (Lord Houghton) do we get a hint of the Rogers of tradition: 'Old Rogers goes on breakfasting but is a good deal estranged from me. I rather think he is the loser by it.' And again when, after a serious accident at the age of 87, Rogers's memory and faculties began to fail, 'Rogers is quite easy in his mind, and not the less so because Luttrell is dying too.' That Rogers was more than a little jealous of Milnes is likely. Milnes was young, wealthy, a poet, with already a great reputation as a host; but the passages throw quite as much light on Milnes as they do on Rogers. For some five years, lonely and half-forgotten, the old man lived on, confined to his chair until the end came to him as he sat in his drawing-room surrounded by his treasures on December 18, 1855.

It was perhaps Thomas Campbell who summed him up most correctly. A friend of Campbell's complained to him that he had been the victim of Rogers's bitter tongue. 'Borrow money of him', replied the poet; 'he will never say a word against you again.'

HARRIET MARTINEAU

I

SOME few minutes away from the Octagon Chapel in Cole-
gate Street, Norwich, which at the beginning of the nineteenth century used to accommodate the Mayor and Corporation
together with some hundreds of worshippers, stands a little
close known as Gurney Court. Just inside the court are two
plaques, one erected in honour of Elizabeth Fry and the other
to Harriet Martineau, who is described as 'Authoress and pioneer
in opening many new spheres of work for women'. In the house
called Gurney House which faces the road Harriet Martineau
was born on June 12th, 1802. Norwich at that time was a city
of considerable importance owing largely to its trade with
Holland, and the trade brought familiarity with the Dutch
Masters. The Norwich Society founded in 1803 by 'Old' Crome
was an art club of men well acquainted with Dutch painting.
Norwich was the first English city to be associated with a school,
and the names of Cotman, James Clark, Vincent B. ('Young')
Crome, the Ladbrookes, Thistle, and others remain a source of
local pride. Norwich claimed also to be a literary as well as
an artistic centre. Few of the names of her great figures convey
much to the readers of to-day, except perhaps that of Mrs.
Barbauld. W. T. Sayers the German scholar, Smith, Enfield,
Alderson, are forgotten. Even William Taylor, the centre of a
coterie which was regarded with serious admiration by his contemporaries, is hardly remembered. Miss Martineau indeed
late in life remarked rather harshly that Norwich was a rival to
Lichfield itself in the time of the Sewards for literary pretension
and the vulgarity of pedantry. But it is certain that she was born
in no sleepy backwater, but rather in an environment which
took itself, its religion, its duties, and its pleasures with despe-
rate seriousness. She was the sixth of the eight children born
to Thomas Martineau, a maker of camlet and bombazine.[1] The

---

[1] Camlet was originally an eastern stuff composed of camel's hair and silk. It

family was of Huguenot origin, long settled in the city. Generation after generation they had been surgeons, and they were consistent Unitarians. Her mother, born of more modest north of England stock and always conscious of the fact, had the stronger character. Knowledge of French was the hall-mark of culture in the Norwich of those days, and this knowledge she appears never to have acquired. From her daughter's account of her she was vigorous, determined, sarcastic, capable, and severe. We are told significantly that in her house servants and tradespeople met with 'rather old-fashioned treatment'. But she and her husband were conscientious parents, anxious to do their best for their children, and even from her own account Harriet must have been a difficult child. She had poor health and, as she admits, a bad temper. It is a common enough state of affairs—a child naturally affectionate, a parent consistently well-meaning, and yet a gulf of misunderstanding between them. The mother was always restrained in her manner: enjoying good health herself, she never realized that her child was often tortured by bad nerves and by indigestion. Dr. Martineau, after the appearance of the *Autobiography*, told a rather different story. He says that Harriet was resentful and seemed almost a stupid child. The picture he draws of the mother is decidedly more favourable. But the two stories are in fact not contradictory: they are both true. Harriet, who was always a most dutiful daughter, never spoke out to her parents, believing they would never understand even if she did. Nor were relations with the other children much better. Her elder brother taught her music and was not too kind. Her shyness, her morbid introspection, made her afraid of everybody; and, as such children are, she was full of dreams and imaginings. Fortunately, being a Unitarian, she was spared the fear of Hell.

When she was eleven she was sent to the school of Isaac Perry, who, having lost many of his boy pupils on becoming a Unitarian

had come to mean a type of light cloth made of various materials. Bombazine is twilled dress-material which used to be used for mourning, made of worsted, sometimes mixed with silk or cotton.

convert, was prepared to take in girls. She gives us a quaint picture of the school, where she read Cicero, Virgil, Horace, and later Tacitus. She describes Perry standing with his powdered hair and raised forefinger reproving a bad exercise and beginning, 'You perceive, Ladies'. It is clear she was well taught. When Perry's successor in the school translated from the *Aeneid* and told his pupils to put the translation back again into Latin, Harriet's version was found to be exactly the original, except that she had *annosa* instead of *antiqua*. She tells us that she even thought in Latin, that she was good at arithmetic, and developed a devotion to the works of Shakespeare and Milton. But the school failed, and at thirteen she returned to continue her education at home. The following three years were clearly an unhappy phase. She worked at Latin, French, history, music, and needlework which proved a lifelong interest to her. It was her mother who taught her to make clothes, to make shirts, and to plait. At about this period there appeared the first symptoms of the deafness which was to handicap her for the rest of her days, an affliction which she bore with such consistent fortitude. It is more than probable that when people complained that she was dull and stupid as a child it was due to deafness in its incipient stages, and it was certainly deafness that made the adolescent girl appear priggish, self-centred, and jealous of her sisters. The deafness gave her a feeling of isolation and the isolation made her unhappy, but her mother never seems to have inquired into the cause of her unhappiness; only gradually did she herself or anybody else realize that she was becoming deaf. When in 1818 she was sent to Bristol to a school kept by her mother's brother, it was because the state of her nerves clearly showed that she needed a change. She was happy at the school and happy in the society of clever cousins, but she was homesick and in the following year returned to Norwich in no better health. Harriet Martineau was still only seventeen, but her character and personality were developing rapidly, and, even more, her views on politics and religion. She grew up during the period of disillusionment which followed the close of the Napoleonic Wars. There was revolution in the air: Castlereagh and Canning were unpopular, Cobbett's influence was at its height. It is not surprising that politics and parties were matters of interest to her from a very early age. And religion interested her no less. From her infancy she had been religiously minded: in religion she had found her chief happiness, and this tendency had been intensified during her stay in Bristol, where she had come under the influence of Dr. Carpenter, who, though he had no very definite religious teaching to impart, nevertheless became her hero and turned her thoughts to philosophy. She, being a Unitarian, naturally read Priestley and went on to Hartley and to Locke. From Locke she proceeded to study the Scottish metaphysicians, Beattie, Reid, and Dugald Stewart. From the time that she was eleven she had puzzled over the problem of the existence of evil, and it was a chance remark of her brother James, her one companion and friend among the members of her family, which led her on to the first definite phase in her religious development. She remained firm in her belief in a special Providence which noted all things, but she became convinced of the certainty of the action of laws and that the workings of the Universe cannot be broken by human will. From this it followed that her prayers began to take on a new form. Gradually she ceased to ask for external benefits or for anything except spiritual good. Christian prayer, it seemed to her, could find no authority in the New Testament. The only petition in the Lord's Prayer that savoured of free-will doctrines was 'Give us this day our daily bread', but she remarks that the whole prayer is compiled 'from very ancient materials of the theocratic age'. She remained a Theist but she was henceforth a Necessitarian, or, as it is now called, a Determinist. For her, man's conduct is the fruit of his antecedents and of his environment. All human actions are the results of surrounding circumstances. To better himself he must not seek for any interference from heaven with the natural laws of cause and effect but he must be content to improve his knowledge and to seek good influences. It was her brother James who first encouraged her in authorship. She contributed to the *Monthly Repository*, a Unitarian magazine of small circulation, articles on 'French writers of practical divinity' and on female education. From this time she became less unhappy. Her mother was kinder, her spiritual doubts were for the moment satisfied, and she became gradually conscious of powers hitherto unsuspected. That same year she issued *Devotional Exercises*, morning and evening sermons and prayers for seven days. These meditations and self-communings freely use the phraseology of the Bible, of which she remained throughout her life a careful student.

Meanwhile there came a slump in the trade of the country. Thomas Martineau was no speculator, but his business was of a nature to suffer severely from the general depression. The speculators dragged down with them many a steady tradesman, and he was among the number. The heavy stocks he was carrying depreciated so that he was all but ruined, and not long afterwards he died. It was about this time, too, that there occurred the one romance of Harriet Martineau's life. The matter is dealt with candidly in the *Autobiography*, as well as by her biographers, Mrs. Fenwick Miller and Miss Bosanquet,[1] but even now the facts are a little obscure. John Hugh Worthington was a fellow theological student with James Martineau in Ireland. James introduced him to Harriet, and there developed an understanding between them which never amounted to a recognized engagement. James, who knew his sister's strong character and arbitrary temper, never believed that marriage could bring happiness to either of them. Worthington appears to have been a gentle, hard-working young man who managed to obtain a joint pastorate at Manchester. His studies brought on brain fever. He was nursed at his father's house, and when Mrs. Martineau refused to allow her daughter to visit him she obeyed. The Worthingtons bitterly resented this and believed that her affections had gone elsewhere. In reply to an insulting letter, Mrs. Martineau (not Harriet) wrote and broke off the association. James Martineau believed that she did so at Harriet's desire, since she could not contemplate marriage with a man who had been mad. Worthington died not long

---

[1] *Harriet Martineau*, by Mrs. Fenwick Miller (W. H. Allen & Co., 1884); *Harriet Martineau*, by Theodora Bosanquet (Etchells & Macdonald, 1927).

afterwards, insane. Mrs. Fenwick Miller writes a good deal
more romantically about the matter than does Harriet herself,
and it is probable that her feeling for him never amounted to
more than friendship. 'I am in truth very thankful', says Miss
Martineau in the *Autobiography*, 'for not having married at
all. . . . I am not only entirely satisfied with my lot but
think it the very best for me.' And she was no doubt quite
right.

After the deaths of her father and of Worthington, Harriet
Martineau wrote more and more assiduously stories with moral
purpose suitable for schools, as well as poems and essays. When
her health broke down she was put under a doctor brother-in-
law at Newcastle, where from her couch she continued to write,
and when she was not writing to do needlework. The famous
preacher, W. T. Fox, had taken over the *Repository* with the
object of improving its literary quality, and he called upon her
services which she gave him at first gratuitously. Articles sent
to other papers in London were returned to her, and these, too,
he gladly accepted, and finally offered her £15 a year for as
many contributions as she cared to provide. The year 1829
brought yet another disaster, the failure of the house of which
her father had been the head, which left the family practically
penniless. The spirit in which she took the blow is shown in a
letter to her mother: 'If it will gratify you to hear from your
children, I have pleasure in expressing what we all feel, that if
we should be able to go through this trial better than some, it is
to you chiefly that we owe it. We have by you been trained to
habits of industry and economy which will now prove our best
wealth.' She therefore settled down determinedly to make her
living with her pen. She does not appear at this time, or indeed
at any time, to have been greedy for fame. All through her life
Harriet Martineau seems to have done the work that she felt
herself called upon to do at the moment, and to have thrown
herself into it whole-heartedly; but there was no conscious effort
to make a reputation. She wrote for Fox a number of stories
which were collected and called *Traditions of Palestine*, and a
further volume of devotional exercises. Fox, who was ready

to help her, seems to have had no idea that she was ever likely to find a large public. Her mother disapproved of her staying in London, where she had gone to be in direct touch with publishers, and Harriet, then twenty-seven, obediently returned to Norwich. Her next effort was to compete for three prizes offered by the British and Foreign Unitarian Association for essays designed to convert Roman Catholics, Jews, and Muslims to Unitarianism. Though sent in under three different pseudonyms and at different times, she won them all, and the immense encouragement which this afforded made clear to her the direction in which her capacities lay. In later years she came to write of these essays with bitter contempt. 'If either Mohammedans or Jews have ever been converted by them, such converts can hardly be rational enough to be worth having.' The prize-money at least gave her a holiday in Ireland and some leisure to read. She thought out a scheme for a series of tales which should illustrate the principles of political economy. With characteristic industry she set herself to study the works of Adam Smith, Malthus, and Ricardo. The England of the moment was a country cursed with high taxes, falling trade, bitter feeling between class and class, a discredited royal house, violent political agitation, widespread misery, and social unrest. With the purpose of combating this state of affairs, which she contended was due largely to ignorance as well as to selfishness, she wrote one or two stories and sent them round to various publishers, but they were not accepted. Finally Charles Fox, brother of W. T. Fox, undertook responsibility for them and fell in with her scheme of periodical publication. His terms were not very generous, but she accepted them. His caution was perhaps not unreasonable, for the project found no support from the economists. James Mill definitely discouraged it, and to the end John Stuart Mill spoke of Harriet Martineau as a tiro in political economy. But her success was instantaneous. The original 1,500 copies issued in February 1832 were sold out in ten days, and for two and a half years the tales continued to appear. Harriet Martineau had leapt into fame.

II

It is with curiosity that the reader takes up the nine neat green volumes into which, in sets of three, the stories have been collected. These nine were followed by two others dealing with the Poor Law, and yet two more which were concerned with Taxation. The separate stories which appeared month by month in handy little buff covers are each followed by a summary of the principles which the particular story is intended to illustrate. The greater part of volume 9 consists of a short treatise on political economy. The books remain for the most part unnoticed on the upper shelves of public libraries and can be picked up from time to time for a few pence on the stalls of second-hand dealers. Few, perhaps none, of those who write about Harriet Martineau can claim to have read them through. And yet nobody can look through these volumes even casually without realizing that many of the stories are good ones, and it is certain that when they first appeared they found eager readers among those who never troubled much about their application. The first story, *Life in the Wilds*, tells of South African settlers, robbed and stranded, making the best of things and gradually, like the Swiss Family Robinson, obtaining a high standard of comfort once more. The lesson drawn is that wealth is obtained by the employment of labour on material supplied by nature. The only limits that can be assigned to the operations of labour are those of human intelligence. Labour is economized by division of labour. The next tale, *The Hill and the Valley*, shows that to encourage labour is to increase capital, and that increased capital brings more demand for labour. Machines which economize labour increase the demand for it. This story shows admirable character-drawing in the account of the destruction of machinery in a Welsh valley and the abandonment of the works. *Brooke Farm* is an account of a village on the eve of an inclosure. We are told of the indignation of the villagers at the loss of their rights to the common land. But Miss Martineau points out that large capital well employed produces proportionately more than small, and the story describes how the waste is planted, the

soil enriched, the breed of beasts improved. We are encouraged
to draw the complacent moral that the interests of capitalists best
determine the extent to which capital should be employed, and
that any interference on the part of the law is unnecessary and
injurious. *Demerara* shows that Protection taxes people at home
and is the cause of ruin and misery in protected colonies. There
are fine scenes in this story, and the hero is the high-minded
slave so often depicted in the contemporary works of Libera-
tionist writers. The conclusion which the reader is invited to
draw is that free trade in sugar would banish slavery, since
competition would induce economy both of labour and of capital
which would ensure the substitution of free labour for slave
labour. *Ellie of Garveloch* and *Weal and Woe in Garveloch* are
two stories, the scene of which is laid in a small island off the
west coast of Scotland. The increase of rent is a symptom, not
a cause, of wealth. When the islanders look forward to the day
when they will pay no rent at all, it is pointed out to them that
there will be no landlords. The land will be in the hands of the
cultivators, prices will fall, large areas will go out of tillage,
less food will be raised, conditions will relapse. In the second
story we hear how a fishing company has brought population
to the island and that the population has become greater than
the means of subsistence which the island can supply. This is the
first of the Malthusian stories. The teaching of Malthus clearly
inspires much in the succeeding volumes. Harriet Martineau's
standpoint is set forth with candour by one of the characters.
The remedy is to be found, he says, in a condition of things when
'marriage is less general and takes place at a later age, at least
among the middling classes whose example will, I trust, be
soon followed by their poorer neighbours. . . . There is hope
that the poor will in time be more eager to maintain than to
multiply their families.' It is passages like this which show that
Miss Martineau's point of view is not that of a sentimentalist,
but of an acute intelligence interested to the exclusion of any
other feeling in what she believes is good and efficient government. It is this story which roused the indignation of Croker,
who called her (among other things) a female Malthusian.

A Manchester Strike propounds the doctrine of the wages fund, and that conditions of labour may be improved by inventions and discoveries which create capital by avoidance of waste of capital (saving instead of striking) and by adjusting the proportion of the population to the capital available. In looking through these stories it is easy to see how much their economic philosophy owed to the political ideas of the times. John Stuart Mill put his finger on their weakness when in 1833 he wrote to Carlyle: 'Miss Martineau reduces the *laissez-faire* system to absurdity as far as the *principle* goes, by merely carrying it out to all its consequences'. The same doctrine is developed in *Cousin Marshall*, the scene of which is set in a cathedral city. The arbitary distribution of the necessities of life is injurious to society, whether in the form of private almsgiving, public charity, or legal pauperization. Miss Martineau denies any right to subsistence. All encouragement to the increase of population should be withdrawn. Charity should be diverted to enlightenment of the mind and not to relief of bodily wants. 'Every blanket given away', remarks one of the characters, 'brings two naked people, and every bushel of coals, a family that want to be warmed.' The same spirit inspires the story called *Ireland*. There, too, population is growing too fast and the establishment of an alien Church is a great evil. A poor rate would make matters worse. Absentee landlords at any rate pay their taxes and there is an estate manager on the spot, wherever the landlord himself may be. She sees hope for the country in agricultural improvements and in the remedying of political grievances. The later tales, it has been generally conceded, show on the whole greater powers of description and are of more general interest than the earlier ones. International exchange is dealt with in a tale of Holland in the seventeenth century. The doctrine of free trade is set forth in a story dealing with French silks. Gold as a medium of exchange is the subject of a tale of Siberia. Australia shows the virtues of emigration and provides material for an attack on penal colonies. A story of Western America points out the results of unproductive expenditure. *The Three Ages* is an ambitious effort showing London first in the time of Wolsey and More, then under Charles II, and finally as it was at the time of writing. The moral is the need for economy, a trite topic at any time. *Life in Sheffield,* with its descriptions of bread riots, sets forth the need for free trade in corn. Ceylon is shown as a colony suffering from attempts to confine its trade to the mother country. Restrictions on buyers in the colonies and sellers at home can only mean, so Miss Martineau stoutly maintains, loss to the Empire. In yet another tale she sets out to show that interference with such ports as Newcastle or Shields is bad for the State, and that any attempt to dictate the particular direction in which citizens must seek the rewards of industry is a violation of the duty of the State to the individual.

From all this, it will be apparent that Harriet Martineau, if as regards free trade she was in advance of public opinion, was nevertheless, in her general point of view and habit of mind, very much of her time. When Croker said her stories were absurd trash and that he was shocked and disgusted, he undoubtedly represented a public wider than, and different from, the readers of the *Quarterly Review.* But the stories took the public fancy and pleased many who cared little about economics. Later in life Harriet Martineau herself spoke rather contemptuously of them, as she was inclined to do of all her early work and discarded beliefs. She came to believe that there is no science of politics and that social affairs proceed according to general laws no more and no less than natural phenomena of every kind.

Harriet Martineau in her *Autobiography* gives an account of the way in which the remarkable success of her stories made her a literary lioness, and she describes her experiences with a certain good-humoured and rather caustic contempt. The heavy work of seeing her monthly tales through the press necessitated her residing in London, and with her mother she settled in a small house in Westminster. Her correspondence assumed large proportions. People sought her advice and various public causes put forward claims for her support. She wrote a hymn for the Polish exiles, vaguely suggestive to modern ears of

Kipling's 'Recessional'.[1] She was admitted to the prize-giving
at London University by Lord John Russell, a privilege hitherto
withheld from women. She owed this perhaps to Brougham,
who spoke of her enthusiastically as a little deaf girl from Norwich, though in fact she was tall and already thirty years of age.
Brougham's attempts to patronize her were always resented, for
she thought poorly of him and never hesitated to say so. She
received cards of admission to Almack's. Ministers called upon
her. But she was always very much on her dignity and refused
to visit Lansdowne House because she was asked there as an
authoress. Even after Lord Lansdowne had asked and obtained
an introduction, she continued her refusal to accept invitations
because her mother was not included. Rogers she was content
to know, and we hear of him attending her party in company
with Hallam, Fanny Kemble, and Mrs. Gaskell. Moore, on the
other hand, she refused to know owing to a 'ribald song' addressed to her in *The Times*, of which song he was reputed to
be the author. Harriet Martineau described a party at which he
sang. 'He screened his little person behind a lady's harp, and
all the time she was playing, he was studying me through his
eyeglass.' For the most part she speaks of her distinguished
acquaintances with complete detachment. When she approved,
it was a very judicial approval. There is a vignette of Princess
Victoria which has escaped the ironic pen of Mr. Lytton Strachey.
'Lady Durham told me how one evening the little girl (then
eleven years old) came with a hop, skip and jump from the
inner drawing room to show her Mother the next paper with

[1] God! Scorched by battle fires we stand
   Before Thee on Thy throne of snows,
But, Father, in this silent land
   We seek no refuge nor repose:
We ask, and shall not ask in vain—
'Give us our heritage again!'

Thy winds are ice-bound in the sea;
   Thine eagle cowers till storms are past,
Lord! when those moaning winds are free,
   When eagles mount upon the blast,
O, breathe upon our icy chain,
And float our Poland's flag again!

the advertisement of the "Illustrations of Taxation" whereby her pleasure was extended when she thought the series was just done.' Jeffrey's manners, she says, were artificial, but he was generous and sympathetic. On the other hand, he would take advantage of the weakness of vain women, which showed levity, cruelty, and unmanliness. Hallam she found a capital gossip but apt to say rash and heedless things. Her respect for him continued to grow, though she never sympathized with what she considered his reverence for people of rank. Lord Campbell was then 'plain John Campbell', but 'plain John was wonderfully like the present Lord, flattering to an insulting degree, and prone to moralizing in so trite a way as to be almost as insulting'. Stanley, Bishop of Norwich, she found 'a nervous, good-natured indiscreet rattle'. Monckton Milnes she speaks of with affection as of a loyal friend who hid the depth of his feelings beneath an appearance of worldliness and whose cynicism disguised his generosity. Macaulay was no favourite of hers. He had, in her estimation, no heart, and was a signal failure in politics. His review articles ought to have abolished all confidence in his honesty. His history, she adds unkindly, as an historical romance would have been read with almost unmixed delight. Bulwer is described 'on a sofa, speaking and languishing among a set of female votaries'. The poet Campbell's sentimentality was too soft, his craving for praise too morbid, to let him be an agreeable companion. The Kembles she found to be full of knowledge and accomplishment, with genius and cultivation, but yet with an incurable vulgarity clinging to them. The picture she draws of the Carlyles is a friendly and attractive one. The pages of the *Autobiography* devoted to her visits to Cheyne Row and to the character sketches of her host and hostess, as well as of Sterling, Leigh Hunt, and Mazzini, whom she met there, show her at her best. She seems to have understood the Carlyles and to have been able to see the warm-hearted genius behind the sour dyspeptic. It is a little sad that in the case where, for once, she wrote with whole-hearted appreciation and graciousness, we should have in Carlyle's own *Reminiscences* the impression that Harriet Martineau herself left upon her host's recollection. He appears to think that what he called 'the poor whinnering old women' who crowded into the little house in Fludyer Street turned her head. In the notes put together after his wife's death he speaks of Harriet Martineau's nigger fanaticism and of her being 'constantly in spectacle'. He finds, as the years pass, that her books and her actions are full of ostentation. 'We saw', he says, 'the ever self-sufficient Harriet in the company of common friends still once or twice: with pleasure rather than otherwise: but never had more to do with her or to say to her. A soul clean as river sand, but which would evidently grow no *flowers* of *our* planting.' Many of her friends were glad enough to make use of her services. Mrs. Fry asked her advice as to how most effectively to fight pauperism by legislation, a query which still awaits a satisfactory answer. Lord Althorp, then Chancellor, sent her information that should help to prepare the public for his forthcoming Budget. One of her strangest anecdotes is that she, who habitually used an ear-trumpet, could yet always hear Malthus, who had a hare lip and mispronounced his consonants, without it. Her gallery of character-sketches is indeed very extensive and includes Sydney Smith, Roebuck, Miss Mitford, Guizot, Eastlake, Miss Edgeworth, Urquhart, Hartley Coleridge, Godwin, the Brownings, to name only a few. She was in fact recognized on all sides except by herself as a woman of genius. The fame enjoyed by Harriet Martineau during the time that her stories were appearing is an incident without parallel in the literary history of the country.

III

The strain of writing her stories, often against time, in addition to the lionizing which was always distasteful to her, led Harriet Martineau to contemplate a holiday once they were completed. She felt she needed a rest and she admits also that she was glad to get away from her mother. No daughter could have been more loyal and dutiful, but it was difficult if not impossible to be a public figure of importance in political and social circles and at the same time to be obedient to the wishes of a companion who was disposed to exert her maternal authority to the full, who moreover had never been particularly sympathetic or understanding. At the suggestion of Lord Henley she determined to visit the United States with the idea of interesting herself in various social questions, including Poor Law administration. Her studies and her intensive reading of the last few years had clarified and fixed her views on many, perhaps on most, matters; and when she landed in New York in September 1834 she received a welcome which might well have turned the head of any one who did not possess her rare poise and self-possession. Her fame had preceded her, and Americans were then as now eager to receive and to fête a distinguished foreigner. She had letters of introduction from leaders in public life in England to the most influential figures in the States, and she soon found that whereas the Unitarians at home were a small dissenting community of little consideration, they were on the contrary in America a strong and powerful body. Between her arrival and her departure in August 1836 she visited all the New England States and went south to Virginia, the Carolinas, and New Orleans. She made a journey up the Mississippi and saw the Great Lakes and Pittsburg. In the 'Memorials' which Mrs. Chapman appended to the *Autobiography* perhaps too much space is given to this event in her life; and in the *Autobiography* itself, written many years later, Harriet Martineau is possibly disposed to emphasize unduly her sympathies with Garrison and the anti-slavery movement and the personal dangers which she ran. The intensity of her feelings on the subject in middle age tends to colour the portraits she draws of the great men with whom she was brought into contact. The Madisons, Clays, Calhouns, and Porters were warmly devoted to her, but she was able to regard them all with the same amusingly detached objectivity which she had brought to bear on the distinguished men and women who had sought her society at home. Clay, she tells us, never satisfied her of his sincerity: Webster's folly and treachery were worse than any double dealing of Clay's. As to the Presidents, Fillmore and Pierce, she 'refuses to waste indignation upon them'. Everett was 'a mountebank who talked of freedom before a people who could remember Jefferson and

Wesley'. Of the aged Chief Justice Marshall she speaks with reverence; but though she enjoyed the hospitality she received and the almost universal popularity she met during the earlier part of her stay, her comments and criticisms alike in her *Autobiography*, in *Society in America*, and in *Retrospect of Western Travel* are for the most part acrid and harsh. The women, except the abolitionists, fare little better than the men. Mrs. Sedgwick, whose kindness is acknowledged, is yet blamed for worshipping 'that parchment idol' the Act of Union. She and her family are set down as timid and prone to flattery, and her novels and travels 'had better be passed over with the least possible notice'. Mrs. Gilman, a devoted southern admirer of Harriet Martineau, is held up to contempt in the *Autobiography*, and in extreme old age wrote indignantly to repudiate various statements made concerning herself. That remarkable woman, Margaret Fuller, already dead when the *Autobiography* appeared, is castigated for her pedantic methods of thought, her confirmed bad manners and self-delusions. Only her Italian life at the very end gave true revelation of her character. On the other hand, there is Mrs. Chapman, Harriet Martineau's literary executor, one of the most fanatical abolitionists. Lord Morley, in his essay on Miss Martineau, rightly censures Mrs. Chapman's lack of tact, taste, style, considerateness, and sense of proportion. It was Crabb Robinson's complaint of her that she was discontented if you did not go all lengths with her views. Harriet Martineau was always susceptible to good looks, and Mrs. Chapman's beauty and enthusiasm appear to have upset her usual balanced good sense. That her sympathies were with the abolitionists before she started is no doubt true, but it is none the less true that they captured her. As late as December 1834 she wrote home that she had never given an opinion on their politics since she came; and in May 1835 she could still write that, hating the institution of slavery, she was full of hope that 'the day of liberty is rapidly approaching, notwithstanding the mutual quarrels of colonizationists and abolitionists and the hard thoughts which the friends and masters of the slaves entertain for each other'. It was only at the end of the year, November 18th, 1835, that she said a few words at an abolitionist meeting: 'in your *principles* I fully agree', from which date her experiences were less easy, though it is fair to say that she seems to have been treated with perfect consideration and courtesy to the last. If she ran any danger at all it was in the north and not in the south. Harriet Martineau was incapable of deliberate misrepresentation, but her enthusiasm for the abolitionist cause henceforward knew no bounds and the *Autobiography* suffers accordingly.

She returned hearing herself as much talked of in America as in England, and her books on her experiences, although inevitably they gave pain in various quarters, brought her a good return, with a portion of which she purchased a small deferred annuity. She was now no longer a lioness but a figure of widely recognized literary eminence, and for the next few years she proceeded with her invariable seriousness and industry to do the work which came her way, though she could never hope to equal the success of the *Tales*. The year 1837 saw three volumes published on America and 1838 three more. Between these two works she issued four *Guides to Service*, the Maid of All Work, the Housemaid, the Lady's Maid, and the Dressmaker. It was an outstanding quality in Harriet Martineau that she was a most efficient housewife. She not merely controlled everything, she could do everything: cooking, needlework (in which she excelled), filling the lamp, and cleaning the windows. Finished with America for a time (another American book was still to come), she turned to fiction. *Deerbrook* is not one of her successes. It is a story of two sisters from Birmingham who pay a visit to the country. The local doctor falls in love with one of them, but believing her affections to be engaged elsewhere, he marries the other. The sister who had originally attracted him comes to live with them. Trouble comes as might be anticipated, though the lines on which the story develops are hardly those which a modern novel-reader would anticipate. The doctor loses his popularity with the villagers and gives his support to a political candidate of whom the squire does not approve. His practice is ruined and they almost have to face starvation. Then the lover of the unmarried sister comes to learn that the doctor's affections had originally been engaged by her, and he throws the girl over. Only an epidemic which restores the doctor to the goodwill of the village and the fact that the lover comes to his senses, and the further fact that the doctor and his wife find that they really care for each other after all, enables the book to end happily. That it is a comparative failure is attributable to two causes. For once, Harriet Martineau was dealing with matters in regard to which she knew nothing. Her love-scenes are ridiculous, as is the whole psychology of the story. But the chief cause is personal to herself. Her splendid courage is apparent when the difficulties under which she was living and working are realized. In the house with her were her mother, who was becoming increasingly blind, an old aunt who made serious demands on her time and patience, and a brother whose failure to make good the losses sustained by the family had led to heavy drinking. Further than that, her own health broke down. She found herself compelled to return from a continental journey before it was concluded, to the home of a brother-in-law who was a physician in Newcastle. She made the journey from London by water, and among her fellow passengers was Arthur Stanley, the future Dean. Stanley in writing to his father describes the impression she made upon him, that with her masculinity of intellect she was yet essentially feminine. Arriving in Newcastle, she characteristically refused to be a burden on her sister's household and took rooms at Tynemouth facing the sea. There she remained during five years of complete physical inactivity, of most active literary work, and of almost incessant pain.

IV

Harriet Martineau lived and died in the belief that she had disease of the heart. It is now clear that her trouble was a dermoid cyst, ovarian in origin. While it remained in the pelvis it was the cause of her troubles: when it shifted to the abdomen, as it did later, it ceased to cause her acute discomfort for many years during which it grew slowly. It is a tragic fact that the condition is one which was easily operable. From this time forward she lived, even when not actually ill, under the shadow of illness. It cut her off even more than her deafness from social life. Away from her family (who were more of a trial to her than a pleasure) and from her friends, she lived increasingly in her work. Well aware of her abilities, though without exaggerated estimate of them, she set herself to serve mankind by instructing where she thought instruction was called for, helping with her pen such causes as she deemed worthy, encouraging, admonishing, elucidating. From her sick bed she wrote *The Hour and the Man*, an infinitely more successful and readable story than *Deerbrook*, inspired no doubt by her interest in the anti-slavery movement. Though in the form of a romance, the *Autobiography* tells with what care and thoroughness she collected the materials for what is in fact an account of Toussaint L'Ouverture. Then, because she felt up to no great mental effort, she designed and carried out a series of children's stories called the *Playfellow*, and the modern generation of children, which can still very sensibly find pleasure in Miss Edgeworth's *Rosamond* and *Harry and Lucy* and in Mrs. Sherwood's delightful *Fairchild Family*, might do worse than read the *Peasant and the Prince* and the *Crofton Boys*. There is also *Life in a Sick Room*, a series of essays which set forth the thoughts which came into her mind as she lay on her couch month after month looking out on the sea and the mouth of the river. The hints and suggestions with regard to nursing no doubt provided a foundation for her friendship with Florence Nightingale. In later years Harriet Martineau calculated that during what she called her passive period she was responsible for sixteen volumes.

It was in 1844 that she found herself unexpectedly restored to some measure of health following mesmeric treatment, to which she had submitted herself at the suggestion of Bulwer and others. This was the cause of a breach with members of her family, including her brother James, and she remarks plaintively that she had more than her share of persecution for the offence of recovery from a hopeless illness by a new method. Her offence was, of course, not that she had recovered but that she wrote about it, and that later on in her writing on mesmerism she attributed effects to the wrong cause. Thenceforward, mesmerism became one of the chief interests of her life. She discovered that she herself had mesmeric power and used it therapeutically in various cases. Mesmerism brought her into touch with Henry Atkinson, who, though he finds no place in the *Dictionary of National Biography*, undoubtedly impressed many of his contemporaries, such as Emerson, Margaret Fuller, and Charlotte Brontë, only less than he impressed Harriet Martineau. They did not actually meet until after her recovery from her long illness, though he had already advised her on the subject of mesmeric treatment through his friends the Basil Montagues. The friendship with Atkinson, a well-to-do and attractive man some years her junior, brought a new element into her life. Many have found more than a trace of eccentricity in Harriet Martineau's intense individualism, her interest in phrenology, her desire to leave her skull and brain for dissection, her advanced views (as they then seemed) on women's rights, her spiritual pilgrimage which led her from Unitarianism to Positivism and Free Thought. In her own opinion, it was her earlier years which were the winter of her life: its spring only began after she had left Tynemouth, apparently cured. A journey to the Lake District determined her to settle there: she bought the ground and built the house, and having done so she accompanied some friends to the East, the best possible evidence of the completeness of her recovery. She visited Paris, Marseilles, Malta, Cairo, and the Nile. She made long journeys on horseback to Sinai and Petra and then proceeded to Palestine and Syria. Her book, *Eastern Life, Past and Present,* is more than a mere travel record; it is a story of the Egyptian, Jewish, Christian, and Moslem faiths, showing each as a stage in man's development, first the pantheon of Gods, then a Trinity, then a single God, all the divine beings displaying the attributes of man in exaggerated form. There is no reason to think that at this period Harriet Martineau knew anything of Comte, but her progress from theology to metaphysics was in line with the ideas which underlie his system.

She was now forty-five and an independent woman for the first time. She had, as it were, found herself. Her health could never be robust, society had no attraction for her, her deafness made her

more and more the centre of her own world. She could not throw
her ideas into the common stock, but, lying on her couch busy
with her pen or her needle, she could enjoy the company of those
with whom she found herself in sympathy or who were prepared
to share her views. Henceforward, with but little exception, her
physical life was confined to the home she made for herself at
Ambleside. Here she lived from 1847 until her death, and there
is something at once fine and pathetic in the picture of that eager
mind ceaselessly occupied with public questions, playing an
important part in their discussion and solution from the quiet
retreat of her lakeland home. The Knoll stands in two acres of
hilly and well-wooded ground. From a terrace in front of the
house there is a view of the valley, of the roofs of Ambleside, and
a glimpse of Lake Windermere. On the terrace she loved to sit
and talk, sometimes with a mild cigar, recommended originally
as a cure for deafness. The house, of gray stone, is gabled, and
Mrs. Chapman has described in detail the interior arrangements.
The drawing-room on the right of the entrance was furnished
to a great extent by presents. To quote only a few, the carpet
was the gift of Jacob Bright, the marble-mounted sideboard that
of Crabb Robinson, an almanac from Darwin, an ebony *papeterie*
from Florence Nightingale, a gold inkstand from Lord Durham,
Richmond's well-known crayon likeness of her on the wall, a
pastel from Lady Byron, an engraving after Raphael from Mrs.
Carlyle, another from Mrs. Jamieson. Across the hall on the
left was the study with its red carpet and curtains, on two sides
of which was her library, which in its composition indicated the
breadth of her interests. Many of her books were presentation
copies. In the bay window was her working table and behind it
her sofa: busts and pictures contributed by friends found places
here and there. It is interesting to know that her fame was such
that during the holiday season she suffered from the curiosity of
tourists who invaded her garden and flattened their noses against
her window. Her deafness[1] made this the more intolerable since
she would suddenly become aware of a strange face looking in

---

[1] She was also without the sense of smell. Once only was she able to taste roast
mutton, and found it delicious.

upon her. What she would have endured in days of excursion trains and motor-cars it is difficult to say; but it is probable that neither her personality nor her work would have made the same impression on a later generation that they made on her own. She built a cottage near her home and placed in it a Norfolk dairy-maid. There was also a poultry yard and a piggery, and a cow-shed occupied by beasts known to fame by reason of the fact that they were liable to be the subjects of their mistress's mesmeric experiments. The first ten years at The Knoll were probably the happiest of Harriet Martineau's life. She took pride in her home and an active interest in all that surrounded her. She was on the best of terms with her neighbours, the Arnolds and the Wordsworths. She gives an amusing sketch of William Words-worth, of whom she remarks that the heart element in him was not strong. His advice on how to treat visitors is well known: 'You must say "If you like to have a cup of tea with us, you are welcome: but if you want any meat, you must pay for your board".' Macready, who visited her when her home was in course of erection, comments on her brown, healthy appearance and her firm, almost manly stride. 'What a truly great and excellent-hearted woman that is', he had written in his diary not long before. 'How little, how very little does one feel before her virtue and wisdom.' The conventionally-minded Macready was, as might be expected, one of the many who shook their heads later on over mesmerism, and remarked, 'Alas, alas', about her atheistical opinions. Not only did she appreciate her neigh-bours but she encouraged them to appreciate her. Her small farming experiments were undertaken in order to show them what could be done. She lectured to them on sanitation, on her travels, and on the history of England and of the United States. She wrote a guide book to the Lakes; and though her relations with the clergy were not always easy, we hear of no quarrels. All accounts agree that Harriet Martineau was one of those women who, plain in youth, appear almost handsome in middle life. The early portrait by Evans in the National Portrait Gallery shows a thin-faced woman with a large and straight mouth and piercing black eyes. Richmond's drawing, also in the Gallery, shows a fuller face, hair parted in the middle covering the ears in the fashion of the time, displaying a fine forehead; a general impression of authority and benevolence. James Payn describes her greeting when he called at The Knoll. Her brown hair with a little grey in it was arranged with peculiar flatness over a low but broad forehead. She was of middle height, inclined to stoutness, and as she stood in her porch with a smile on her kindly face and her trumpet at her ear, she impressed him as gentle and motherly. Benevolence indeed had its part in Harriet Martineau's character in spite of her arbitrariness. It was Mrs. Wordsworth who declared that in her household economy she was a model, for she made those who served her happy, and set an example of activity to her neighbours. There is something pathetic in the account of the wedding of her housemaid Jane. 'A more graceful lady I never saw. She presented me with a pretty cap of her own making for the wedding morning; and would let nobody else dress me.' It is difficult to realize that Harriet Martineau herself was only fifty. Side by side with such pictures one must place that drawn some years later by Charles MacFarlain, the journalist and traveller. MacFarlain was an ultra-Conservative and was suffering under a sense of grievance when he described her as a rampant rationalist, a prophetess of mesmerism, an ill-favoured, dogmatizing, masculine spinster. He was disgusted with her personal appearance, her loquacity, and her positiveness. 'Compared with her, Brougham's face was charming.' This only shows in extreme form the indignant and resentful opposition which a personality like that of Harriet Martineau is bound to arouse among the conservative-minded. In politics, in religion, in economics, in science, in her social creed, she fearlessly, almost recklessly, stood for new ideas, and if it involved unpopularity and misrepresentation she willingly paid the price. Plato relates how Socrates compared his relation to the Athenian State with that of a gnat which worried a noble horse. Harriet Martineau was at bottom a woman devoid of self-importance; but she regarded it as her duty to write what in her view it was to the good of her fellow countrymen that they should hear.

It was during these happy days that her best work was done, her *History of the Thirty Years' Peace* (1816–46) and her translation of Comte's *Philosophie positive*. The History is perhaps the most important of all her books, though Mrs. Browning regretted it as a waste of her fine intellect. To write impartially of contemporary events is no easy task, and Harriet Martineau made no attempt to disguise her personal views. The first volume had been written by Charles MacFarlain and George Craik and had appeared periodically at the time of the repeal of the Corn Laws. In 1849 she continued the book from the point at which it had been left, and each of the two volumes was completed in six months. The reader who to-day takes up this handsome work with its maps and its steel-engraved portraits will find it a readable record of the period with which it deals, written in a flowing and unmannered style which is at the same time never slipshod or lacking in dignity. In the 1,300 pages there are no indications that the book was written far from libraries and with no means of personal consultation with the many still living personalities who played their part in the story. From this book, so admirably put together, so wide in its scope, we can judge the abilities of Harriet Martineau, both as a writer and an artist. Her record of the thirty years wanders far afield to India and to South America, and it includes careful vignettes of men and women who in any direction have made contributions to the history of the period; but she draws her threads together at the end and she makes it clear that 1846 indeed closed one chapter and opened another, and that, upon the whole, peace had brought its blessings and victories not less renowned than war. To have completed the work in so short a time was possible only by intense application, and a day carefully parcelled out. Harriet Martineau rose at 6, walked until 7.30, and then breakfasted. Her household affairs were settled by 8.30 and from then she worked until 2, when she dined. The rest of the day was given to reading and to her heavy correspondence. Her industry was indeed dauntless. Her abridgement of Comte's *Philosophie positive* runs to three volumes of 400 pages, and for English readers it remains the standard work. A Mr. Lombe of Norfolk,

personally unknown to her but an admirer of Comte, sent her
£500, of which she took only £200, and when the work was
finished she insisted on dividing the profits with her publisher
and with Comte himself. The record of the field covered by her
work is so wide that it is not surprising that in days long before
women took up journalism the figure of Harriet Martineau,
far away at Ambleside but with a pen ready to write upon any
matter, historical, philosophical, industrial, and to support
energetically those political, social, and ethical causes which
commended themselves to her, should have attracted public
attention. She wrote on the Jews, on educational reform, on
America. She wrote a sketch of Indian History and of British
administration up to the Mutiny, and at a later date she planned
'suggestions for a Future Government of India'. Agricultural
subjects she made particularly her own, and she issued a volume
of collected essays on *Health, Husbandry, and Handicraft*. She
quarrelled with Dickens and *Household Words* because of an
article which she considered contained unjust reflections on the
Catholics; but her book *The Factory Controversy: a Warning
against Meddling Legislation*, which is a stout protest against
interference by Government in private enterprise, shows that
she remained a staunch individualist and Utilitarian. When one
glances through the mass of Harriet Martineau's work during
these busy years, the question inevitably suggests itself, what
might she not have done in other circumstances, if she had
been born two generations later, if she had enjoyed good health,
if she had not been handicapped by deafness, and, as a result
of that deafness, by loneliness and a certain intellectual self-
sufficiency, a certain hardness and dogmatic narrowness of view.
It is hard indeed to estimate what part she would have played.
Her qualities and her defects arose each out of the special circumstances of her life. She could probably never have worked
effectively with others. She could never have developed the
committee mind. She was an individualist in an age of individualism, and it is profitless to inquire how so rigid a philosophy
of life might have adjusted itself to a world which faces its
problems in a totally different spirit.

Harriet Martineau, no doubt, placed very high among the services which she rendered to humanity, the publication in 1851 of the *Letters on the Laws of Man's Nature and Development*, a correspondence between herself and Mr. Atkinson in which the most important letters are his and not hers: indeed he wrote 225 out of the total 291. The purpose of the letters was to discover whether there could be found a real basis of a science of mind. They sought to discover, along Baconian and inductive lines, the laws governing man's nature and development. Personal partiality perhaps made her see beauty and eloquence where less prejudiced readers could only find wordiness and obscurity. Many of her friends, including Charlotte Brontë, considered the publication ill advised and liable to leave her own views open to misrepresentation, as indeed it did. Feeling in many quarters was very bitter, and many who were not angry were censorious and deplored her association with Atkinson and his ideas. Lady Eastlake relates how she attended a mesmeric séance given by a practitioner who had been in touch with Harriet Martineau, and that she found it 'fearful nonsense and impious flippancy'. James Martineau, under the title of 'Mesmeric atheism', reviewed the book; and though his attack was upon Atkinson and not upon his sister it caused a breach between Harriet and her favourite brother which was never healed. It would seem that she had just ground for complaint, for however much Dr. Martineau might dislike mesmerism, it had no more to do with theology than had her theories about phrenology, which no doubt seemed as fantastic to him as they did to most other people. The book in fact was not atheistic. Atkinson said in explicit terms: 'I am far from being an atheist. I do not say there is no God but that it is extravagant and irreverent to imagine that [First] Cause a person.' Harriet Martineau says much the same. 'There is no *theory* of a God, of an Author of Nature, of an origin of the universe which is not repugnant to my faculties; which is not (to my feelings) so irreverent as to make me blush, so misleading as to make me mourn.' They were both of them in fact agnostics long before Huxley had invented the term. Her usually sound sense may well have been at fault in the matter, led away by her feelings for Atkinson and by her admiration of and her sympathy with the line of approach he adopted, which was in such full harmony with her own methods and ideas. She remained as unmoved by obloquy and insult as she had been in the past by popularity and praise. Hypnotism as a therapeutic agent, though used increasingly on the continent, has made slow progress in this country. Not until 1892 did a committee of the British Medical Association report favourably upon its use, and not until 1907 was the Medical Society for the Study of Suggestive Therapeutics set on foot. The Martineau-Atkinson letters were published at an unfortunate moment, a moment when spiritualism was becoming a craze and Mr. Sludge the Medium a well-recognized type. Even more important, perhaps, was the discovery of the anaesthetic usefulness of chloroform, which provided a satisfactory substitute for one of the more obvious uses of hypnosis. The treatment meted out to Harriet Martineau by her relatives and by the public generally must be recognized as having been grossly unfair. In this matter, as in so many others, she was in advance of her time. As always, she had spoken what she believed to be the truth; and modern psychological medicine would freely admit that when she claimed to receive and to give benefit by hypnotism in such cases as her own there was real substance in the claim. When the storm died down it left Harriet Martineau with an increased reputation for eccentricity. Of Mr. Atkinson little more is heard. A man of perfect sincerity and seriousness of mind (C. J. Holyoake describes him as looking like an evangelical bishop), his death at Boulogne about 1890 was quite unnoticed.

So the years passed until 1855, years of strenuous work and of happy isolation. In 1855, however, Harriet Martineau's health suddenly failed and the doctors informed her that her days were numbered. Indomitable as ever, she returned home and set about writing the story of her life. So keen was her feeling that she was working against time that she wrote of her later years first. It is generally considered that the *Autobiography* hardly shows Harriet Martineau at her best. Her life

had been one long fight: against ill health and deafness, against
prejudice and misrepresentation—a fight, too, on behalf of many
unpopular causes, and one that had been waged with financial
resources so modest as never to free her from the necessity of
earning her daily bread. The tone of the book shows a certain
acerbity, her critical opinions tend to be harsh, and she writes
as one who is still in the midst of the battle rather than as one
who contemplates the drama of her life in the world from afar.
Her own work she summarizes with detachment; if she errs at
all it is in underestimation of her capacities. She recognizes the
religious impulse which from first to last lay behind her activities
and that she was stimulated to write by an impelling need for
utterance. 'With small imaginative and suggestive powers and
therefore nothing approaching to genius, she could see clearly
what she did see, and give a clear expression to what she had to
say. In short she could popularize while she could neither discover nor invent.' The *Autobiography* concludes with a general
view of the world as she saw it, aged 53. She castigates the
administrative incompetence which the Crimean War then being
waged had made manifest. She notes that 'benevolence towards
the helpless and our interest in personal morality have grown
into a sort of public pursuit'. But she considers that, while undertaking by law to provide against personal vices and certain
special social contracts, the public has overlooked the fact that a
system of national education is long overdue. She looks for
reform of the land laws and for a progressively democratized
constitution. Outward conformity to Christian practices she
believes to be on the decline, and she looks for the day when the
last of the mythologies will vanish before the flood of greater
light. 'The world', she concludes, 'as it is, is growing somewhat
dim before my eyes: but the world as it is to be, looks brighter
every day.' With buoyant hopefulness and contentment she
settled herself to die.

V

But the doctors were mistaken, and in fact she lived on for
another twenty-one years. She survived even the friendly

surgeon who had undertaken at their joint request to forward, when the time came, her brain and skull to Mr. Atkinson. During this final period she was increasingly an invalid in hourly expectation of death, but yet working steadily so long as power of work remained to her. She would write a vigorous article or plan something for her neighbours at the same time that she could hardly speak for weakness. During the Crimean War and after, Florence Nightingale found a stout ally in Harriet Martineau in her campaign against War Office inefficiency. 'No harm can come of an attempt to shame the Horse Guards. I have consulted my Editor and if I can obtain a sufficiency of clear facts I will gladly harass the C-in-C as he was never harassed before.' This is a good example of her as the journalist militant. She contributed to the Reviews articles on 'Meddlesome Legislation', on female industry, on the anti-slavery cause, Russia, women's dress. Dickens and the more advanced humanitarian writers of the time she held to be wrong in demanding of Government what Government has no business to undertake. In this spirit she opposed the Factory Acts and, in the *Edinburgh Review* for October 1869, the tyranny of trade unions. The American Civil War blew into flame her constant anti-slavery sympathies, and letters and articles followed one another across the Atlantic in a steady stream. Relations with her American friends were strained after the seizure of the Confederate Commissioners while under the protection of the British flag, and she was ready at all times to deal faithfully with them, as with everybody, when she thought they were wrong. Mrs. Browning remarks without resentment that in her political letters to America Harriet Martineau 'has set me down, with her air of serene superiority'. 'The sin of the North is protection,' she wrote, 'as the sin of the South is slavery.' Such sayings inevitably created a soreness, but it passed when her friends remembered the invalid woman in her lonely house still working with all the strength that remained to her. Her chief occupation during the years that followed was her journalistic work on the *Daily News*. Her leading articles numbered in all 1,642, and she continued them until 1866, when her gradually failing health

demanded that all public work should cease. Harriet Martineau
had lived by her work, and her savings had at no time been considerable. Both Lord Grey and Lord Melbourne had at different
dates suggested that she should receive a pension, but she preferred to retain her independence. Again at the end of her life the
matter was raised once more by Mr. Gladstone, but she refused
to entertain such a proposal. She was helped financially by the
kind initiative of Robinson of the *Daily News*, who collected and
published a number of biographical sketches which had appeared
in his paper. The book passed through four editions and remains
to-day one of the best known and most readable of Harriet
Martineau's works. It is journalism of a high order, written
in that limpid style which the writer knew how to combine with
conciseness of form and lucidity of statement. The biographies
are divided into six sections: royal, political, professional,
scientific, social, and literary. It has been truly said that they
might have been equally well divided into two sections instead
of six: those of whom she approved and those of whom she did
not approve. Her honesty never allowed her even for a moment
to confuse what in her belief was right and what was wrong.
Even an obituary notice must tell nothing but the truth. So of
Lord Lyndhurst she wrote: 'He is not and never will be regretted except by the partisans of the old English Toryism.' She
remarked of Lord Campbell that some of the welfare he had
earned for himself 'was a poor substitute for blessings and enjoy-
ments relished with an even greater keenness than his by poorer,
more modest, refined, and honoured men'. Macaulay's life was
'cold and barren as regards the higher part of human nature'.
In Croker, an old enemy, she castigates 'the mingled violence
and casuistry of his temper and his entire unscrupulousness in
matters both of feeling and of statement'. She quotes with
approval the saying of Macaulay: 'Croker is a man who would
go a hundred miles through snow and sleet on the top of a coach
in a December night to search a parish register for the sake of
showing that a man is illegitimate or a woman older than she
says she is.' She censured in Thackeray his obedience to the call
of the great, and *Vanity Fair* aroused her 'moral disgust'.

Landor, Whewell, Palmerston, De Quincey, Lockhart, Sidney
Herbert come off better, but they do not escape some trenchant
criticism.   On the other hand where she approves it is with her
whole heart, and Humboldt, Lady Byron, Hallam, Mrs. Wordsworth, and Joseph Hume are outstanding in a not very long list.
The last cause which aroused her public support was Mrs.
Josephine Butler's agitation for the repeal of the Contagious
Diseases Acts, but up to within a few weeks of her death she
continued to write long letters to her friends. 'I cannot think
of any future as at all probable', she wrote to Atkinson on May
19th, 1876, 'except the "annihilation" from which some people
recoil with so much horror. . . . I remember the passion with
which W. E. Forster said to me "I had rather be damned than
annihilated". If he once felt five minutes' damnation, he would
be thankful for extinction in preference.' Her mind remained
unclouded and her spirit undaunted when she at last faded out of
life on the evening of June 27th. For some reason she was not
buried at Ambleside, where so much of her life had been spent
and where she had found rest and happiness, but in the family
grave at Birmingham, where she lies with four Martineaus who
had predeceased her, including her mother.

    A career such as that of Harriet Martineau is inevitably
liable to various interpretations. The works of Mrs. Chapman
and of Mrs. Fenwick Miller are certainly too whole-hearted in
their praise. Lord Morley's essay is detached and censorious
in its standpoint. Her latest biographer, in a book wittily and
brilliantly written[1] as 'an essay in comprehension', brings out
successfully the unity and consistency which lie behind a career
in many respects unique. At the time of her breakdown in
1855 Matthew Arnold wrote:

> Hail to the spirit which dared
> Trust its own thoughts, before yet
> Echoed her back by the crowd!
> Hail to the courage which gave
> Voice to its creed, ere the creed
> Won consecration from time!

[1] *Harriet Martineau*, by Theodora Bosanquet (Etchells & Macdonald, 1927).

It is disconcerting to find him some years later writing to Dean Boyle of Salisbury: 'I do not want to overpraise a personage so antipathetic to me as Harriet Martineau. . . . What an unpleasant life and unpleasant nature.' Harriet Martineau was no doubt not always easy to understand, or her friend Florence Nightingale could hardly have written to her niece, on hearing of her death: 'The shock of your tidings to me was great, but oh, I feel how delightful the surprise to her! . . . She is gone to our Lord and to her Lord; she is in another room of our Father's house.' It is possible to imagine the rather grim smile with which Harriet Martineau herself would have received this tribute. It was nevertheless Miss Nightingale herself who at a later and less emotional moment summed up Harriet Martineau's career most truly. She was an apostle of freedom. She believed in freedom equally in the social, legislative, administrative, religious, and economic spheres: freedom for the American slave, poor law reform, land reforms which would improve the lot of the agricultural labourer, freedom for women to play their part in the public life of the world, freedom for them from humiliating and degrading regulations. Democracy for her meant liberty. She lived in an age when, in order to make mankind happy, it seemed that one had only to extend more liberties and reproduce elsewhere the British constitution. It is evidence of her clear-sightedness that though her philosophy was that of her own time she realized, as is shown by her article on 'Trade Unions' in 1859, long before most other writers, that liberty and democracy are not always synonymous terms. She saw the human race, as she remarks in the obituary notice she wrote of herself, advancing under the law of progress. Succeeding generations have found the advance less steady and less regular than she expected. Dogmatic religion, which she believed to be in its last stages, still remains strongly entrenched all the world over, though there is certainly in most quarters more tolerance for honest opinions honestly held than was the case in her day. Of the rights of women she is justly regarded as a pioneer. Her insistence in later years on being known as 'Mrs. Martineau', though unmarried, was a significant gesture, and it is perhaps to be regretted that her lead back to the gracious custom of an earlier age has not been followed. She explained and illustrated the teachings of others with ability and enthusiasm. She made their principles her own, and courageously applied them in her own attitude towards all the issues with which during her long career as a writer she was called upon to deal.

A sun-dial still stands in the modest garden at The Knoll bearing a motto chosen by herself. The motto sums up the philosophy which, from first to last, inspired her life: 'Light, come visit me.'

CHRISTINA ROSSETTI

·⟨═══════⟩·

IN the inscription placed on the walls of Casa Guidi by the
Municipality of Florence, the poet Tommaseo describes Mrs.
Browning as one 'che fece del suo verso aureo anello fra Italia e
Inghilterra'. In a different sense but with equal truth the same
may be said of the Rossetti family. They too, father, mother,
and children, link our England to his Italy. Gabriele Rossetti,
curator of the antiquities of the Naples Museum, was one of
those who extorted a constitution from King Ferdinand (Bomba).
When that monarch, relying on the support of Austrian soldiery,
cynically withdrew it not long afterwards, Rossetti with difficulty
escaped with his life. Exiled at 42, he became Professor of Italian
at King's College, London. A prolific writer in prose and verse,
he remained to the end an ardent patriot; but whereas his earlier
work was devoted to the cause of liberty and reform, his later prose
was connected with the poems which, in varying degree but always
unmistakably, inspired his children—the *Divina Commedia* and the
Vita Nuova. His son has left a crayon drawing of the old man in the
year before his death, seated at his desk wearing a black cap and
an eye-shade, snuff-box at hand, closely scanning some document
through his glasses—a very Rembrandtesque figure. In Vasto,
his birthplace, the chief piazza now bears his name, and a tablet
to his memory has been placed on the walls of the cloisters of
Santa Croce at Florence. His wife Frances Polidori was grand-
daughter of Alfieri's secretary and niece of the John William
Polidori who, as a young man of 21, was Byron's travelling
companion and physician. Long before Byron returned to
England they had parted company, but Polidori's tragic death
some four years later was a real sorrow to the poet. It is impossible to have even a slight acquaintance with the voluminous
literature which has gathered round the Rossettis without realizing the central position in the story occupied by the 'just, liberal
kind, forgiving, steadfast Mother'. W. M. Rossetti quotes a
saying of hers as being at once sound and characteristic. 'I

always had a passion for intellect and my wish was that my husband should be distinguished for intellect and my children too. . . . I now wish that there was a little less intellect in the family, so as to allow for a little more commonsense.' To these two were born four children. The eldest was Maria Francesca, whose *Shadow of Dante* is at once an introduction to his works, a commentary, and an analysis.[1] Christina calls her sister 'a dear saint' and maintained that it was only the domestic responsibilities which devolved on the eldest in a household where means were limited which prevented Maria from developing gifts and enjoying a reputation equal to that of the rest of the family. Maria is a somewhat shadowy figure throughout. We hear of her teaching Italian, copying out her sister's verses, tending her sick relations, always gentle, helpful, and in her quiet way stimulating, until in the early seventies she disappears into an Anglican sisterhood and fades out of the story. The second was Dante Gabriel, summed up by his brother as 'honoured among painters as a painter and among poets as a poet'. The third was William Michael, whom many still happily remember in his old age as carrying into our own times the punctilious courtesies of a bygone day; for he lived into his ninetieth year and saw the end of the Great War. Art critic, poet, biographer as well as civil servant, he was, above all, the historian of Pre-Raphaelitism and of the Rossettis. The mutual affection and the discriminating admiration which bound all these members of the family together is shown nowhere more clearly than in the great regard they had for him. W. M. Rossetti himself quotes the amusing instance of his *Democratic Sonnets*. The others felt, no doubt rightly, that however agreeable these sonnets might be to the Muses on Mount Helicon, they were less likely to give satisfaction to his superiors at St. Martins-le-Grand. Gabriel points this out in a letter to Mrs. W. M. Rossetti, not venturing to speak to his brother direct 'lest his first impulse should be to resent it as an encroachment', and he followed this up with a short note to William himself 'With the ut-

---

[1] Her *Shadow of Dante* is reprinted by Messrs. Longman in their well-known 'Silver Library'.

most humility and only at the absolute call of brotherly love'. It is the more remarkable that this incident occurred at a time when Gabriel's health was quite broken, and within a year of his death.

The fourth was Christina. Her earliest memories must have been of the Italian refugees who thronged the house in Great Portland Street where in 1830 she was born. Visits to the cottage of her grandfather Gaetano Polidori near Little Missenden made a lasting impression upon her, and gave her that love of animals and of flowers which plays so large a part in her poetical work. The grave beauty of her face at twenty is to be seen in her brother's *Ecce Ancilla Domini* in London, and it was as a 'pure and docile-hearted damsel' that she impressed the youthful Holman Hunt. In comparison with the rest of the family she read little, and one may picture her as a delicate, introspective girl, almost painfully conscientious in regard to her family obligations, writing out from quite early years little poems in her notebooks. It was her grandfather Polidori who first printed her verses privately when she was 14. Again when she was 17 he printed a paper-covered volume of sixty-six pages with a quotation on the title-page from Metastasio, whose work, strangely enough, greatly attracted her.

It was on January 13th, 1851, that W. M. Rossetti drew up the rule of the Pre-Raphaelite Brotherhood. This incident, far from marking the beginning of the movement, which had been in existence since 1848, marks rather the beginning of the end. Between her 18th and 23rd year Christina was in the closest association with a body of young men whose activities will always form a chapter in the history of British art. (She was the poetess of *The Germ* under the pseudonym 'Ellen Alleyn'.) In addition to the two Rossetti brothers, Millais, and Holman Hunt, there was F. G. Stephens, who early abandoned the practice of art and was known for something like forty years as the distinguished critic of the *Athenæum*, and James Collinson, who severed his connexion with the P.R.B. on joining the Roman Catholic Church. His place was taken by W. H. Deverell, who died before his considerable powers had had time to develop.[1]

---

[1] It was Deverell who introduced Miss Siddal, his model, to Gabriel Rossetti.

Thomas Woolner, another of the poets of *The Germ*, later famous as a sculptor, was lost to the movement when, at twenty-seven, he went to Australia. Others too, though not members of the P.R.B., were closely associated: Coventry Patmore, who contributed to *The Germ* and secured the intervention of Ruskin on behalf of the movement; W. Bell Scott, Rossetti's friend, whose *Autobiography* contains reminiscences and criticisms of the Pre-Raphaelites which do not lack pungency; and above all Ford Madox Brown, whose teaching and practice, though he stood outside the movement, had done so much to inspire it. As to the origins of the P.R.B., there is the story told by W. M. Rossetti in *The Pre-Raphaelite Brotherhood* on the one hand, and the work of Holman Hunt's old age, *Pre-Raphaelitism*, on the other. Whenever it may have begun and whoever may claim to be its founder, the end of the movement can be dated November 8th, 1853, when Gabriel wrote to his sister, on Millais's election as an A.R.A., 'So now the whole Round Table is dissolved', and Christina wrote a poem in sonnet form (more or less) which ended:

> And he at last the champion great Millais
> Attaining Academic opulence,
> Winds up his signature with A.R.A.
> So rivers merge in the perpetual sea:
> So luscious fruit must fall when over-ripe:
> And so the consummated P.R.B.

But, though she was among them, even in youth Christina lived a life apart. If she appears, it is in spite of herself. It is remarkable that, though her character and her genius were never unrecognized and indeed were fully appreciated, in all the writing covering this period there is little said about her. She was merely there. This no doubt was due in part to her ill health, but also to the fact that throughout her life she had no interests outside her family, her religion, her charities, her poetical work. In her later years her friendships became increasingly restricted. There is no record that relations were renewed with Millais or with Holman Hunt, though there was no reason on either side why they should not have been.

She joined her mother in carrying on a day school, first in North London and later at Frome, but the effort met with little success and the family returned to the house of W. M. Rossetti where in 1854 the father died. From the beginning of 1854 London was her home, and it is one of the strangest and saddest things about her that, having Italy in her blood, she saw Italy but once. Rome, Florence, Naples, Venice she never visited. Her six weeks' tour afforded time for no more than a glance at the sub-Alpine region round Milan, approaching through France and the St. Gothard and returning by the Splügen and the Black Forest. Her only other journey abroad had taken place four years earlier, when W. M. Rossetti had accompanied his mother and sister to Paris and Normandy. Sir Edmund Gosse remarks that 'there is hardly a solitary touch in her work which betrays her transalpine parentage'. It is true that nowhere do we find in it the 'Italianismo' of her father or her brother William. Lover and student of Dante as she was (and in a lesser degree of Petrarch and Tasso), his work was no inspiration to her as it was to Maria and to Gabriel. For all that, it is to be remembered that her Italian poems cover practically the whole of her life—as early as 1846 and as late as 1890. Like nearly all her work they are subjective, and they show a familiarity with the idiom of the language in every variety of metre to which no ordinary English student could aspire. Sir Edmund's statement is, no doubt, broadly speaking correct, but there is yet one great exception in the self-revealing 'Italia, io ti saluto!' with its pathetic third verse:

> But when our swallows fly back to the South,
>   To the sweet South, to the sweet South,
> The tears may come again into my eyes
>   On the old wise,
> And the sweet name to my mouth.

Her brother realized that could she have lived in Italy she would have been a happier woman. 'I can remember', he says, 'the intense relief and pleasure with which she saw lovable Italian faces, and heard musical Italian speech at Bellinzona.' The poem

En Route dated June 1865 (they had reached home on June 26th)
is equally touching:

> Farewell, land of love, Italy,
>   Sister-land of Paradise:
> With mine own feet I have trodden thee
>   Have seen with mine own eyes:
> I remember, thou forgettest me,
>   I remember thee.

And again,

> Take my heart, its truest tenderest part,
> Dear land, take my tears.

At thirty-five, therefore, Christina Rossetti returned to England
never to leave it again. There is a chalk drawing of her at this
period by her brother in which the severity of her costume and
of the hair, parted in the middle and half covering the ears, only
heightens the spiritual beauty of the face itself, the oval contour,
the large wistful eyes, the long graceful neck. Illnesses followed,
and within a few years Graves' disease left its mark on her
appearance; but in spite of this her biographer[1] states that in
later middle life she 'looked unquestionably a woman of genius'.
She had lost the slimness of youth and her face in repose was
heavy: but nevertheless we can picture the arresting personality
of the woman in the simple black silk dress and black lace cap
with a touch of white only at neck and wrists, her dark hair
streaked with grey, her deep hazel eyes, her broad brow, her
olive complexion, her low musical voice, and the beauty and
precision of her enunciation. Of her life there is little to record.
What little can be said is told with loving care by Mr. Mackenzie
Bell, himself a poet and, like Christina Rossetti, a humanitarian
in the broadest sense: like her, too, full of courage and not un-
acquainted with suffering. Between Gabriel and his sister there
was uninterrupted affection, understanding, and admiration. The
whole romantic episode of the courtship of Miss Siddal must
have seemed strange to her. Christina and 'Guggum' can have
had little in common. The life in subsequent years at Cheyne
Walk must have seemed no less strange. But quarrelsome and

[1] *Christina Rossetti*, Mackenzie Bell (Hurst and Blackett, 1898).

rude as he could be with others, Gabriel fully reciprocated the
devotion with which he inspired all the members of his family.
She was his constant correspondent and was with him at the end
at Birchington. We hear of Christina at Kelmscott during the
years when Gabriel was joint tenant with Morris. At Kelmscott,
as everywhere and always when she was not required for some
service, she lived her own life, contented with her own interests
and her own thoughts. It may truly be said of her, as was said
of a very different character, that she was never in the way and
never out of the way. Amid all the criticisms, sometimes rather
acrid, she was exempt. Where friendship might be interrupted
or even broken, she was always spoken of with regard. Her whole
life indeed was permeated with religious and devotional feeling.
Two opportunities of marriage, one when she was twenty and
another fifteen years later, were set aside, in the first case
because the suitor though a Christian was not an Anglican, and
in the second because he was not a believer at all. The first was
with Collinson, a colourless personality who became a Roman
Catholic and even contemplated taking Orders. Almost without
their having noticed it, he slipped out of the Pre-Raphaelite
circle. He married, he exhibited from time to time at the
Academy, and he died in 1883. Then later, when her youth was
almost past, she might have married Charles Bagot Cayley, who
had studied under her father and was employed in the Patent
Office. Cayley is known as the translator of the *Divina Commedia*. 'Attempting most and aiming highest he reaches also
furthest' was the verdict of her brother William, a verdict which
has failed to find general support. Readers of Dante continue to
prefer the blank verse of Cary or the *terza rima* of Plumptre.
Frederic Shields remembered Cayley at Torrington Square and
described him to the present writer as an elderly, unattractive
scholar. For Christina this was certainly the deeper attachment
of the two. Only after her death did her brother William find in
her writing-desk a series of short Italian poems in every variety
of metre covering the six years during which this second
friendship ran its course, came to its end, and left its scar, *Il
Rossegiar dell'Oriente*. Here more than anywhere we have the real

Christina Rossetti, her mastery of metre, her power of melody, her selfless spirituality of outlook, the ever recurrent note of self-sacrifice. One may hazard the conjecture that she was perhaps never so much in love with her lover as with love itself.

During her later years her output was considerable: stories for girls, volumes of prayers, a commentary on the Book of Revelation, studies on the minor Church Festivals. Her best work, it is generally conceded, appeared in the volume *Goblin Market and other Poems* issued in 1862. This, together with two other volumes, the *Prince's Progress* (1866) and *A Pageant* (1881), was rearranged and reissued as *Poems* in 1890, four years before her death. Here are to be found, in addition to the longer poems already mentioned, most of the lyrics and sonnets which have already their assured place in any anthology of English poetry: *Remember, When I am dead, my Dearest, The Convent Threshold, Amor Mundi, Up-hill, A Birthday, Rest.* W. M. Rossetti regarded the *New Poems*, collected by him in 1895, as containing much that was up to the level of her average, and not a little that was up to her best work. This opinion has not generally been held in other quarters; and yet a re-reading of the *New Poems* leaves an impression that her brother's high opinion was not without its justification. Christina, like most poets, no doubt wrote too much, and it is impossible, in a volume of nearly 400 pages consisting mainly of short lyrics, to pick out half a dozen as being incontestably superior to the rest. In addition to the Italian poems there are many, especially those written between the years 1860 and 1865, of a haunting pathos and beauty. There is *The Summer is ended*, and *En Route*, and *Sleeping at last*, and *Sunshine*. Every one must make his own choice. One of the last things she ever wrote sums up her philosophy of life:

> Heaven overarches you and me
> 　　And all Earth's gardens and her graves,
> Look up with me, until we see
> The day break and the shadows flee.
> What though to-night wrecks you and me
> 　　If so to-morrow saves?

It has been suggested that her work has affinities with that of seventeenth-century mystics, Donne, George Herbert, Vaughan, and Treherne. The atmosphere of mysticism certainly pervades Christina Rossetti's work. She saw in everything the manifestation of the Divine. For her, life and death were part of a whole, aspects of an underlying unity. One feels, as it were, that death is looming behind in most of her poems, except in those which themselves deal with death. When she writes of death it is as being the gate of life. There is no doctrine or philosophy consciously and deliberately put forward. It is merely an atmosphere. Others have detected the influence of the writings of Keble and Newman. This too is possible, though she had no high opinion of Keble's poetical gifts. The political atmosphere in which she had spent her youth discouraged any tendency she might otherwise have felt towards the Church of Rome; her sympathies were always what we should call to-day Anglo-Catholic. But the probability is that her poems were written merely because she felt impelled to write them. There was no underlying purpose but merely a subconscious instinct. Christina Rossetti knew little and cared nothing about 'schools'. Her gifts were the result of her own ancestry, her own experience of life. They owe little to her literary preferences or her particular attitude to religious questions. She spoke her thoughts, as Mr. A. C. Benson has said, 'not because they were improving, but because they were beautiful'.

It was in 1874 that Christina Rossetti together with her mother and her two aunts moved to No. 30 Torrington Square, in which she spent the last twenty-one years of her life. The tall, narrow, basement house in the rather drab square was indeed no home for a poetess, except that Miss Rossetti could be singularly independent of environment. Here her mother was her chief care, until in 1886 she died. One of the aunts lived on another three years, and the other survived bedridden, in what would normally have been the dining-room, until within eighteen months of Miss Rossetti's own death. When time and health permitted she interested herself in district visiting and in a Factory Girls' Club. She occupied the first-floor front room, some treasured possessions about her, not many books: busy with simple things such as making scrap-books for hospitals. She received few visitors, and latterly, as her terrible illness, cancer, developed, hardly anybody at all. Her death on December 29th, 1894, attracted comparatively little attention. The papers were full of Gladstone's 86th birthday and of the Armenian Atrocities.[1] But within three days there came from 'The Pines' an appreciation characteristically generous and enthusiastic.

A soul more sweet than the morning of new-born May
Has passed with the year that has passed from the world away.

And Swinburne adds:

There is none to sing as she sang upon Earth,
Not one.

She is buried at Highgate with the father and mother to whom she was so devoted. Here, too, lies the most romantic and pathetic figure among them all, Gabriel's wife. The story is well known how at the last moment he had placed the manuscript of his poems in her wonderful red-gold hair as she lay in her coffin; and Sir Hall Caine has related how, on an autumn night some seven and a half years later, a fire was built, the coffin was raised, and the poems were recovered.[2] The modest headstone has no room for Christina's name, which appears on a slab at the foot of the grave. This would not have been displeasing to one who had written:

Give me the lowest place: and if for me
The lowest place too high, make one more low.

Poets, even good poets, are generally more praised than read, and this is true of Christina Rossetti as of others. But where many reputations contemporary with her own have disappeared, hers has remained steady. The field she covered was comparatively narrow, her point of view never varied, her powers did

---

[1] *The Times* gave her half a column under 'Obituary' which included many other names besides her own.

[2] Adjacent is the tomb of Mrs. W. M. Rossetti and W. M. Rossetti himself, as well as of Oliver Madox Brown ('Nolly'), whose premature death was widely recognized as a tragedy of the first order.

not develop as the years passed. But within the limits which she deliberately set herself few poets, certainly no woman poet, has written in our tongue with the musical and metrical power or with the depth and sensitiveness of feeling which were hers. Within these limits her supremacy remains to-day unchallenged.

THE *ITALIENISCHE REISE* OF GOETHE

I

(1)

PROFESSOR C. H. HERFORD has set forth with incontestable authority and consummate skill the influence of the Italian Journey upon the work and the character of Goethe.[1] To regard his Italian Journey as finally closing his naturalistic and realist period, and as transforming him during the latter half of his career into an idealist, is an interpretation which he considers is at once superficial and incorrect. He sums up the influence of the Journey in a single phrase. It meant for Goethe the difference between things learnt and things seen. What he had seen combined for the future with what he had learnt, to which we may perhaps add as an important element what he had himself attempted to do in drawing, painting, and modelling. After his return to Weimar he continued to learn, and it is this combination of learning (and, as Goethe himself admits, of unlearning) and of experience which made him in his later years the great poetic realist.

Professor Herford traces the influences of the Journey on Goethe's psychological development; what is attempted here is the much simpler task of following him on his travels.

It is not necessary to do more than sketch in a very few words the situation which he left behind him in Weimar on September 3rd, 1786. Goethe was 35 years of age and had already resided there for eleven years. Those who are acquainted with the Weimar of to-day can only with difficulty picture to themselves Weimar as Goethe first knew it. The population is now some 40,000. In 1775 it was about 6,000—a walled city containing some 700 houses. There were no street lamps, there was no park, and few of the other open spaces which now make the city so attractive. The population was poor. There was no intellec-

---

[1] *Goethe's Italian Journey*, Taylorian Lecture, by C. H. Herford (Oxford, 1897).

tual or commercial life. Weimar at that time indeed had few
attractions beyond its site in the green Ilm valley surrounded
by the Thuringian hills. It seems probably more romantic in
retrospect than it did to many who were called upon to live out
their lives as members of a stagnant and isolated community.
To those who know the busy and commercial Frankfort of to-day
it is hard to realize that in leaving it for Weimar Goethe was
leaving a medieval city of infinitely greater charm and beauty
and an intellectual environment beyond all comparison larger
and more stimulating. Goethe came to Weimar on a visit. He
transformed it and made it his home for half a century. That
he should gladly have accepted the invitation of the Grand Duke
is understandable. Life in Frankfort had lost its attraction; his
heart had never been in the law. His relations with his father
were not close enough to retain him. Lili he could bring himself neither to marry nor to give up; he had fled from her to
Switzerland, and had come back. The social life of Frankfort had
meant little to him. He was famous, but it was only too apparent
with what difficulty he was able to work amid the distractions
of every kind that surrounded him. Weimar he knew had little
to offer, but it could at least give him the two experiences
he wanted above all: the opportunity to develop his work and
the chance to live at the centre of things. For him it was not
enough to live: he wanted to live in such a way, in Aristotle's
phrase, 'as to get the best out of life'. It was this that attracted
him in the Grand Duke's invitation, but it is to be remembered
that just as the town had little in itself to attract, so also in 1775
there was little on the social and intellectual side. There was the
Dowager Duchess Anna Amalia, a typical eighteenth-century
figure, still young though her son was 18, pleasure-loving, a
friend to learning and to the Arts. The Duke Karl August, when
he and Goethe first became associated at the time of his marriage
to the Duchess Luise, was much of a Bohemian, and he remained
through life an active, cheerful, genial personality. His friendship with Goethe brought out the best in him. He devoted him
self to an extent then rare to the affairs of his Duchy. He could
make himself happy in almost any society—amongst soldiers,

philosophers, or peasants, and unlike his uncle, Frederick the Great, it was in German and not in French literature that he interested himself. The University of Jena must always remain greatly in debt to the Grand Duke and to his mother, and it is one of his outstanding qualities that in spite of occasional quarrels with Goethe his friendship had that characteristic which is rare in the friendships of princes—constancy.

Of the great figures which have made Weimar famous one only was there already when Goethe arrived, Wieland. Professor of Philosophy at Erfurt, he had been invited to come to Weimar as tutor to her son by the Grand Duchess, and he always held his place in the inner circle of her friends. His welcome was cordial, and his consistent friendship in the years ahead always received the appreciation it deserved. When Goethe arrived he found the Residenzschloss in ruins, and the Grand Duke residing in the Fürstenhaus. Whether he had originally come only on a visit, or whether it had all along been his intention and that of the Duke that he should settle in Weimar, is uncertain. In any case after a short period of rather boisterous amusement the poet settled down, and there gradually formed around him and the Ducal household that cluster of names which has made Weimar so famous. Herder[1] came at Goethe's suggestion. The history of their relations is a stormy one, and long before Herder's death they had come to mean nothing to one another. Herder, soured by his experience of life, often ill, highly sensitive, was jealous of Goethe just as Wieland was jealous of him and of his friendship with Herder. There was Major von Knebel, a Court official of romantic temperament who gradually won Goethe's great regard, and Musaeus, who collected German folk-lore and laid out a flower-garden. There was Bertuch, the Duke's secretary, who translated Cervantes and concerned himself with the finances of the theatre, and the Chamberlain, von Seckendorf, a musician and an actor who had translated *Werther* into French before Goethe arrived. There was also Bode, the translator of Montaigne, Sterne, Smollett, and

[1] See *Herder and his Times*, by Henry W. Nevinson, 1884; also *Goethe: Man and Poet*, 1932, by the same writer.

Fielding, and Corona Schröter, who played the leading part in
the theatricals and who was the cause of an awkward moment
in the relations of Goethe and the Grand Duke. Finally there
was Frau von Stein. Goethe's friendship with Frau von Stein,
platonic though it was, was far the greatest romance of his life.
A married woman with a family, her influence upon him was, at
any rate in the early years of their friendship, entirely good. He
seemed to lose the morbidity of *Werther* and his tone became
more healthy and virile. Weimar held him. The Duke gave
him a house and made him a Privy Councillor. Little by little
the duchy came to look upon him as Finance Minister, War
Minister, and, in practice if not in name, President of the Council.
The story of the years at Weimar before 1786 is a story of much
hard work, which many others could no doubt have done equally
well. As Goethe said himself, he was meant to be a private
person but Fate compelled him to be concerned with the administration of a State. It must be remembered, too, that though the
duchy was small it consisted of four isolated regions. Apart
from Weimar itself there was Jena and the University, Eisenach,
and Ilmenau, now known merely as a pleasure resort, where
Goethe interested himself in mining development.[1] This involved much travelling, the consideration of industrial questions,
and of political and academic appointments, in addition to the
duties which were bound to confront a finance minister face to
face with an extravagant young Prince who was at the same
time his own close personal friend. Behind it all there was Frau
von Stein. The opinion of Herr Ludwig that she surrendered
herself to Goethe is not generally shared. Perhaps Goethe's
own conduct is the best evidence against this view. She
stimulated and encouraged him, but as the years passed he found
increasingly that an unsatisfied passion was a poor background
for his busy life. He was a poet, he had come to Weimar in order
to do the work he could not do at Frankfort, and he found that
the work remained undone. His greatest projects were un-
finished and indeed to a large extent untouched—*Iphigenie*,
Wilhelm Meister, *Tasso*, *Egmont*, *Faust*. Life at Weimar seemed

[1] At Ilmenau he spent his last birthday.

to have failed him. He had loved but it had become a torture, friendship had become an embarrassment. There were jealousies and misunderstandings, and the public work that had at first brought him honourable satisfaction ceased to please. Apart from these personal reasons there was the reason, perhaps sufficient in itself, that he had that urge which men in northern Europe have so often found irresistible. He wanted to see the sun. His decision was taken at Karlsbad, where he had been staying with the Duke, Herder, and Frau von Stein. They left him there, and the day afterwards he wrote a letter to each of them, but in no case did he give any indication of what his intentions were. On the following morning, accompanied only by his servant Siedel with a trunk full of manuscripts and little other luggage, he set out on his journey southwards. Once more Goethe found safety in flight.

(2)

The *Italienische Reise* starts from Karlsbad. There are those who complain that it is ill constructed, and they are right, for there is no attempt at construction. But many will agree with Mr. Nevinson that it is in spite of these limitations one of Goethe's most interesting works. The names of those to whom the letters were sent which form the background of the book are not given, but it is understood that they were Herder and Frau von Stein. The book must be read with three important considerations constantly in mind. The first is that what he tells is incomplete. He does not appear to have drawn upon his correspondence with the Duke or with the Duchess Anna Amalia or with von Knebel. Secondly, in writing to Frau von Stein and Herder he naturally tells them only what he thinks they would have been interested and pleased to hear. We know for a fact that there was much in his Italian experiences that he did not tell them, and if we did not know it we should still infer it. Thirdly, and this applies more particularly to the period of his second stay in Rome, he depended on his memory, and perhaps on the memory of others, when he came in his old age to prepare the book for publication.

The journey by post from Munich direct to Rome took sixteen days in 1786. Goethe's journey was much more leisurely.
Anxious to get away and to enjoy the luxury of an incognito he
called himself Herr Möller. He rushed up into the mountains,
but once he reached the plain of Lombardy and could feel himself
indeed in Italy his progress was slower. He did not proceed
direct to Rome but turned eastward, and with no undue haste
made for Venice, where he spent a fortnight. Only on leaving
Venice did the call of Rome become irresistible. During the last
stage, indeed, the city drew him like a magnet, and he hurried
on his way with little interest in anything but the route ahead.
Altogether he spent not 16 but 54 days between his setting
out and his arrival. The route he took was the Brenner Pass
which unites Munich and Verona. Nothing could well have been
more precipitate than this phase of the journey. Leaving
Karlsbad at 3 a.m. on September 3rd he was in Ratisbon, 108
English miles away, 39 hours later.[1] In Ratisbon he spent some
hours. He saw a performance by the pupils at the Jesuit school,
noted a rare stone of a porphyritic nature, and was off again at
midnight, arriving at Munich at 6 a.m. Munich he had already
visited in student days. The weather was wet and cold, and
bitter winds were blowing from the mountains, which were
hidden by clouds. He found time for not more than a fleeting
visit to the Museum and at 5 the next morning was off again,
remarking truly enough, 'What do I not pass over both on my
right and on my left in order to carry out the one thought which
has become almost too fixed in my soul!' The Brenner is the
lowest of the passes over the main chain of the Alps. The route
was used by the Romans, but the route along which Goethe
passed, the first modern road over the Alps, had been constructed only in 1772. It proceeds due south by the Isar valley,
and Goethe remarks rather unexpectedly to those who were

---

[1] In 1762 Adam Smith stated that a coach journey between London and Edinburgh
of 400 miles took from 12 to 14 days. After MacAdam had revolutionized road-
making in the early nineteenth century, the journey was accomplished in less than
2 days. The increase in speed between the pre-MacAdam coaches and the post-
MacAdam express post was greater in proportion than the increase of speed
between the express post and the express trains of to-day.

brought up on Campbell's poem *Hohenlinden* that the river flows slowly. Past the mountain lakes Kochelsee and Walchensee the route cuts into the mountains, rising to some 2,700 feet at Mittenwald, where he spent the night. Starting again at 6 in the morning he soon reached Scharnitz, then as now the Austro-German frontier, and entered the Tyrol. At Zirl he reached the river Inn and was in Innsbruck by 2 p.m. Here he seems to have made no stay at all, and merely remarks on the gay crowds who thronged the streets, celebrating the birthday of the Blessed Virgin. He pushed forward and spent the night at the inn at the top of the pass. The diary of these two days is very full. He was impressed, as every traveller must be, by the sight of mists rolling amongst the mountains, by dark outlines cut sharply against the clear sky, and by foaming waters in rocky chasms. But he writes mostly as a scientist of the influence of the mountains on atmosphere and temperature, and with his Linnaeus at hand he notes with delight trees and plants, hitherto unknown to him, and geological formations which impressed him as strange and beautiful. Side by side with these very sober observations, his pleasure at his hardly-won freedom is undisguised. 'I now detach *Iphigenie* from the bundle and take her with me as my fellow traveller into the beautiful and warm country of the South. The days are long and there will be nothing to disturb reflection while the clearest objects of the surrounding scenery stimulate [the poetic sense] and call it forth more quickly and more vividly.' From the Brenner, Goethe proceeded with what he calls 'frightful rapidity'. Leaving at 7 the next evening his coach proceeded down the valley of the Etsch, now called the Eisace. The postillions were asleep, and the horses found their own way among the familiar windings of the long route. At daybreak he notes his first vineyard. 'I felt an inward joy that a favourable wind blew behind me and seemed to hurry me towards the object of my wishes.' Bolzano was reached in the morning, and in the evening Trento. The next day, the 11th, found him at Rovereto, where for the first time he found himself in an exclusively Italian-speaking community: 'How delighted I am that the language I have always most loved

now becomes living, the language of common usage.' Rovereto
was a town that loved to welcome famous travellers. Eighteen
years before it had fêted the young Mozart. Two years later it
received Cagliostro. Fortunately 'Herr Möller' was able to
avoid the welcome which would have been accorded to the illustrious Goethe. So rapid a journey must have been an exhausting
experience, but there is no mention of fatigue in the Diary. It
was, however, at Rovereto that, feeling he was indeed in Italy,
Goethe ceased to hurry forward, and instead of proceeding south
to Verona he deliberately turned eastward to Torbole at the
northern end of Lake Garda. Here he became frankly a tourist
and amused himself by rowing on the lake. The long, narrow
northern half of Garda is not unlike a Norwegian fiord, with
cliffs going down steeply to the water, and small villages
where streams enter the lake. At Malcesine he was forced by
the wind to land, and proceeded to sketch the ruined castle, just
as he had already made an attempt to draw the innkeeper at the
Brenner. On this occasion, however, he was stopped by the
Venetian officials (for he was already within Venetian territory),
and was only saved from arrest by a kindly podestà who had
known Frankfort, to whom Goethe could give information about
various Italian families and residents in that city—a Republic,
as Goethe was careful to point out, just as Venice was. The
little adventure does not appear in the least to have upset his
calm. He writes in praise of the people, the scenery, and the
agriculture, and in this happy frame of mind he proceeded to
Verona, where he arrived on September 10th.

The railway era, which brought so many places for the first
time to public notice, must have proved disadvantageous to the
old cities which lie on the road between Milan and Venice—
Brescia, Verona, Vicenza, and Padua. The changes of the last
thirty years have no doubt familiarized many foreigners with
them, who previously would have made the journey direct, but
until the motor-car restored the roads Verona was visited rarely,
Padua very rarely, and Brescia and Vicenza hardly at all. At
Verona Goethe broke his direct journey to Rome and began in
leisurely fashion to proceed towards Venice. His flight was at

an end. He no longer felt the urge to press forward, though later on that urge was to come upon him once more. Feeling that he was indeed in Italy and that his incognito was complete, he could enjoy himself at last. He therefore allowed himself to pass the greater part of a week in Verona. Here he was thrilled at the sight of the Arena, the first important ancient monument he had seen. To this he returned again and again, watching from the top the crowds in the piazza below, noting how carefully it had been restored, and admiring the arcades on the ground-level filled with shops. In order not to be conspicuous, he dressed himself in the costume of the locality. Of many of the sights which attract the modern visitor to Verona he makes no mention. He says nothing of the Lombardian cathedral, the church of S. Anastasia, considered by many to be one of the most beautiful gothic churches in Italy, the noble tombs of the Scaligers outside S. Maria Antica, and, perhaps most famous of all, far from the centre of the town, the Romanesque church of San Zeno Maggiore. The gothic made no appeal to Goethe and he was content to pass it by.[1] There is indeed something refreshing in the determination of this traveller to look only for what he wants to see and to admire only what pleases him. Apart from the Arena he mentions the Porta Palio, a gate in the Doric style of which Vasari says that the Venetian Signori equalled here the buildings of the ancient Romans. Goethe had the advantage of seeing pictures arranged, not as now in a Pinacoteca or civic museum, but in the churches and the private galleries to which they belonged. Here again he displays his characteristic independence of opinion. He writes with enthusiasm of Tintoretto and speaks with veneration of Veronese, but he is impatient of the sacred subjects which they were almost invariably compelled to portray. From Verona he proceeded to Vicenza, and the three days spent there were an outstanding incident in his journey, for it was at Vicenza that he came under the spell of Palladio, an influence which affected his judgement during the ensuing months and certainly pre-

---

[1] His admiration for gothic architecture, so strong at Strassburg, did not survive his return to Frankfort in 1771.

vented him from appreciating Venice as he might otherwise have done. Goethe arrived at Vicenza already a great admirer of Palladio, and well acquainted with engravings of his work. The building known as Casa del Diavolo (Palazzo Giulio Porto), which for some reason he believed was Palladio's own residence, he had always regarded with 'an especial predilection', nor is Goethe's partiality difficult to understand. Palladio, who has been called the founder of modern architecture, did in fact revive the style of the ancients, and it is on this outstanding quality that he depended for his effects—not on decorative detail but on the perfection of his proportions. Since the period of the Gothic Revival it has undoubtedly been the practice to underrate Palladio.[1] This is perhaps because his work at Venice is more familiar than his work at Vicenza. Vicenza, where he built palaces, shows him no doubt to greater advantage than Venice, where he built churches. Further than that, his art for all its virtues is derivative. It is based frankly on classic models, even though it is now conceded that he followed the Augustan Vitruvius less and his own genius to a greater degree than used to be believed. Goethe says of him enthusiastically that he was a man really and intrinsically great, whose greatness was manifested in what he produced. His outstanding difficulty was to adapt the orders of columns to buildings for domestic or public use. 'With what success', he remarks, 'has he not worked them up together!' The visitor to Vicenza to-day will perhaps be more ready to accept this valuation than those generations who were taught to admire almost exclusively the work of the architects of the Middle Ages, to value the work of the fourteenth, fifteenth, and sixteenth centuries, and to think little of that of the seventeenth and eighteenth. It was claimed that the earlier was more real, more devout, came more from the heart, and that the latter was not merely imitative but devoid of spiritual impulse. All such argumentation would have left Goethe cold. He had come to Italy imbued with classicism and he had eyes for the classic and for little else.

[1] It is significant that in the Index to the great 39-volume edition of Ruskin his name is not even mentioned.

The Basilica (Palazzo della Ragione) is perhaps the greatest work of Palladio. Around the original Town Hall he erected a double colonnade, the first Doric the second Ionic, of great dignity and beauty, and the Palazzo Chericati, now the Museum, which also shows the two orders in double colonnades, displays his work at its best. Goethe was also pleased with the Rotunda,[1] which stands magnificently on a hill to the south, looking across the city and the valley to the Alps—a square building with a low dome in the centre, approached on each of its four sides by a flight of steps and six Ionic columns.[2] That same evening he attended a debate in a Society which appears to have resembled those Debating Societies which were more popular fifty years ago than they are to-day. The question debated was 'Which has been more serviceable to the fine arts, invention or imitation?' —a question which was bound to be of interest in the city of Palladio. As might be expected, imitation appeared to have the more supporters. In addition to these sights Goethe found 'indescribably beautiful' the Olympic Theatre, a building ill adapted for modern plays or indeed for plays at any time, but interesting in its elaborate architectural ornamentation with streets indicated in perspective on either side of the stage.

And so, immensely impressed with Palladio, to whom he refers again and again, he hastened to purchase drawings of his work and then proceeded to Padua, where he arrived after four hours. Here, too, though he stayed but a couple of days, his visit was of importance in the history of his own development, and here again his Diary reads strangely to the modern traveller.

Those who can spend a day at Padua, and few unfortunately do more than that, hasten to the Arena Chapel, where it is possible to study the work of Giotto more favourably than at Florence or Assisi. There is the huge Sant'Antonio ('Il Santo') with its domes, an almost startling apparition to the traveller who comes upon it suddenly. In front of it there is the famous equestrian statue of Gattameláta by Donatello. None

---

[1] Chiswick House, in which Fox died in 1806 and Canning in 1827, was in its original design modelled on the Rotunda.
[2] Goethe, who is rarely inaccurate, calls them Corinthian.

of these sights does Goethe even mention. He praises the Mantegna frescoes in the Eremitani, and he is impressed, as nobody can fail to be, by the Salone, 'the Hall of Audience' as he calls it, in the Town Hall; 'such a huge enclosure that one cannot conceive it, much less record it to one's memory', a building surrounded by wide loggias with arcades and shops beneath. The great chamber is over 250 feet long and proportionately high. The only church mentioned by Goethe is S. Giustina, a Renaissance structure far from the centre of the town. He was also pleased with the huge piazza near by, then known as the Prata della Valle, a piazza almost deserted except during the Fair, but which he appreciated because of the oval area, surrounded by water, which is adorned with statues. There is indeed so much to see in Padua that, greatly as one may respect Goethe's determination to see only what he wanted to see, it is hard not to feel that there was a certain perverseness in his attitude, a perverseness which became still more marked when he reached Venice. Two remarks in the Diary about Padua are specially significant. One is that he found time to visit the anatomical theatre at the University, an early evidence of what later on in Rome became for a time an absorbing interest. The other is a reflection which came to him while walking in the Botanical Gardens. 'About ordinary plants as well as about other objects that have been long familiar to us, we do not think at all, and what is looking without thinking? Amidst this variety which comes upon me as quite new, the idea that all forms of plants may perhaps be developed from a single form, becomes more lively than ever. On this principle alone it would be possible to define orders and classes, which it seems to me has hitherto been done in a very arbitrary manner.' Goethe himself in his old age regarded his services to science as comparable in their importance with his distinction as a poet, and his scientific discoveries are three in number. There was first the discovery in 1784 of the intermaxillary bone in man. This bone is the centre bone of the upper jaw and contains the incisor teeth. Goethe argued that if man has teeth in common with animals he must also have the bone that animals possess. In adult man the bone is hardly perceptible, but it is clearly to be seen in the skulls of infants. During his lifetime the importance of this discovery and its implications were not recognized, but it certainly gives Goethe his place among those who have made a substantial contribution towards the theory of evolution. Then side by side with anatomy and osteology there was optics, which resulted in his book on the theory of colours (*Die Farbenlehre*, 1810). In this book he opposed the accepted Newtonian doctrine that white light is made up of the seven prismatic colours. He contended that white light is not 'composed' at all, but homogeneous. He contended further that colours are no more than various combinations of the simple ingredients of light and darkness. He who was always searching for a fundamental unity which lay behind diversity of phenomena, who sought it in anatomy and in botany, looked for it also in the field of optics. Goethe in later life passionately supported his views in this matter as against the generally accepted theories, encouraged, no doubt, by the support of Hegel and Schelling. His remark to Eckermann shows the partiality so commonly displayed by those whose theories do not receive the support their authors consider that they merit. 'The Newtonian explanation', he says, 'is too stupid, and a good head-piece is incredibly damaged when it meddles with stupidities. Do not trouble yourself about the Newtonians.' The third service he would claim to have rendered had regard to the metamorphosis of plants; and in the Botanical Gardens at Padua, enclosed in a special building, may still be seen the Palma di Goethe (*Chamaerops humilis*), planted somewhere about 1585, his visit to which was the occasion of the remark already quoted. Here again he showed himself a forerunner of the evolution theory. Seeing so many plants, many of them for the first time, it occurred to him that the only reasonable basis for a really scientific botanical classification must be the theory that they had originally evolved from one. He noted the modifications between the stamina and the leaves of the blossoms, and between the leaves of the blossoms and those of the stem, and he called the leaf the fundamental type of plant organism. But he did not find what he always hoped to find, the original and primitive plant from which all others derive.

And so, after two days at Padua, he set off for Venice, proceeding thither by water. To reach Venice by water is still the most attractive method of approach. Ruskin has described the experience with great truth and depth of feeling in the beautiful final paragraph of Volume I of the *Stones of Venice*. Even in Goethe's Diary and letters we can find a trace of emotion:

Now it stood written on my page in the Book of Fate that on the evening of the 28th September about 5 o'clock German time I should see Venice for the first time as I passed from the Brenta into the Lagunes, and that soon afterwards I should actually enter and visit the strange Island City, the heavenly Republic.

(3)

It is good that Goethe should have written like that, and all the more so seeing that his notes on Venice are on the whole disappointing. He seems never to have really appreciated the city. He was there for sixteen days, and his letters to Weimar which are full of detail make little mention of St. Mark's or of the Doge's Palace, except incidentally. There is no reference to the Piazza or the Piazzetta, though it was there that Goethe could best have studied, and no doubt did study, the habits of the people and the colour and beauty of Venetian life. He never appears to have visited the two churches which to succeeding generations have appeared as exceptionally worthy of attention: S. Giovanni e Paolo, a huge Gothic structure containing the tombs of forty-six Doges and of the Bellinis, and the Frari, another large, brick, gothic church full of pictures and of tombs including that of Titian. He mentions the mosaics at St. Mark's, for instance, on the tenth day of his stay, but nowhere is there any description of the church itself. It is indeed almost laughable how carefully Goethe guards himself against contamination with the Gothic, so much so that it must be clear that the *Italiänische Reise* only recalls what he chooses to relate and that it gives no complete account either of what he saw or of what he did.

It is quite impossible to believe that he was not really impressed with the beauty of St. Mark's, to which generation after generation had made its contribution, or that he did not appreciate the crowds, the costumes, the lights, the gaiety, the constant movement on the Piazza. There are clearly reticences in the record as printed, and Goethe was no doubt careful what he related to Frau von Stein. The completeness with which the classical obsessed him is shown by an entry in the Diary after having seen a portion of the entablature of the Temple of Antoninus and Faustina in Rome which was preserved in the Palazzo Frasetti, now part of the Town Hall. This induced the following outburst : 'It is indeed something very different from our queer saints piled up one above the other on little consoles after the Gothic style of decoration. Something different from our tobacco-pipe-like shafts, our little steeple-crowned towers, and foliated terminals. From all taste for these I am now, thank God, set free for ever.' It must be recognized that with his love for the classical, stimulated by his old enthusiasm for Palladio and greatly increased by his recent visit to Vicenza and to Rovereto, he failed to appreciate the beauty of Venice. He had come with no prejudices : indeed, remembering his father's delight, he was prepared to succumb to its spell. That the spell did not work is to be regretted for the further reason that Goethe arrived at a most interesting moment. His account of Venice, such as it is, gives us the last picture that we have from a distinguished foreigner of Venice on the eve of her fall. Reading the cool and unenthusiastic accounts from his Diary and letters it is hard to remember that he is portraying the romantic life familiar to us in the paintings and writings of the later Venetians. When Goethe visited Venice Longhi had only been dead 24 years, Canaletto 18, and Tiepolo 17, Guardi was still alive, Goldoni lived on another 7 years and Gozzi another 20. The Doge whom Goethe saw was Renier, the last but one, a man who had bribed his way to office and made money by selling posts. He was not unpopular, for he was kind and affable, and Goethe was struck by the dignity of his appearance and his dress. The description which follows of the Doge attending officially High Mass at S. Giovanni, now suppressed, is of some historic interest.

When the gilded barks which carry the princes and a portion of the nobility approach the little square, when the boatmen in their fine liveries are plying their red-painted oars, when on the shore the clergy and the religious fraternities are standing, pushing, moving about, and waiting with their lighted torches fixed upon poles and portable silver candlesticks; and then, when the gangways covered with carpets are placed from the vessels to the shore, and first the full violet dress of the Savii, next the ample red robes of the Senators are unfolded on the pavement and lastly when the old Doge adorned with his golden Phrygian cap in his long golden *talar* and his ermine cloak steps out of the vessel, when all this, I say, takes place in a little square before the door of a church, one feels as if one were looking at an old worked tapestry, exceedingly well designed and coloured. To me, northern fugitive as I am, this ceremony gave a great deal of pleasure.

This vivid vignette of Venetian life, unfortunately the only one that Goethe gives, shows how even on the verge of dissolution the Republic retained all the forms of its ancient splendour. Within two years Doge Renier was to give place to Doge Manin, and nine years more saw the end of the Republic.

On arriving in Venice Goethe had set to work with all a tourist's enthusiasm. He bought a plan, he walked through the town, and made a tour in a gondola so that he could claim on the second day to have visited the remotest parts. But he was from the first unfavourably impressed with the dirt and the smells, and he mentions them again and again. They appear greatly to have interfered with the enjoyment of his visit, and within two days of his arrival he was amusing himself by sketching out sanitary regulations. 'One always feels inclination', he says, 'to sweep one's neighbour's doorstep.' After his look around the city he hastened to visit two of the buildings of Palladio, whom he calls that 'heavenly genius'—the Carità and the Redentore. These two he describes with a detail which he accords to no other buildings. The Accademia now occupies the conventual buildings of Santa Maria della Carità. The work of Palladio, which so delighted

Goethe, is merely a façade in a court. Goethe had, as we have seen, during the previous few days made careful study of Palladio's drawings and plans, and this accounts for his hurrying off to inspect one of them which on paper had specially pleased him. Though not a tenth part of the building had been completed, and Palladio's plan still remained unachieved, Goethe was enthusiastic as to the way in which the artist had based himself on the ancients in the hope of reviving their ideas. The Redentore, a landmark standing on the Giudecca, was preferred by Goethe to S. Giorgio Maggiore, a preference which is not generally shared. S. Giorgio is at least easier to reach than the Redentore, and visitors to the city have learnt to appreciate its beauty, and particularly the beauty of its campanile, from the mingled praise and criticism of Ruskin.

Goethe entered freely into the life of the city. He attended the Opera and saw a tragedy by Gozzi, a Venetian dialect comedy, a farce called *The English in Italy*, and the translation of the translation of the *Electra* by Crébillon, but he does not seem to have been impressed. He enjoyed the singing of the gondoliers. He found Veronese 'charming' and the horses on the front of St. Mark's 'glorious', but as a rule it needed the antique or copies of it to kindle any fire. During the last few days he visited the Lido, where he enjoyed his first view of the sea. 'We walked straight across the isthmus. I heard a hollow murmur. It was the sea! I soon saw it. It crested high against the shore as it retired. It was about noon and time of ebb. I have thus at last seen the sea with my own eyes.' The loneliness of the Lido pleased him. He wandered about collecting plants and shells in which he tried to dry some of the fluid of the cuttle-fish—happy, no doubt, to get away from the dirt of Venice. Even his second visit in 1790 does not appear to have modified his impression. At the end of the *Italienische Reise* there are a number of paragraphs headed 'Modern Restorations in Venice contemplated 1790'. Once again, as in the body of the book, he avoids criticism of the mosaics at St. Mark's. He says merely that 'of the oldest mosaics I have yet seen nothing to attract my attention'. The best old Greek paintings, he says, are to be found in the church

of the Greeks, S. Giorgio dei Greci, a church hidden away among
the small canals and *calle* behind the Riva degli Schiavoni. Once
again the traveller has reason to regret that in Venice so many
of the pictures have been collected in the Accademia, for this
church to-day contains little of interest. Goethe points out that
the idea of the holiness of a picture in itself came to an end with
Giovanni Bellini, and he notes the secularization of the work of
the great Venetians which in the time of Veronese permitted the
inclusion of beautiful women spectators in the delineation of
religious subjects to which artists were still compelled for the
most part to confine themselves. On leaving, Goethe has little
to say of Venice itself. What had made him happy was the
climate and the inspiration he received from the buildings he
had seen. The romantic Venice of Longhi and Goldoni and
Casanova—the torches, the masks, the flambeaux, and the crino-
lines—appears hardly to have touched him. Venice sent him
back to the ancients; he was grateful to her for that. He had
left her, he admits, without reluctance, but he took with him a
memory of her 'rare and unique image'.

(4)

The journey between Venice and Rome occupied fifteen days,
and except for a short stay in Bologna Goethe pushed forward
as quickly as possible. The first stage to Ferrara was made by
water, a no doubt attractive experience in comparison with the
discomforts of travelling by coach over poor roads. Goethe
started early in the morning of October 15th and arrived in
twenty-four hours, a journey which by train to-day takes less
than three. He enjoyed the experience, though he admits there
was little to see. By the time it was light the packet-boat was
probably already in the Po, and sailed its way up-stream through
flat, fertile country for the most part hidden by the thick vegetation which covered its banks. Ferrara, which stands some three
miles south of the river, appears to have had no interest for
Goethe, and he only remained there for a day. The Diary contains perfunctory references to the Ducal palace, the great
fortress which stands surrounded by its moat in the centre of

the city, one of the finest buildings of its kind in Italy. He saw the tomb of Ariosto in S. Benedetto, which tomb, some fifteen years later, was removed by the French to the Library of the University. He visited also the tomb of Tasso. This seems to have made no impression on him, perhaps because he doubted, not without reason, its authenticity, but the work of Tasso had always attracted him, and he cannot have failed to compare his own experiences at the Court of Weimar with those of Tasso at Ferrara. His *Tasso*, which in its prose draft he brought with him to Italy, was not finished until some years after his return home. The work, the career, and the personality of the unfortunate poet were the object of his interest and study during a long period, and it is strange that Ferrara and its associations seem to have moved Goethe not at all.

From Ferrara a short day's journey brought him to Cento, which remains to-day both in character and in population very much what it was when Goethe saw it. He liked its cheerfulness in comparison with the gloom of Ferrara, and he was pleased to find himself in the birth-place of Guercino, one of those painters whom the eighteenth century admired more than the nineteenth. Goethe calls him intrinsically bold as a painter, masculine, sensible without roughness—an opinion which is accepted by the high authority of Sir Charles Holmes—until in his final phase under the influence of Guido Reni he became sentimental and insincere. Many who may regret Goethe's unwillingness to appreciate anything but the classical and who cannot share his enthusiasm for Palladio may nevertheless wonder whether the views of the nineteenth century in regard to such a painter as Guercino may not call for reconsideration at the hands of the twentieth.

The following morning after another short journey Goethe is in Bologna, where he spent three days. He does not appear to have cared for Bologna, and when the time came for him to go he remarks: 'Whether I have to-day left Bologna or whether I have been driven out of it I cannot say. Enough that I eagerly availed myself of an earlier opportunity of leaving it.' Once again he saw what he wanted to see. He was delighted with Raphael's 'S. Cecilia', now in the Pinacoteca, a picture in which

the Saint stands surrounded with her earthly instruments of
music lying broken at her feet. When Goethe saw it, it was in
the north transept of S. Giovanni in Monte, from which it was
removed in 1796. He makes no mention of the church, which is
Gothic. 'The picture was exactly what I had been told of it',
he says, 'but now I have seen it with my own eyes.' He was no
doubt familiar with copies and etchings of the work. The days
before photography must have brought many delightful surprises
to the traveller which he cannot hope to enjoy to-day, and perhaps
some disappointments, too. On the other hand there is definite
loss in the disappearance of the eighteenth-century fashion of
having copies made of the works of the great masters and also,
some may think, of decorating houses with plaster casts. At
Bologna as at Venice and Vicenza Goethe was glad to get away
from the crowds in the streets. He went up 'the Tower', no doubt
the Torre Asinelli, which is 4 feet out of the perpendicular. He
advances the theory that in days when every great family had
a tower it was a mark of distinction to possess one which was out
of the straight. This ingenious suggestion appears at first sight
to obtain some support from the fact that the adjacent and un-
finished Torre Garisenda, a monument of a rival family, leans
as much as 8 feet. The balance of opinion, however, is that it is
the result of earthquakes, or, as in the case of Pisa, that the
foundations sank in the course of building. Contemplation of
the wonderful view enjoyed in solitude, and of the pictures for
which the city is famous, more particularly the works of Francia
and of Guido Reni, was what he most appreciated in Bologna.
On the third day he rode about in the neighbourhood of the city
examining rocks and stones, and returned in the evening with
specimens weighing a quarter of a hundredweight, some of which
are to be seen in the Goethehaus at Weimar. That same evening he was informed that a *vetturino* was about to start direct for
Rome. He eagerly seized the opportunity, hurriedly made his
arrangements, and together with his servant, whom he rarely
mentions, Herr Möller started off. There were to be no more
stops. The journey to Rome, which in its first stage had been a
flight, which later had become a more or less leisurely progress,

once again quickened its pace. From this moment he made
what can only be called a headlong rush towards his objective.

The road from Bologna to Florence over the Appenines had
been constructed in 1762. Goethe found it a tedious journey
and the inns inadequate, but he was agreeably surprised once
he got on the southern slope by the high cultivation among
the lower hills, and by the glorious view of the Arno valley in the
early morning. The journey of sixty-three miles took him the
best part of three days. To Florence Goethe devoted not more
than a few hours, but it must be remembered that he had con-
tracted for a through journey, and that it was his intention, an
intention which he fulfilled, to stay there on his return. He took
a hasty glance at the city, the cathedral, and the Boboli Gardens,
which stand on high ground on the south bank of the river overlooking the city. He merely remarks of them that they are most
delightfully situated and that he hastened out of them as fast as
he had entered them. In his mood at that time it is more than
probable that had he remained a week he would not have visited
S. Croce or S. Maria Novella, or that he would have had eyes
for the Fra Angelicos at the Annunziata or Orcagna's Tabernacle
at Or San Michele. As he hurried along he makes acute observations as to the trees and the methods of farming and generally
as to the agriculture, with which he had hitherto been unfamiliar.
He gives an account of a conversation with an Italian travelling
companion which shows how little an educated man knew about
Protestantism. Goethe sagely remarks: 'I could not but admire
the wise priests who sought to parry and to distort whatever was
likely to enlighten or to vary the dark outline of their traditional
dogmas.'[1] Of Arezzo he says nothing. He stayed a few days at
Perugia, of which he remarks that 'the sight is beautiful and the
view of the lake in the highest degree refreshing'. This no
doubt refers to Lake Trasimene, seen on the way. He appears
to have been detained at Perugia and to have been unwilling to
notice anything. 'Before I get to Rome I can open my eyes
no more.' Having learnt from his Palladio that there was at

[1] The writer remembers the wife of a French Préfet who asked him, 'Do Protes-
tants believe in God?'

Assisi a Temple of Minerva he left his carriage when it got near
to that city, and arranged to rejoin it at Foligno. Alone he
followed the rising road which leads from S. Maria degli Angeli
into Assisi, noticing on the left, with aversion, 'the vast mass of
churches piled Babel-wise one over another in one of which rest
the remains of the Holy S. Francis of Assisi'. The Temple, now
a church, he describes at great length, for it was the first temple
building he had seen. This refusal to visit S. Francesco is perhaps
the most famous incident in Goethe's journey to Rome. The
cult of S. Francis and the fame of the frescoes by Giotto in
the Lower Church combine to make it a matter of wonder to the
modern pilgrim to Assisi that Goethe, having inspected S. Maria
della Minerva in the little Square, should straightway have
retraced his steps down again into the valley. Those who have
followed his course since he left Munich will feel no such surprise. It is only an outstanding instance of his exclusive interest
in the classical, combined no doubt with his strong distaste for
and mistrust of the Church. On his way back from the city his
conduct was regarded as so unusual as to be suspicious. Four
men, two of whom were armed, stopped him on the road and
asked him why he had not visited S. Francesco, no doubt
suspecting him of being a smuggler, and showing a strong
inclination to arrest him as such. Only after explaining that
he was an architect was he allowed to proceed on his journey
to Foligno, where he lodged in what he describes as Homeric
simplicity with a humble family. Once off the main roads,
travelling in 1786 was still a matter of considerable hardship, as
Goethe's Diary and letters constantly attest. Foligno, Spoleto,
and Terni all lay off the main road from Perugia to Rome which
went straight to Narni and Civita Castellana, and it is clear that
Goethe did not travel through to Rome in the same carriage.
Spoleto it was worth his while to see, for the great aqueduct
which spans the valley between two hills is one of the most
impressive monuments of ancient Rome and one of the very few
which has remained in constant use to the present day. Terni
and Narni he passed without comment. From Terni he wrote
excitedly: 'I do not even undress any more in order to be

ready to start as soon as possible in the morning.' The precipitous road leading up to Narni, the beautiful little piazza with its cypress-trees and the panorama over the rich plain, all this was passed in the early morning before it was light. Civita Castellana evokes only some geological notes. Soracte was the first natural feature that told him he was near Rome at last.

The *Italienische Reise* gives no indication of his feelings as he entered the city. He reached Rome on October 29th, and his letters of November 1st make clear that his reticence is due to depth of feeling. All through the years the first view of Rome has been to generations of pilgrims a thrilling experience. The slight hill on the top of which the *vetturino* used to point with his whip and say 'Ecco Roma' is still to be identified; even after the turn of the century the guard of the Milan express rushing through the night gave a thrill to his passengers by walking up and down the corridor calling out 'La Bella Roma!'[1]

Little emotion is to be found in Goethe's Diary except his remark: 'To-morrow evening I shall be in Rome, even yet I can scarcely believe it possible, and after this wish is fulfilled, what shall I wish for afterwards?' His journal shows more feeling: 'I can say no more than that I am here. Now only I begin to live and I reverence my Guardian Angel.'

---

[1] The rather pedestrian verse of Rogers expresses something of what many others besides Goethe have felt:

> I am in Rome! Oft as the morning-ray
> Visits these eyes, waking at once I cry,
> Whence this excess of joy? What has befallen me?
> And from within a thrilling voice replies
> Thou art in Rome!

And in his poem on the Roman Campagna, more finely:

> Once again we look; and lo, the sea is white with sails
> Innumerable, wafting to the shore
> Treasures untold; the vale, the promontories,
> A dream of glory; temples, palaces,
> Called up as by enchantment; aqueducts
> Among the groves and glades rolling along
> Rivers, on many an arch high over-head;
> And in the centre, like a burning sun,
> The Imperial City!

II

(1)

'It was only as I passed under the Porta del Popolo', wrote Goethe, 'that I felt certain of reaching Rome.' On arrival his Diary notes, 'I have sent for Tischbein.' On the 30th he moved to Tischbein's house, No. 18 the Corso, then No. 20, which to-day bears a plaque, and this remained his head-quarters during his first stay in the city, from October 1786 to February 1787. Even before moving to Tischbein's house Goethe, like any other tourist, found time to rush round the city in order to get a general view of the ruins and of St. Peter's.

Tischbein was some two years younger than Goethe and felt for him during the early days of their acquaintance an almost passionate admiration and gratitude. This was no more than Goethe's due, for it had been thanks to him that originally Tischbein had been enabled to go to Rome by the Duke of Gotha, who had made him a regular allowance. Tischbein had repaid Goethe by sending him from time to time copies of works by the great masters, but they had never met. As months passed their friendship became clouded, but the fault was perhaps not so much with Tischbein as with Goethe, who in the beginning had exaggerated ideas of Tischbein's personal qualities just as he had of his artistic abilities. 'What most holds me in Italy is Tischbein. . . . I live three-fold in Tischbein's person . . . now indeed do I begin to live and Tischbein is my *genius*.' Mr. H. W. Nevinson describes Tischbein as a pretty fair painter, and his reputation to-day is that of a conscientious artist of the second class. He is not represented in the National Collections in Berlin or Dresden or Munich, but his work is to be seen in many public galleries throughout Germany, notably in Hamburg, Oldenburg, Gotha, and of course Weimar, more especially in the Goethehaus. For Goethe the time spent in Rome was a glorious and exhilarating interlude. He was still young enough, having thrown aside the troubles of Court life and the responsibilities of power, to enjoy his incognito. He found himself able to live a simple Bohemian existence, to work at what he wanted, and to do what he wanted in the society of friendly and admiring young Germans. But he did not always remember that Tischbein had his living to get, that he was a poor man often in search of a patron. Tischbein on his side, always subject to the calls of his profession, was at Goethe's feet. In after years he used to relate the unforgettable impression which Goethe made upon him at their first meeting. Goethe was standing at the fireplace, wearing a green coat, and he said merely, 'I am Goethe', to which Tischbein replied, 'I thought you would look like that.' It was Goethe's composure which most impressed Tischbein on this occasion. He had expected him, owing no doubt to the tone of his recent letters, to have been more highly strung. Tischbein at first had lived in the Via Balbuino, which runs like the Corso itself to the Piazza del Popolo, and he moved to the Corso with the couple from whom he tenanted his rooms. In these rooms there lived also two other young German artists, Georg Schütz and Friedrich Bury. Schütz was hardly a serious student, but he appears to have been a cheerful young man 31 years of age whom Goethe was perhaps predisposed to like from the beginning, since he came from Frankfort. We hear of him travelling about with Goethe, amusing him with his talk, and sitting to him for his ears, which his friends held to be more attractive than those of the Apollo Belvedere, and colouring carnival masks. He was evidently in a position to take life easily, and was called *Il Barone* by the Romans, a recognizable type. Bury was only 24 and had lived in Rome since he was 17. In his case art was the serious business of his life and he appears to have had the artist temperament. In later life he earned some distinction as a portrait-painter, came to Germany, and made a chalk drawing of Goethe, not very successfully, when he was 50. A third friend was Heinrich Meyer, a Swiss from Zürich, aged 26, who had already copied antique busts in Spain, and who was working in Rome along the same lines. Meyer was a serious young man, modest and retiring, entirely given up to his work. He was essentially a connoisseur. It was he who induced Angelica Kauffmann to buy a picture by Daniele da Volterra discovered by Tischbein, and it was he who in the following year urged her, this time unsuccessfully, to buy an antique statue from Naples. Angelica would probably have been willing enough, but they had to reckon with her husband, Zucchi, who was notoriously mean. Goethe's relations with Meyer never varied. For the rest of his life they were in constant touch. It was the most lasting and to Goethe perhaps the most valuable of the friendships made in Rome.

Another close acquaintance was Karl Philipp Moritz, who having written a book of his travels in England had been sent to Rome at the expense of his publisher in order to produce another work on similar lines. He arrived in the city about the same time as Goethe, but they did not meet until the beginning of December, and a few days after the meeting he had the misfortune to break his arm. There is at Weimar a rough sketch by Tischbein of Moritz being tended by Goethe while Tischbein himself prepares the dressing. Goethe's special affection for him is shown in one of his letters: 'What during these last forty days I have experienced and learnt as nurse, confessor, and private secretary to this patient may prove of benefit to me hereafter.' Moritz was clearly a lovable man, somewhat neurotic, subject to fits of depression. Goethe was always ready to learn from him, while at the same time there was something protective and even fatherly in his attitude. Moritz was a serious student of sculpture and mythology. As a philologist he was later of great help to Goethe in preparing his version of *Iphigenie* in verse, and they discussed together very frequently Goethe's ideas in regard to the origin of plants. And then there was Angelica Kauffmann, 'Fra Angelica' as he playfully calls her. This was a long friendship which did not suffer diminution as did his friendship with Tischbein. She was a woman who had attracted to her *salon* not only artists but musicians. Goethe had the impression, no doubt a correct one, that she was not particularly happy: 'She is herself weary of painting for sale, but her old husband finds it profitable that she should do so.' Angelica Kauffmann played a larger part in Goethe's second stay in Rome than during the first, but he never appears to have doubted her essential goodness or to have failed to appreciate her charm.

At any rate to start with, Goethe was delighted with the Bohemian atmosphere which he found with Tischbein, though later he tired of it somewhat, as he always tired of Bohemianism. The rooms were apparently comfortable enough, and he only asked for himself very modest accommodation, but it was a curious feature that the sitting-room, it appears, should have had a hole in the ceiling through which the landlords could look down, which they were always welcome to do.

By far the most famous of Tischbein's works is a portrait he painted in 1787 of Goethe in the Campagna, now in the Städelsches Institut at Frankfort. This shows Goethe sprawling rather than reclining on various fragments of classical ruins, his body covered, except for his right leg, with a long cloak, three-quarter face, wearing a large wide-awake hat. The composition is artificial, and the pose is very self-conscious. Two other works of the same artist, less well known, probably represent him more faithfully as he was at this time. One is a water-colour drawing given by Herr Ludwig in his *Life*, of Goethe looking out on to the Corso through half-opened shutters. Only his back is to be seen, but it is the back of a man still young, wearing knee-breeches and slippers, half dressed, his arms resting on the sill. The whole sketch in its pose suggests intense concentration of interest, and in the lines of the figure the suppleness and strength of a man in the prime of life. The Campagna picture might be that of a man of 50. This sketch might well represent a man of 25 instead of 38. The other, perhaps more interesting, is of Goethe in his room, a tall, slight youthful figure, leaning over the table, poised on one leg while he draws, probably in charcoal, the large Juno's head now in the Goethehaus, the purchase of which caused him such delight. Under the table is the landlord's cat, and under the shelf propped up by heavy books and weighed down by the Juno is his modest trunk. Goethe, as Tischbein shows him, is concentrated, happy, and youthful.

For Goethe, Rome was the Holy Land of Art and Mankind. From his father he had learnt to love Rome, and the need to see the city had come upon him almost as an illness. The Rome etched by Piranesi, who had died only eight years before, was, as

we know, not the real Rome. Piranesi did not pretend any more
than Turner pretended that his work was a faithful representation
of what he saw. The Rome he drew was the Rome of his imagining, based on the Rome with which he was so familiar. There
was no deliberate dishonesty or calculated untruthfulness. Architectural features he copied with care, but he did not hesitate to
embellish with appropriately picturesque detail, and he allowed
himself wide latitude in dealing with what was broken or incomplete. Goethe arrived well acquainted with his work and
remained, at any rate during the early part of his stay, his
enthusiastic admirer. The Rome of Piranesi was real enough
to Goethe, and indeed as he saw it the city must have been
very beautiful, even though its beauty was of decay. Except
during Carnival time, when the Corso was full of excitement and
activity, there was little social life. There were long proces-
sions of seminarists, priests, and monks in the streets. The city
contained 800 churches and 284 convents. A description given
by Peter Beckford, who visited Rome some twenty years after
Goethe, probably represented fairly enough the Rome of 1786.
'Cardinals, Monsignori, and Abbés', he says, 'had become the
representatives of the Scipios, Catos, and Brutuses. Only the
horses still showed something of the restiveness of a Gracchus
or the vice of a Catiline.' Among the diplomatic representatives
at the Papal Court there was a certain amount of entertaining
after sundown. People walked or drove in the Corso, and artists
then as now were to be found living in or near the Piazza di
Spagna and patronizing the cafés of the Via Condotti. There
were public whippings of malefactors, and the remains of those
who had been publicly drawn and quartered were left lying about
like butchers' meat. Assassinations were frequent, and the dirt
of the streets and of the houses too was beyond words. Nearly
twenty years later Chateaubriand, when he occupied the top
floor of the Palazzo Lancelotti, says that his white breeches were
sometimes literally black with fleas. The ruins, it is true, had a
picturesque beauty which to-day they have lost, when sheep and
cattle grazed among the wild fig-trees, and goats roamed over
the Capitol. How dense was the foliage which covered the

palaces, monuments, temples, baths, and tombs is indicated
truly enough by Piranesi and by Pannini. The Colosseum had
been put to one use after another. The builders of new Rome
had made havoc of what the Barbarians had spared. The saying
non Barbari sed Barbarini is literally true. Living for everybody was poor, and the joys of Carnival were a matter of eight
days only. Goethe remarks: 'The people of Rome are the
children of Nature. Amidst pomp and honours of all kinds,
religion and the arts are not one jot different from what they
would be in caves or forests.'

He eagerly seized the opportunity to live an artist life with his
artist friends, who respected his incognito as did everybody
else, though his presence in the city came to be gradually known.
One of the first things he did was to see the Pope celebrate Mass
in his private Chapel in the Quirinal Palace, a spectacle which
aroused his latent Protestantism. The Pope was the unfortunate
Pius VI who was to see the Castle of S. Angelo in the hands of
the French, the city given over to the Republicans, and was himself to die in exile at Valence. During his first few days it was
the Rotunda (Pantheon), S. Peter's, and the Apollo Belvedere
which aroused Goethe's keenest enthusiasm, though he has
praise also for Guercino, Titian, and the *stanze* of Raphael.
There is already noticeable a new attitude of mind: the strange
and rather absurd prejudice which during his journey had closed
his eyes and his mind to nine-tenths of what was to be seen,
became less marked. His mind, in fact, was open again. He had
come to Rome in order to learn; as he put it later to Brun, he
had come to plunge into the contemplation of the beautiful and
to lose himself in so doing. Bielschowsky in his monumental
Life remarks that Goethe's appreciation was confined almost
exclusively to painting, and that too within very circumscribed
limits. Careful readers of the letters which make up this part of
the *Italienische Reise* may think this is too sweeping a statement
when they remember what he has to say about Domenichino
and the Caracci, Guercino and Titian, but it is true that he does
not appear interested in Renaissance sculpture and that both the
Church itself and the religious subjects of many of the pictures

continued to repel him. There is no record that he spent his time
with Italians or that he talked anything but German. The days
passed happily enough, devoted at one moment to painting, at
another to architecture or to sculpture or to botany or to the
literary work he had brought with him. This was even more
true of his second stay than of the first. It is impossible to read
his letters without realizing that much of the pleasure he found
in Rome was due to the fact that he was able to do what he
wanted and to do it at his own time. It was during his first stay
that he set himself seriously to study the work of Winckelmann.
Goethe had hoped when he was a boy of 19 to make his acquaintance at Leipzig, when the startling news arrived that he had
been murdered at Trieste. 'Yesterday', says Goethe under date
December 16th, 'many of Winckelmann's letters which he wrote
from Italy fell into my hands. With what emotions did I not
begin to read them.' Thereafter his references to Winckelmann
are inspired with enthusiastic reverence. Winckelmann's work
in the University Library at Halle and later in Count Bünen's
Library at Dresden had equipped him with artistic knowledge
which was already organized and systematized at the time when
he was put in charge of Cardinal Albani's collection at Rome.
His career in the city had begun after he had passed through
trying years of semi-starvation and intensive study. He had
been received into the Church, and it is as a cleric that Casanova,
in error, refers to him. The moment of his coming to Rome
was the moment when Pompeii was yielding up treasures hitherto unsuspected in number or value. The fame of this collection
brought fame also to the scholar who arranged it, and Goethe
soon found himself with his *History of Ancient Art* in constant
use. Winckelmann is an outstanding figure among the scholars
who have taught that Greek art and Greek literature should be
studied side by side, and it was one of his sayings that 'imitation of the ancients is the shortest way to perfection in the fine
arts'. Goethe's admiration for Winckelmann remained lifelong,
tempered though such enthusiasms were always liable to become
by the passage of years. 'We sometimes find Winckelmann
merely groping about', he remarked to Eckermann in 1827, 'but,

what is a great thing, his groping always leads to something. He is like Columbus when he had not yet discovered the New World, yet had the presentiment of it in his mind.' Looking back we may now see that the classicists, of whom Winckelmann was the outstanding figure, went too far in their purism and in their exclusive concentration on the antique, and it is sad that in the case of each of those three names which meant so much to Goethe— Vitruvius, Palladio, and Winckelmann—later times have placed a different valuation on their work; but it was Winckelmann who helped Goethe to realize that behind Rome lay Greece. He came to feel that he must see the originals from which so much in Rome was merely derivative. He must go south, and if not to Greece then to Naples and to Sicily. 'How much has Winckelmann done', writes Goethe on January 13th, 'and yet how much reason has he left us to wish that he had done still more. With the materials which he had collected he built quickly in order to raise the roof. Were he still living he would be the first to give us a re-cast of his great work.'

Meanwhile, Goethe was content to enjoy Rome like any other visitor from abroad, and between his arrival at the beginning of November and his departure immediately after the Carnival on Shrove Tuesday 1787 he saw at his leisure and in his own way all that was to be seen. Apart from the major sights to which reference has been made already, he tells of a visit to the Pyramid of Cestius and an evening on the Palatine. The immensity of the ruins of the palaces of the Caesars impressed him as it must impress everybody, but his letter characteristically does not give an idea of what he saw, but merely of the sensations which the panorama evoked in him.

There is nothing little here although indeed something occasionally to find fault with. Something more or less absurd in taste; and yet even *this* partakes of the universal grandeur of all around. . . . To me at least it seems as if I never before rightly estimated the things of the world as I do here. I rejoice when I think of all the blessed effects of all this, and what I am to be in the future. . . . I am not here to enjoy myself after my own fashion, but to busy myself with the great objects around, to learn and to improve myself before I am 40 years old.

A few days later, and in a less sententious mood, he did what travellers continued to do until about sixty years ago: 'We could not resist the temptation to cram our pockets full of the granite, porphyry and marble slabs which lie here in thousands.' He visited the Capitol again and again, and describes with more than his wonted enthusiasm the Colosseum at night.

At night it is always closed. A hermit dwells in a little hut inside it and beggars of all kinds find homes beneath its crumbling arches. The latter had lit a fire in the arena and a gentle wind bore down the smoke to the ground, so that the lower portion of the ruins was quite hidden by it, while above the vast walls stood out in deeper darkness before the eye. Presently the smoke found its way up the sides and through every chink and opening while the moon lit it up like a cloud. The sight was exceedingly glorious.

He writes with delight and enthusiasm of a 'find'. The Obelisk of the Trinità del Monte was in process of erection during his visit, and he describes how he obtained from his wig-maker what was evidently a portion of a large key with cameo-like figures carved upon it; but keen sightseer though he was, once he had obtained his general view of the city he settled down to study carefully only those things which appealed to him most. He refused to spend time upon sights which were not to his taste, and we find no reference to the great basilicas other than St. Peter's or to those other churches which attract most travellers, S. Clemente, S. Prassede, S. Maria sopra Minerva, and S. Pietro in Vincoli. There is only the slightest reference to the great medieval palaces, no reference at all to the Castle of S. Angelo or the catacombs, the fountains, the gates, the bridges. And if he saw what he liked, he lived as he liked. Goethe was no hermit in Rome, and starting with the small circle to which Tischbein introduced him, his letters show that he steadily increased the number of his friends, though still confining himself, no doubt as part of the price of his pseudo-anonymity, to Germans.

(2)

So much we may say of Goethe the traveller and the tourist in Rome living among his circle of friends. But behind it all there was always the complication he had left in Weimar, the matter of his relations with Frau von Stein. He had come to feel their relationship an insupportable strain. His ardour had died down, and he hoped as men have hoped before and since that because he personally was ready to allow their passion, which had always been retained within prescribed limits, to evolve into no more than a friendly comradeship, she on her side would be equally ready. To begin with, it is true, in spite of his flight and secrecy, which any woman in her position would justifiably have resented, he continued to write like a lover, and until he reached Rome he wrote daily. His Diary was written for her, but its arrival was delayed, and in any case a travel diary was hardly likely to soothe her bewilderment and indignation. The Diary which was sent to her from Venice reached her only at Christmas. She had thought that he was lost, perhaps killed in the mountains. However the fault arose, he gave her undoubtedly much useless suffering. Sometimes even yet Goethe seemed to feel an irresistible need of her company, and had she written to him in Rome when at last she knew his address, in a tone which was calculated to touch his sensibility, he might well have responded and returned, but she wrote him the wrong sort of letter if she wished to retain his love. He had persuaded himself that the perusal of his Diary had brought her pleasure, and that she was following his experiences with affection and enthusiasm. Her letter, which reached him within a few weeks of his arrival in Rome, told him, it must be inferred (for all her letters later on were returned to her at her own request), that she wished to hear from him no more. This came upon him as a blow, strangely we may think; but after he had fled, his nerves frayed by her treatment of him, he certainly had no desire for a rupture, and his letters to her from Rome are pathetic in their humility.[1]

Gradually the inevitable happened: his letters receiving no response became fewer as time passed. During his second stay in Rome his affections became directed into new quarters, and

[1] Some of the most touching are quoted by M. Alexandre Bérenger in his *Goethe en Italie*, based on his journal and letters, to which I am much indebted.

when he returned to Weimar he returned full of gratitude and affection for what she had been to him in the past, but their old relationship had no renewal. Frau von Stein was 45 and it was a new Goethe who had come back. Before long he found peace and for many years happiness in the simple fidelity of Christiane. This as we know was regarded by Frau von Stein as the occasion for a final breach, and their friendship came thus to its end.

This complication, then, lay behind his happiness during his first stay in Rome, and though there is no evidence of it in the *Italienische Reise* it must have done not a little to mar his enjoyment. Perhaps it accounts to some extent for the feverish intellectual activities which characterized these months, for while he was living as a tourist Goethe crammed into his days the most varied interests and activities. He drew, he painted, and if he did not know it before he learnt the limitations of his own genius. He studied anatomy. 'I have not without labour', he says, 'gained a tolerable knowledge of the human frame, for the continued examination of the ancient statues is continually stimulating one to more perfect understanding of it.' He was delighted with an anatomical figure displaying the whole muscular system. 'Its beauty is really amazing. It might pass for some flayed demi-god, even a Marsyas.' Above all there was the work that he had brought with him, *Iphigenie* and *Tasso*, and to these he devoted himself with energy. The new version of *Iphigenie* must have been quickly completed. It was not approved when later he came to read it at Weimar. His friends preferred the earlier prose version. They did not appreciate its classic spirit, nor does it appear to have pleased in Rome, though Goethe gives an account of a reading there which undoubtedly explains how it was that Angelica Kauffmann gained and held his affection. Madame Angelica and Hofrath Reiffenstein were the auditory, and even Signor Zucchi had asked to be present because it was the wish of his wife. While it was being read over, he worked away at a great architectural plan. 'The tender soul of Angelica listened to the piece with incredible depth of sympathy. She promises me a drawing of one of the scenes which I am to keep in remembrance of her.' It would appear that Moritz had an important part in encouraging Goethe to write this version during his illness.

(3)

The question of going farther south does not appear to have been in Goethe's mind when he arrived in Rome. It had originally been his intention to return home direct, but quite early in January the project began to take shape. His friends urged that having seen so much he ought to see more. The Duke was content not to press for his return. Tischbein was ready to go with him, and we may infer that Goethe expected that he would continue to be his companion until they came back to Rome, though there is no suggestion that Tischbein gave any definite undertaking on the point. It is quite certain that Goethe's study of Winckelmann impressed him with the fact that there were things to see in Naples and in Sicily at least as interesting as in Rome, and, for a student of the antique, artistically even more important. Quite early in his stay, therefore, Goethe determined to leave Rome after the Carnival, and to this arrangement he adhered. He wanted to go, as he says, 'in order to cleanse his soul from the sadness of so many ruins'. Rome was full of memories. In Naples he would see a living city. Carnival meant little to him, and he writes contemptuously of its mummeries: 'incredible tumult, but no joy'. When he heard that Vesuvius was in eruption he was keen to get off: 'I can scarcely endure to wait until it shall really be my lot to witness such grand phenomena.' He was sorry to leave Moritz still an invalid, and sorry no doubt to leave others who had been his companions, but the urge to be off was upon him, and Tischbein whose picture of him was well advanced was coming too. With Tischbein by his side he felt that nothing in Rome need detain him, especially as he had already made up his mind that he would go back there and make a further stay before finally returning to Weimar. On February 22nd, therefore, in high spirits he set out for the south.

III

(1)

The railway journey from Rome to Naples is to-day a matter
of some five hours, and the line runs by Cassino and Capua,
following more or less the course of the Via Latina. The other
more westerly route to Naples was in Goethe's time by the Via
Appia, which followed the coast for the greater part of the way.
Even to-day along that route the line goes as far only as Terra-
cina, beyond which service is by diligence. This latter route
is rather longer, but has for the most part few gradients. It was
the road in general use in the eighteenth century. Goethe and
Tischbein reached Velletri on the evening of the 22nd, and starting thence at 3 in the morning they arrived at Fondi by night-
fall. Tischbein was not merely Goethe's companion but his
guide, for he already knew Naples, and he helped Goethe to
enjoy the journey. Goethe indeed showed himself very appreciative of the unfamiliar vegetation, the wonderful views of Terra-
cina and the sea beyond, the interest of the Pontine marshes and
the volcanic formations. He noticed the blue vapour hanging
just above the ground, and remembering the warning that they
must not go to sleep, the journey took on something of the
nature of an adventure. From Fondi they came down to the sea
at Gaeta, and following the coast to Formio they struck inland.
It was another day full of interest, Tischbein continually sketching and Goethe fascinated with the views of islands and capes
and the ruins of ancient villas, aqueducts, and tombs. He delighted in the orange-groves and in the new and exciting
treasures to be found on the shore : not merely a starfish, the
first he had ever seen, but stones thrown up by the water—
serpentine, jasper, quartz, porphyry as well as blue and green
glass and marble of all kinds. That night they slept in a large and
cheerless inn. There is no mention of other travellers on the
road (probably on account of the season), but the inn as described by Goethe was clearly a recognized stage on the Rome–
Naples Road. The next day, the 24th, they started at sunrise,
and in bitter cold and crossing some volcanic hills arrived at

Capua at noon. After their midday halt they proceeded through the level country of corn and vineyards, thrilled by the sight of Vesuvius on their left, and they finally arrived in Naples and went to an inn in the Largo del Castello. The castle must have been the Castel Nuovo, so called to distinguish it from the Castello S. Elmo on the high ground behind the city, The disappearance of the old name is no doubt the work of United Italy, which in Naples as elsewhere has renewed the names of so many squares and streets. Goethe's early impressions were ecstatic as he made his hurried inspection of the bay, the city, the castles, and the streets, and even found time on his first day to go out to Posilipo. Within the next two days he got in touch with two men, each of whom had no little influence on his immediate future—the painter Hackert, who showed himself both now and afterwards in Rome a kindly and helpful friend, and the Prince of Waldeck. The Prince's feelings for Goethe were from the first most cordial. He wanted him later as a travelling companion in Greece, and he engaged a sculptor to execute a bust of him in marble. It was the Prince who was the unwitting cause of the coolness which later on developed between Goethe and Tischbein. Tischbein saw in him a patron, and Goethe resented that the Prince should receive consideration before himself. The trouble did not develop at once, and Goethe appears to have enjoyed Naples quite as much as he had enjoyed Rome, though no doubt in a different way. As compared with its free open situation he exclaims excitedly: 'the Capitol and the basin of the Tiber look like a cloister built on a bad site.' He wrote those words a few days after his first attempt at the ascent of Vesuvius. The day was cloudy, but the steam from the crater was so dense that it was impossible to approach it, and Goethe's guide deserted him. Tischbein apparently had refused to accompany him. He was no scientist and Vesuvius did not interest him, besides which the Prince of Waldeck wanted him to accompany him to Baiae. This was the first occasion on which Goethe's wishes and what Tischbein considered his duties were at variance.

When a few days later Goethe made his second attempt at Vesuvius, it was in Tischbein's company. He went, as Goethe

admits, out of good fellowship, and Goethe remarks that to an
artist concerned with the beautiful it is not difficult to understand
that 'such a frightful and shapeless conglomeration of matter
continually preying upon itself must have appeared utterly
abominable'. Tischbein gave up before reaching the crater, but
Goethe, attracted by the presence of danger, went to the top and
glanced for a moment into the chasm. A fortnight later, hearing
that the mountain was in eruption, he made yet a third excursion
in order to watch the lava pouring down. The spectacle once
again fascinated the scientist in Goethe, whose venturesomeness
and enthusiasm in collecting specimens of lava had to be restrained by the guide. Pompeii and Herculaneum were of course
visited. Systematic excavation at Pompeii did not begin until
long after Goethe's day. About forty years previously the discovery of various statues and utensils had led to the uncovering
of the theatre and adjacent parts, and the work had gone on
spasmodically since then, more particularly with the idea of
finding valuables. Though Goethe was able to admire the bright
colouring of the houses and the gay arabesques on the walls of
such homes as he saw, he paid no second visit, and he speaks of
the 'strange and in some degree unpleasant impression which
the mummified city leaves on the mind'. Excavation at Herculaneum has only been undertaken on an extensive scale in our
own day, since the town lies beneath a solid bed of lava with
which only modern mechanical appliances can hope successfully
to deal, and then only with difficulty and at great cost. Here again
the search for valuables was the original incentive for the work.
Goethe saw what was to be seen by torchlight at the bottom of
a pit. He found it a strange experience, but he none the less
expressed a hope, which was not fulfilled, of returning there again.
But in truth the time spent in Naples was not spent in sightseeing. He was enthralled by the beauty which surrounded
him—the panorama, the vegetation, the climate. 'Were I not
impelled by the German spirit and desire to learn and to do
rather than to enjoy', he writes, 'I should tarry a little longer
in this school of a light-hearted and happy life and try to profit
by it still more.' And again, 'If in Rome one can readily set

oneself to study, here one can do nothing but live.' There follows immediately an entry which must be given in full:

Sir William Hamilton, who still resides here as ambassador from England, has at length, after his long life of art, and long study, discovered the most perfect of admirers of nature and art in a beautiful young woman. She lives with him: an Englishwoman about 20 years old. She is very handsome, and of beautiful figure. The old knight has had made for her a Greek costume, which becomes her extremely. Dressed in this, and letting her hair loose, and taking a couple of shawls she exhibits every possible variety of posture, expression and look, so that at the last the spectator almost fancies it is a dream. Standing, kneeling, sitting, lying down, grave or sad, playful, exulting, repentant, wanton, menacing, anxious—all mental states follow rapidly one after another. With wonderful taste she suits the folding of her veil to each expression, and with the same handkerchief makes every kind of head-dress. The old knight holds the light for her, and enters into the exhibition with his whole heart.

Three years previously Emma Hart had been handed over by Charles Greville to his uncle, Sir William Hamilton, in return for payment of his debts. Sir William married her in 1791. On returning from Sicily, and after having enjoyed much hospitality from Sir William Hamilton, Goethe remarks, rather more critically: 'Our beauteous hostess seemed to me by no means richly endowed in respect of mind. . . . the promise of her fair figure was by no means made good by any expression of voice or language betokening equal wealth of soul.'

Goethe's letters give many evidences that he found it hard to make up his mind when to start for Sicily. Sometimes it looks as if he considered giving up the idea altogether. For this it is probable that Tischbein was responsible, and it was certainly a heavy blow to Goethe that Tischbein felt himself unable to accompany him. Tischbein had already thrown aside his work in order to be with Goethe. He was a poor man who found life expensive, and he was perhaps not good at saving. It is to be remembered that Tischbein was not a highly educated man, and that though he gave Goethe hero-worship he never understood him and never seems to have realized his greatness. Goethe

on his side was wounded that Tischbein was always anxious
to find wealthy patrons, in which he was no doubt inspired by
the success of his brother Heinrich, who was Court painter to the
Grand Duke of Hesse Cassel. Even before they had met, Tischbein had written to Goethe for introductions, and it is clear that
there was in him little of the idealist. Goethe's pride was
wounded still further when later on he went off with the Prince
of Waldeck, and never rejoined him as he had promised to do.
The breach is easily understandable, and there is much to be said
in excuse and explanation of Tischbein's attitude. On March
19th, two days before Goethe sailed, Tischbein recommended
as travelling companion a young painter named Kniep, a man
with little experience but clearly of great personal charm. His
combination of deference, good spirits, and good humour did
much to make the journey in Sicily a great success. Goethe on
his side appreciated his admiration, thought well of his draughtsmanship, and made an arrangement to purchase a number of his
sketches.

(2)

On March 29th, accompanied by Kniep, Goethe set sail for
Palermo, and after experiencing every sort of weather arrived
there on April 2nd. They were back in Naples on May 17th.
The weeks in Sicily were well spent, for after a fortnight in
Palermo they proceeded to Segesta, Castelvetrano, Girgenti,
Catania, Taormina, and Messina, whence they returned. Palermo
delighted Goethe and he spent a full fortnight there. He found
it, as he said, a Paradise. They lodged quite close to the sea front
at the bottom of the Corso. One of their first excursions was to
Monte Pellegrino, the great limestone hill which stands to the
north of the Bay of Palermo under the summit of which is the
Grotto of S. Rosalia. Goethe seems to have been greatly
impressed at the scene—the loneliness, the voices of priests in
the cave, and the recumbent marble figure of the Saint herself.
Though he called upon and was courteously received by the
Viceroy in the Palazzo Reale he failed to visit the Capella Palatina
with its wooden ceiling of Moorish work, its marbles, and its

famous mosaics, nor does he appear to have seen, although he must have passed by, the even more beautiful Cathedral of Monreale. Mosaic work did not interest him, as we know, and he was content to treat the finest examples of it in and near Palermo as he had treated it at Venice. A whole day on the other hand was given to a visit to the Villa Palagonia at Bagheria, a town some eight miles to the east of Palermo, where members of the Bourbon Court had their country properties. Goethe writes with the greatest contempt of the grotesque figures and monsters and the puerile fancies, the maddest rococo, with which the house was decorated. The only explanation of his visit is perhaps that he had heard so much about Prince Palagonia's eccentricities that his curiosity was whetted, a curiosity fully satisfied when later on he came across the Prince himself collecting, with the assistance of a courier, money for the slaves in Barbary. His most interesting experience in Palermo was perhaps his visit to the family of Cagliostro. It was already fairly generally believed that Cagliostro was by birth Giuseppe Balsamo, born of poor parents in the city and educated at a monastery where he picked up some rudimentary knowledge of chemistry and medicine. He hung about Palermo, a thorough vagabond, until he was about 26. Since then the city had followed his strange career with interest, especially in connexion with the affair of the Diamond Necklace in 1785. At the time of Goethe's visit he had been released from the Bastille and had proceeded to London, but he was already discredited, and at 44 his great days were over. It was because some lingering doubts still remained in the public mind that Goethe was anxious to get at the facts once and for all. He therefore put himself into touch with a lawyer engaged by the French Government to seek out the origin of Cagliostro, and found that his inquiries left no doubt in regard to the matter. Through his agency Goethe was enabled to visit the family, who appeared to be very poor but decent people. He was introduced as bringing a message from their long-lost son and brother, and after returning to Germany he sent them a sum of money which he was content that they should believe came from their famous relative. This evoked from the aged mother a touching letter of

thanks. It was certainly owing to Goethe that the origin of
Cagliostro became generally known.

On April 16th he left Palermo without having seen, or at
least without commenting upon, the Chapel and the Cathedral.
During his time there, and indeed throughout his stay in Sicily,
he was much occupied with botanical investigation. He was
frequently in the Botanical Gardens and the diaries are full of
geological and scientific observations. The three weeks that
followed were devoted to sightseeing, and Goethe became once
more the enthusiastic tourist. Travelling in Sicily even up to
quite recently was a fatiguing experience once off the beaten
track, but Goethe was never discouraged by discomfort. He
broke his journey at the ancient city of Alcamo and visited the
Temple of Segesta from there rather than from Calatafimi, where
the visitor of to-day finds excellent accommodation in the inn
named after Samuel Butler. Goethe writes of Segesta without
enthusiasm. This portion of the Diary is for the most part
geological and botanical. The sight of the Doric Temple standing alone on its hill, a complete shell, surrounded by the long
grass and the rich Sicilian vegetation, acanthus and asphodel,
wild violets and orchids, and grape hyacinths, is one of the finest
imaginable. It is still approachable only by mule-track, the still-
ness broken by the sound of the bees and the grasshoppers.
Goethe found all this fertility melancholy. He speaks of the
well-preserved theatre with its splendid view over the sea as
insignificant ruins.[1] Clearly Segesta did not attract him. 'I have
actually seen some insects here', remarks Goethe—a curious
remark, for to most visitors Sicily does not lack insects.

From Segesta he travelled south to Castelvetrano and thence
to the coast at Sciacca. At Castelvetrano he passed within eight
miles of Selinunte, where are the remains of the largest temples
to be found anywhere in Europe. The work at Selinunte has all
been done during the nineteenth century, and for the most part
during the latter part of it. It is even yet incomplete, and a keen-
eyed traveller may still make discoveries on his own account.
That there must have been much worth seeing even in 1787 is

[1] Excavation work had not yet been undertaken.

quite certain, but Goethe was in no mood to be interested, and he therefore continued his journey eastward, following the coast-line to Girgenti. Girgenti pleased him better, and he spent there five days. He liked the Temple of Concord, which in com-parison with Paestum was 'as a god compared with a gigantic figure'. The Temple of Jupiter, which was one of the greatest ever built, over 370 feet long and never completed, is little more than a ground-plan and a mass of stone, having later been made use of for constructional purposes. Goethe, like everybody else, was impressed by the huge scale of the building and that he was able to stand within the flutes of a column. He admired most of all the Temple of Juno, which stands, with many of its columns still erect, on an edge of rock. Kniep, of whom he does not say very much, was kept busy sketching at Girgenti, whereas Goethe's scattered notes during this time are more miscellaneous even than usual—archaeology, agriculture, botany, geology, ornithology. There is in them nothing of history and little suggestion of the wonderful beauty of it all. Goethe in Sicily was the scientist, not the poet. From Girgenti they travelled north to Caltanisetta and Castrogiovanni. In Castrogiovanni they were uncomfort-able, but the beauty of its site evokes no comment; in the ancient Enna there is no reference to the Rape of Proserpine. In Goethe's Sicilian notes he speaks neither of Ovid nor of Thucydides. But travelling was difficult, and many of its details were unromantic. Even in the bigger towns where they could get a bed in an inn they had often to find their own provisions. Catania was allotted five days. Here they saw the museum, a collection of coins belonging to Prince Biscari, and a Benedictine monastery. Goethe was, as one might have expected, anxious to climb Etna, but he had to be content to visit the Monti Rossi, which had been formed as a result of the eruption of 1669 of volcanic ashes and stones.[1] On the other hand they spent one day only at Taormina, though he appreciated, as he could not fail to do, the theatre with its famous view of the coast with Etna as a background, and on the other side the panorama of rocks and the Straits and the

[1] The date is given wrongly as 1699 in Goethe's *Travels in Italy* (Bell, 1885), p. 282.

Calabrian coast. It is at Taormina that there occurs a passage
in his Diary which throws a flood of light on Goethe's mentality.
Nobody can read the account of his journey without being somewhat mystified and disappointed that on the whole it is so
uninspired a record, and that he should so often have deliberately
ignored so many of the finest sights. At Taormina he thought
out in detail a scheme which he had long had in mind of a con-
densation of the *Odyssey*. He relates that he sat in a peasant's
garden lost in reverie and that he bought and read eagerly the
Odyssey with immense interest; and he continues:

To describe in lovely colours for the enjoyment of others objects
seen at a great distance from home; to tell of the adventures of travel
and its perils; facing the chance of being looked upon by the young as a
demi-god and by the more sedate as a talker of rhodomontade, all this
caused me to feel so great an attachment to this plan [of a drama based
on Nausicaa] that in thinking of it I dreamed away all the time of
my stay in Palermo and indeed all the rest of my Sicilian tour. It was
this that made me care little for all the inconvenience and discomfort I
met with, for on this classic ground a poetic view had taken possession
of me, and caused all that I experienced or saw to be accepted and
regarded in a happy mood.

This quotation is from a passage written later, but it explains
much and makes it only more disappointing and strange that the
Homeric drama never came to anything. Goethe and Kniep
reached Messina on May 10th and sailed four days later. One
of the many earthquakes from which the city has suffered had
overwhelmed it four years previously. Twelve thousand had
been killed and not a single house had remained uninjured. On
going to pay their respects to the Governor they found him a
choleric old man of whom his attendants and the population
generally stood in fear. To the visitors he was gracious and
extended an invitation to dine with him. Goethe appears to have
forgotten the invitation, and had to be sent for. Arriving there
late he found forty people sitting round an oval table, with a
seat reserved for him beside the Governor, the company silent
and apprehensive. He managed, however, to soothe the old man
by his suave courtesy, and when the ordeal of the dinner was

over, for it was nothing less, he was shown at the Governor's command the Jesuit church, and received an invitation to dine at the Palace during the period of his stay in the town. The Jesuiti appears to have been the only sight in Messina that Goethe visited, and as usual he formed his own opinion as to the reputed value of what was shown to him there. Goethe's record makes clear that there were not merely dangers and discomforts to be faced while actually on the journey, but that even in the cities it was deemed advisable that foreigners should be banded together for greater protection. Goethe grieved the many friendly acquaintances he so easily made by refusing any such assistance. The fact was that he had no intention of staying in Messina, and had indeed arranged to sail for Naples the next day in a French ship. The two days' voyage back was a greater adventure even than the voyage out. The boat was nearly wrecked on the rocks of Capri, sucked along by the current. The sailors were preparing to get her off with poles and anything else that was handy when a breeze arose suddenly, the sails were hoisted, and they moved away into safety. The captain and the steersman had evidently bought the vessel without knowing very much about navigation. It was dirty, uncomfortable, and expensive, and there was little to eat. Goethe asserted himself and urged the tearful passengers to cease screaming and to pray. He was lying below in a semi-torpid condition musing on the story of the storm on the Sea of Galilee, when Kniep ran down to him and told him that the danger was past.

(3)

Goethe arrived in Naples on May 17th and remained there about a fortnight before returning to Rome. His enthusiasm for Naples and the Neapolitans remained unabated, and he quotes with approval the remark of Pliny that the Greeks, always contemptuous of the foreigner, were yet content to pay this country the highest compliment of naming it a part of Greece, Magna Graecia. His friends welcomed him back. Together with Hackert he again got into touch with Sir William Hamilton, with whom his acquaintance was to develop still farther. They inspected once again his collections as well as busts, vases, bronzes, jewels, all lying confused in a cellar. Hamilton had purchased indiscriminately, but Goethe indicates his view that many of the articles they found hidden away had been obtained in other ways than by purchase, and no doubt he was right. It was the custom of visitors, in other respects of the highest principles, who were interested in the antique to help themselves with the connivance of lax and ill-paid custodians to what they could find, so long as it was done not too openly. This state of affairs continued in Italy right up to the middle of the nineteenth century, and in Sicily to an even later date. Emma Hart impressed him no less than before, but he discovered what others were to discover later, that she had no intellectual brilliance.

Perhaps the most important event for Goethe himself during the last days in Naples was that his hopes of finding the proto-plant (*Urpflanze*) were once more stimulated. 'I have come close', he says, 'on the secret of the production of plants and of organization . . . the proto-plant is the most wonderful entity in the World . . . with this model and the key to it, new plants may be multiplied ad infinitum.' This is the vision he had already indulged at Padua, a vision that had come to him again at Palermo, when in the public gardens he saw plants, hitherto familiar to him only in pots and tubs or under glass, growing freely in the open air. One long letter from Naples is exclusively concerned with an account of St. Philip Neri, and at the end of his Neapolitan record he adds a further long note about the Saint, who attracted him by his humour and his humanity quite as much as by his humility.

The last days before his return were happy, but he felt it was time he went back to Rome. In Rome he had enjoyed himself in a circle of friends. In Naples he had moved more freely in society and had accepted invitations. German acquaintances turned up: a lady from Karlsbad, and the Duke and Duchess of Ursel. He was delighted to see them, and in no quarter did he attempt to keep up his incognito. As the time for departure grew near he almost ceased to criticize; the life of the city, its gaiety and its colour, inspired in him a rare enthusiasm. Even the letters to Herder and to Frau von Stein gave indication that like most of his companions he too had found romance in Naples. When the time came there was no slipping away, but rather a punctilious care in paying visits of farewell to all who had entertained him with friendship or hospitality. Vesuvius was once more in eruption the night before he left what he calls 'this incomparable town'. From Kniep he parted with real regret, and Kniep himself, always appreciative of Goethe and essentially warm-hearted, made his way to the customs barrier and took his final farewell of his friend after the journey had actually started. Goethe reached Rome once more on June 6th.

IV

(1)

Goethe's second stay in Rome covers the period between July 1787 and April 1788. The first visit lasted over four months. When he returned he remained about ten. The account of this second visit takes up nearly half the book. It consists mainly as before of letters sent to Weimar, supplemented by a sort of monthly memorandum, written at a much later date, but there are in addition copies of letters received and much material thrown together haphazard. This is little more than the raw material of a book which Goethe might have written on his Italian travels, but which in fact he never wrote. There is a long description of the Carnival of Rome, a rather tedious summary of a paper by Moritz on the plastic imitation of the Beautiful, and notes on Church ceremonies, ballads, street songs, dances, the playing of women's parts by men in the theatre. The work concludes with the critiques and apophthegms concerning Venetian art written in 1790, which have already been mentioned.

On returning to Rome he found himself surrounded by faces which were familiar—Tischbein, Schütz, Bury, Moritz, Meyer, Angelica Kauffmann. Tischbein was still working on his picture, but their relations had definitely entered a new phase, and it is clear that Goethe really never forgave him that he had not gone to Sicily. Their friendship was renewed, but there was a change.

Goethe was quieter, less feverishly excited, than during his first visit. 'I have grown,' he said, 'and the world is real again.' Tischbein no longer saw in Goethe an ideal. The more he saw of him the less easily could he allow himself to be guided by him. On his side it was characteristic of Goethe that the more he saw of people the more critical he tended to become. Tischbein had his own ideas about many things. It grated on Goethe that he thought and talked so much about Holbein and Dürer, when Goethe's own mind was full only of Italians. There remained always much in Tischbein that Goethe found attractive, but he preferred the admiration and the discipleship of Meyer and Moritz to the more independent attitude of Tischbein. Tischbein not only failed to go with Goethe to Sicily but he went off to Naples during Goethe's second stay in Rome. Harnack has stigmatized his conduct as selfish, but it may surely be pleaded in extenuation that Tischbein was bound to think of his work and his career. It was necessary for him to earn, and it was a grief to him that Goethe felt sore. He did what he could to placate Goethe by writing to him from Naples and sending him sketches. He gave him news of his work for the Court. He told him how at Hamilton's desire he had painted Emma as Iphigenia. The letters of Goethe to Tischbein which might throw light on their relations were probably burnt, since Tischbein never kept his papers. Whether with reason or not, Goethe felt himself deserted, and he came more and more to depend on the friendship of Meyer, and, after his arrival towards the end of the year, of Kayser. 'Tischbein', Goethe had written some few weeks before Kayser arrived, 'in confidence be it said, did not join in with me as I expected. He is a real good fellow, but not so pure, so open, so natural as his letters. His character, not to do him an injustice, I can describe only by word of mouth, and what signifies such a description? The life of a man, that is his character. Now I am in hopes of getting Kayser. He will be a great joy to me.' Goethe speaks of Kayser as orderly and sedate, of healthful influence and strict character, with at the same time a true eye for life and society. Born like Goethe in Frankfort, Kayser was six years his junior. They had made each other's acquaintance when Kayser was 17. His father was an organist and he himself a composer and teacher of music even as a youth. He settled in Zurich, and Goethe, with characteristic loyalty to a friend, did what he could to help him. He sent him dramatic work to set to music with a view to its performance at Weimar. Later on Kayser came to Weimar for a short time only, but the idea of co-operation with him remained constantly with Goethe. *Scherz, List und Rache*, the first two Acts of which was given in the spring of 1785, had been the fruit of their collaboration, but Kayser was dissatisfied with his part in it. He had managed to get to Italy in the previous year, and in reply to Goethe's invitation he came out again and brought the manuscript with him. A piano was obtained, and Kayser's earnestness taught Goethe to appreciate Italian music as he had not done before. Their relation, indeed, was the sort of relationship that Goethe always appreciated. He could learn something from Kayser, at the same time that Kayser became his whole-hearted admirer and follower. In Rome with Goethe and his artist circle he was therefore supremely happy, working, studying, and composing music for *Egmont* and the lighter dramatic works of Goethe, of which there are four in all. Only later did Goethe realize that the libretto for an operetta was work not well suited to his genius.

Few among those in Goethe's circle were his seniors, but Hofrath Friedrich Reiffenstein was at the period of Goethe's stay between 50 and 60, a business man already a resident in Rome during many years, cultivated, hospitable to all visitors to the city, and highly esteemed socially. He served the Courts of Russia and Gotha as their agent in regard to art purchases. Goethe got to know him not long after his arrival in the city, though it was only during his second stay that Reiffenstein became his friend. There was perhaps something a little pompous about Reiffenstein, and Goethe's young companions were inclined to laugh at him, but he was a man who was always ready to be helpful: 'my influential friend' Goethe called him, when after his return to Weimar Reiffenstein obtained for him a cast of the skull of Raphael. Their friendship no doubt developed side by side with Goethe's friendship for Angelica Kauffmann,

for Reiffenstein had long been intimate with Zucchi and his wife.
Angelica Kauffmann, a few years Goethe's senior, had a special
place of her own in his affections, and everything he says about
her amply bears out her reputation as a woman of remarkable
sweetness and serenity of character. Herder later on, it is interesting to note, found her personality and her environment no
less attractive. He was far from willing to accept all Goethe's
friends, but he took to Angelica at once—although no longer a
youthful woman and a highly paid artist, yet living her life 'like
a Madonna'. One of the advantages of his move to the Piazza
Magnanelli was that he could visit her more frequently, and
finally he spent most of his time with her. Herder too almost fell
in love with her. His letters about her tried his wife's patience.
While in Rome he showed signs of jealousy of her friendship
with Goethe, and it was therefore perhaps as well that on his
return he dropped Angelica as completely as Goethe had done
before him. 'The memory of her friendship', says Mr. H. W.
Nevinson, 'was by far the best thing he brought back with him
from Italy.' Angelica Kauffmann, who was already getting on
for 50, lived in a very different environment from most of the
artists among whom Goethe spent his time. She mixed with
the highest social circles in Rome, in addition to being herself
an outstanding figure in the world of art. Goethe no doubt
was attracted to her by the fact that she had known Winckelmann, and was an enthusiastic admirer of his ideas and of the
art of Greece in the age of Pericles. Her house was full of casts,
of classical friezes and statuary, and her own art was permeated
with Greek feeling. All this, quite as much as her qualities of
personality, won for her the admiring friendship of Goethe. But
he soon became conscious that there was behind all her success
an undercurrent of sadness in her life, and that her elderly
husband admired without loving her. It became a habit with
Goethe to visit a picture-gallery with her every Sunday. It
was to please her that Goethe and Bury arranged a concert in
their rooms of the works of Cimarosa. There are frequent
references in the *Italienische Reise* to readings at her house,
notably of *Iphigenie* and *Egmont*. She did not hesitate to let him

know that *Iphigenie* did not altogether please her in its new form, and he consulted her, a rare thing with Goethe, about the supernatural scenes in *Egmont*. He even consulted her about his love affairs. The question has often been raised as to whether he was in love with her, and there was certainly something in their friendship which recalled his relations with Frau von Stein. To judge from her letters Angelica fell under his fascination so far that by the time that he left Rome she was certainly in love with him. He was perhaps never attracted by her in the same way or to the same extent, but he felt for her a mingled gratitude, regard, and affection which made a firm bond between them even though it was not love.

During his second stay, as during his first, Goethe refused to go out into general society. He still remained Herr Möller, though of course his presence in the city was well known. He appears to have made no attempt to talk Italian or even to have learnt the language, but we can nevertheless note certain marked changes which came over him during his last months in Italy. He became more open-minded. Already well acquainted with the city he gave himself up almost passionately to study, and he moved about more freely both in Rome itself and in the neighbourhood. The change in his attitude of mind is well exemplified by what he writes about the Carnival of 1788. In the previous year the whole thing had struck him as almost contemptible: 'One must have seen the Carnival in Rome to get rid entirely of the wish to see it again.' On the second occasion he reflected that it was after all something historical: 'It now assumed in my eyes the character of an important natural production and national event. From this point of view the spectacle interested me. I observed minutely the course of the follies and how everything yet went off with a certain prescribed form and appropriateness.'[1] Then again his whole attitude towards the Church and Church ceremonies becomes less intolerant. There is less aloofness and introspection in his attitude. He is happier: 'I feel in lighter spirits and am grown almost another

---

[1] Appended to his narrative for April which occupies four pages is an account of the Carnival which occupies thirty.

man from what I was a year ago [August 11th].' And again: 'Rejoice with me that I am happy. Indeed I can say I never was so happy as I now am.'

Much of this happiness was due no doubt to absorption in one activity after another, quite apart from his literary work. He continued his botanical studies and carried out experiments with seeds and with twigs cut off the trees. He notes a 'tall shrub-like nettle stalk' on which 'the complete flower has again brought forth from her bosom four complete flowers'. These studies were all undertaken in order to justify the theory set out later in the *Metamorphosis of Plants*, 1790, that everything in a plant including flowers and fruit is a modification or transformation of the leaf. This theory together with the *Urpflanze* theory already mentioned, that all plants are a modification of or development from some original plant, had occupied much of his thought for months past and continued to do so during his second stay in Rome. Another of his most engrossing occupations was drawing. Goethe had amused himself with drawing all his life. Sketching had been one of the great pleasures of his youth. He had even given lessons to his early friend Merck. Merck was a man of acute sensibilities who practised many arts but whose qualities impressed his contemporaries more than they have impressed posterity. He resented, perhaps with a touch of jealousy, the praise which Goethe received on all sides, and it was to Merck, no doubt in order to placate him, that Goethe presented a portfolio of his drawings. At Weimar he had continued to draw and to paint, so that it is not surprising that although he left Kniep to make the sketches of their tour in Italy he himself took up his pencil during his second stay in Rome. His work was directed by Philip Hackert, whose acquaintance he had already made in Naples, a protégé of the Royal Family and a well-known landscape-painter who had already resided in Italy for some years. Goethe quotes a saying of his as having been addressed to another but which might quite well have been addressed to himself: 'Stay with me a year and a half and you will be able to produce works which will be a delight to yourself and others.' Hackert instructed Goethe in architecture and on the human figure, as well as in drawing. He appears to have been frequently in Rome and he accompanied Goethe on more than one of his excursions in the neighbourhood. The closeness of their relations with one another is shown by the fact that when Hackert died in 1808 he left materials for the writing of his biography to Goethe, and that Goethe was willing to undertake the task. The high proficiency obtained by Goethe in draughtsmanship is shown by the sketches which are preserved in the Goethehaus and the Ducal Library at Weimar. He occupied himself also with modelling, in which he received instruction from Trippel, who had been commissioned to make a bust of Goethe by the Prince of Waldeck. Together with his friends he attended lectures on perspective from Verschaffeldt. His progress in his earlier attempts delighted him, but he discovered later, as is so often the case, that success at the start can be deceptive, and after some months of work we find him writing that although he proceeds as far as the knowledge is concerned with accuracy and confidence, he is a little confused in the application. Angelica Kauffmann encouraged him in this as in everything else, and after his return to Weimar he continued to model, but he came finally to recognize that in art 'personal knowledge' does not carry very far. Anatomy was yet another interest to which he devoted himself in Rome, and here again the interest may be said to have been lifelong. Goethe had attended lectures on anatomy at Strassburg when he was 21 and he continued to study later at Weimar. It was anatomy which led him on to osteology and his discovery of the intermaxillary bone in man. We have already noted that during his outward journey to Rome his interest and delight in the human skeleton and anatomy had their important place in the chain of those subjects to which with eager enthusiasm he devoted himself. In addition to drawing and modelling and anatomy he gave much time to music. This was with him a taste inherited and he had learnt early to play the 'cello. During the second stay in Rome his interest in music was greatly stimulated by the arrival of Kayser. It was Kayser who helped to modify Goethe's attitude both towards Church music and to folk-songs. At first he was unwilling to listen to any music other than operatic. Kayser, who was a true musician, succeeded in broadening his attitude of mind in this connexion as well as in others, and to him more than to any other of Goethe's friends we may attribute the larger and more tolerant tone which makes itself felt in the latter part of his record. A few weeks before his departure there is an account of Mass in the Sistine Chapel in the presence of the Pope. Kayser, who accompanied Goethe on that occasion, delighted in the old Spanish motet which was sung, and clearly induced Goethe to realize the beauty of the scene, for he proceeds to write with something approaching enthusiasm of the collection of old music which they had in their house, and also of the music for Passion Week which they heard sung elsewhere. It is significant that Goethe records that during the previous year he had taken a meal in the Chapel and had had a short sleep on the Pope's Throne. His account of this later visit shows how the mood of contemptuous indifference had given place to an eager and respectful interest. Quite apart from the evening party which they gave for Angelica, a party which attracted not a little undesired notice, it is clear that music was one of Goethe's outstanding pleasures during his last months in the city, and that there was nothing he enjoyed more than music in the company of his friends. The society of his friends and no doubt their hearty encouragement induced in him no little restless activity. His enthusiasm indeed was boundless. In August 1787 his hopes ran so high that he wrote: 'My study of art and my authorship both require the time I am yet to spend here. In art I must bring my affairs to such a point that everything becomes personal knowledge, and nothing remains tradition and name, and I will of necessity extort this result in half a year and no-where but in Rome is this to be extorted.' And later in the same letter: 'In natural history I bring with me things you do not expect. I believe I am coming very near to the *How* of organization.'

(2)

All these scientific and aesthetic interests, it must not be overlooked, were secondary to his literary work. He was thinking things out even when he was putting nothing on paper. This is clear from his diaries and letters. Like most creative artists he was often busiest, his imagination most active, when there was little to show for it. This essay must confine itself to the facts of Goethe's stay in Rome, but it would be very incomplete if it did not at least mention the literary work which was the fruit of his Italian journey, and of the ideas which suggested themselves during that time and were developed at a later period. The work actually achieved during the visit to Italy was small. It had been his intention to give up time during his stay to three works in particular, all of them either begun or projected— *Egmont, Tasso,* and *Faust,* but as so often happens his intentions were not altogether fulfilled. His first preoccupation in Italy, as we have seen, was *Iphigenie.* The play in its prose form had appeared originally in 1779 and had been performed in Weimar. *Iphigenie* was his companion all the way to Rome, and he completed his version in verse before he left for Sicily. In the making of his second version he had consulted his friend Moritz, whose prosody in Goethe's words 'shone upon me like a star of light'. Angelica Kauffmann and even Zucchi, as we have seen, thought well of the work, but opinion generally was less enthusiastic. Goethe realized this when letters began to arrive from Weimar recounting how it had been received. 'No one thanks me', he writes ruefully from Caserta, 'for the endless pains I have been at.' *Egmont* fared rather better. Goethe had begun the work in Frankfort in 1774 and had made some sort of sketch of the play at Weimar in 1782. He was inspired to take it up again partly because events which had recently occurred in the Netherlands appeared to repeat the story that was set out in the play.[1] On returning from Sicily he started work upon it, by July 17th he was on the fourth Act, and by the beginning of August he was in sight of the end. On August 11th he was able to tell his friends that it was finished, but he was occupied during the month in

---

[1] In 1787 Frederick William of Prussia invaded Holland in support of the Stadholder and against the party of the Patriots. Egmont had protested against the injustices of Spanish officials sent to administer the Netherlands. Executed by Alva in 1568, he became a Flemish hero. Goethe's play makes no claim to historical accuracy in its details.

putting finishing touches, and he sent it off with a request that Kayser might compose the incidental music. When Kayser arrived in Rome in the late autumn he was able to give the welcome news that it had been well received in Weimar, though by the time letters began to arrive opinion had become rather more critical. Both Schiller and Gervinus considered it too operatic. This critical attitude Goethe resented, and he writes rather tartly: 'The unpoetical lover of art ensconced in his burgess-like comfort is apt to take offence at any part of a poetical work which entails trouble upon him . . . the somnolent reader wants everything to pursue its natural course, little imagining in his obstinate conceit how the extraordinary may be natural.' He was evidently nettled at the criticism (which from the context we may perhaps infer was that of Frau von Stein) that certain passages were too long, sore at what seemed to him to be unfair and moreover to show lack of understanding of what was in his mind. He took the drama round to Angelica. 'Would you had been present', he writes, 'as with such womanly tenderness she opened up the whole play developing one part out of another.' It was this gentle and intuitive understanding that bound her so closely to Goethe. She knew how to treat him, and in this case she treated him like a child who has been hurt.

There is an interesting letter written from Rome during the summer of 1787 to the Duke, in which, in order to justify his remaining there until the Easter of the following year, Goethe sketches out a programme. According to this, *Egmont* is already finished. *Tasso* is to be finished by New Year and *Faust* by Easter. It is fair to conclude that in writing this Goethe was genuinely deceiving himself rather than seeking to mislead his correspondent. Goethe had indeed worked at *Egmont* intensively during July and August, a rare thing with him, and the manuscript had been sent off to Weimar, but the story of *Tasso* is different. *Tasso* like *Egmont* is associated with the Italian journey, but from the first to last it covers many years. Begun in 1780, Goethe did not get beyond the first Act. He worked upon it during the following year, again inspired by Frau von Stein.

The manuscript of the first and second Acts was specially chosen
to take with him to Italy, and in Italy he worked upon it fitfully.
The manuscript was with him during the voyage to Sicily, and
in his cabin during the storm he thought out the plans of his
second metrical version. Only in March 1788 was he able to say
that the plan was at least arranged, and in the following month
he informs his friends that it is his intention that *Tasso* should be
his companion on yet another journey, the journey home. Some
of the most famous passages were composed at Florence in the
Boboli Gardens, but the play was not produced until 1807, when
the close friendship with Frau von Stein was already a thing of
the past. *Faust* owes little to Italy, though it was certainly very
much in his mind all the time. One letter to his friends rather
suggests that at least a large instalment will precede his return,
though another some time later makes it clear that he had found
it hard to settle down to the work. Only a few weeks before he
left Rome he told them that he had drawn up a plan for *Faust*
and consoles himself with the thought that the composition will
have lost nothing by its long suspension of fifteen years. *Faust*
was in every sense the work of his life. From the first inception
of the idea arising out of his youthful chemical experiments to
the completion of the second part covers some sixty years, 1770
to 1831. The only scene which certainly belongs to Rome is
that in the witches' kitchen, which was composed in the Borghese
Gardens. Apart from these more important items, the fruit of the
Italian journey is meagre. There must be added various others,
but even collectively they hold a very modest place in the *corpus*
of Goethe's works. There is *Claudine von Villa Bella* and *Erwin
und Elmire*, libretti for operas, each written many years earlier
and now recast. *Lila*, a composition of rather the same character,
had been composed later, and on *Lila* too he spent some time
making revisions. The coming of Kayser had turned the thoughts
of Goethe and his companions to music, and this is probably
the explanation why he devoted so much time to literary work
which was comparatively unimportant; but the real explanation
of the fact that Goethe's second stay in Rome was, from a
literary standpoint, relatively infertile is that there were, as we

have seen, so many other things which occupied his time. It is Goethe the student, the scientific investigator, the tourist, the man freed from responsibilities, enjoying himself in the society that was congenial to him, with whom we have to deal in Rome. His wonderful eyes missed nothing of what he wished to see, and the mind to which nothing human was alien, was more than fully occupied. It is grimly humorous that he who had fled from Weimar in order among other things to find quiet in which to work, should at the end of it all write to the Duke: 'Everything here distracts me; I am in a hurry to get back in order to be able to write in peace.' He found it difficult in Rome to settle down to literary composition. He admits indeed that all his literary achievements were extorted by sheer force of mind and that he never at any period of his life gave to anything the amount of time it really merited.

The letters to Weimar which make up the greater part of the *Italienische Reise* do not, as has already been indicated, tell all. There is the story of the Milanese Maddalena Riggi, a very simple and harmless flirtation, a mere philandering episode as related in the letters to Frau von Stein and to Herder. Goethe taught her English, and learnt after some time that she was engaged to be married and later that the engagement was broken off. He writes of this episode in a romantically pessimistic vein characteristic of the Goethe of twenty years earlier: 'I found a sad and impossible task thrown on my imagination, the task of picturing those bright features compatible alone with open joyous day, now soiled with tears and marred with suffering; the task of conceiving so fresh and wonderful a figure now in the early spring of her life blasted and emaciated by trouble of soul and body.' The young lady, however, recovered, as young ladies do, attended the Carnival, and was introduced by the kindly Angelica into her circle of friends. We may presume that this story, put together from his letters and from the records which are appended to them written in his old age, is correct. There was another woman, Faustina, to whom he attached himself, daughter of the keeper of an inn near the theatre of Marcellus. It was Faustina who inspired *Roman*

Elegies. She appears to have been a beautiful girl of about 25 at the time of her romance with Goethe. Goethe wrote darkly to Frau von Stein about getting your pleasure where you can find it, and indicated that happiness could be found in Italy and not least in Rome. To the Duke he wrote even more explicitly.

(3)

During Goethe's second stay we hear, as was to be expected, less about sightseeing than during his earlier stay. It is clear that he came to love the Sistine Chapel, and he visited it frequently, both in order to enjoy the ceremonies and to admire the work of Michelangelo. Of Signorelli, Ghirlandajo, and Botticelli he makes no mention, and apart from the Sistine Chapel he has little to say of Michelangelo. Goethe's debt to him is chiefly in regard to human anatomy. It is Raphael and Raphael alone of whom he writes with consistent enthusiasm, whether he is describing the *loggie* in the Vatican, his paintings, his frescoes, or the tapestries. Few things seem to have delighted him more than having been shown Raphael's skull, of which he obtained a cast later on. He ascended Trajan's Column to enjoy the view by day, and he was warm in praise of the sight of the Piazza Colonna by moonlight. On more than one occasion, like any other visitor, he describes a tour through the city with his friends. He does what so many who love the city well have often done—he makes a tour round it just as a stranger with little time at his disposal might be expected to do. He gives an account of a visit to S. Paolo fuori which stands a mile and a half outside the Porta S. Paolo. The great Basilica seen by Goethe was destroyed by fire in 1823, and carefully rebuilt during a long period of years; until quite recently it stood isolated on its rather desolate site, and only a few years ago must have looked much as it appeared to Goethe, though it is to-day surrounded by a quickly-growing artisan population. From S. Paolo they proceeded to Tre Fontane and on the way back they passed the Baths of Caracalla, a huge mass of walls and arches now standing in their own park. In Goethe's day they must have been more picturesque than at the present time. Goethe himself was content not to visit them—Piranesi's representation of them was all that he wanted. It was the Transfiguration by Raphael in S. Pietro in Montorio which pleased them above everything else they saw. The traveller who regrets that in these days he can so seldom see paintings in their proper setting must be glad in this instance that the picture has been transferred from the church to the Vatican Gallery, for it would inevitably have suffered in the revolutionary days of 1849 when the tribune and the campanile were destroyed. The Capitol, the Borghese Gallery, the Cloaca Maxima, the Catacombs, all find mention when the time of departure grew near. The damp and the darkness of the Catacombs were so repellent to Goethe that he preferred to leave his friends to make their exploration, and to await their return above. In the Mausoleum of Augustus he saw without appreciating it the Roman sport of bull-baiting. Perhaps one of the most curious events of his stay in Rome had been his admission into the Society of the Arcadians. He was introduced with elaborate ceremonial rites and received a Diploma which set forth the fame which attached to his work alike in poetry and in prose. This occurred in January 1787. After the concert given in their rooms in honour of Angelica Kauffmann, which received so much public notice, it was more difficult than ever to expect Rome to take Herr Möller seriously. It is indeed remarkable that he nevertheless succeeded to the end in restricting his circle to the intimates he had chosen. It says much for the inherent politeness of the Romans that he was allowed to do so.

His stay in Rome was naturally diversified by short visits in the neighbourhood from time to time. Soon after his return from Naples in the heat of summer he went to Tivoli and later to Albano (through which he had already passed on his way south), Frascati, and Castel Gandolfo. He was at Frascati in September and paid more than one visit. Indeed he had been there already in the previous year. During his September visit he worked hard at drawing and painting, and in the evening he and his friends took walks in order to admire the views by moonlight.

Castel Gandolfo he visited more than once as guest of an English
art-dealer, Jenkins, who occupied the former residence of the
Jesuit General. Jenkins appears to have been a wealthy, hospitable
man and Goethe was very happy with him, although the house
was full of guests. Castel Gandolfo was a watering-place to
which many Roman families came, and Goethe was urged by his
friend Reiffenstein to see the surrounding country before the
holiday season began and the town filled up. At Castel Gandolfo
Goethe found himself compelled to fit in his own plans with
other people's, and he appears to have done so willingly. He
remarks, probably with truth, that at Castel Gandolfo he met
more Italians than he had done during the course of a year.
It was here that the romance with the Milanese lady had its
beginning, and that Angelica Kauffmann showed so much friendly
sympathy.

(4)

But the time came when it was no longer possible to delay
his return to Weimar. Both Frau von Stein and Herder made it
clear that they thought he had been away long enough. His
friend the Duke had treated him with great generosity. During
his eighteen months' absence his salary had been paid regularly,
and no offence had been taken when Goethe dissuaded the
Duchess Anna Amalia from going to Italy for no better reason
than that he did not want to be her cicerone. He made it clear
that he would return only on the understanding that he would
be free from the political responsibilities that had irked him in
the past. He asked in terms that even when he returned he might
be relieved of public duties and allowed to 'find himself', to be
not a servant of the Duke or of the State but a guest. On such
an understanding Goethe was ready to leave; and though it was
saddening to break with so many happy associations, and to do
so for ever, he carried it through with his usual dignity and
courage. 'So soon as I had taken the resolution to go I had no
interest in remaining and should have liked to have got away a
fortnight ago.' As so many travellers like to do, he took as it
were a ceremonial farewell. Once he went round the city with

his friends, and once alone. He mounted the Capitol steps ('la cordonnata'), walked through the Piazza del Campidoglio, past the Statue of Marcus Aurelius, then descended what he calls the 'back steps' staircase leading down the other side, affording a panorama of the remains of ancient Rome. The view which Goethe saw has been described by Friederike Bremer. She speaks of it as 'an immense grave, and out of the grave rose a city of monuments in ruins . . . it was the giant apparition of ancient Rome'. As Goethe saw it the sight must have been overpoweringly beautiful. Since his day generations of scholars, archaeologists, artists, and architects have given time and devoted care and skill to simplifying, identifying, and explaining what in Piranesi's time was little more than a picturesque quarry with names given by popular tradition, often no doubt ludicrously incorrect. Whether the most recent phase of all, the clearing away of large areas of eighteenth-century Rome adjacent to the ruins of the ancient city under an entirely new impulse, the glorification of Fascist Italy and its leader, is on balance an advantage succeeding ages will judge. To some at least it seems that the excuse of improving housing conditions for the workers has been used in order to cover grandiose developments which in some cases involve irreparable injury to the historic continuity of the city. However that may be, Goethe returned through the Arch of Septimus Severus along the Via Sacra to the Colosseum and so to his lodgings. On April 22nd, accompanied by Kayser, he passed through the Porta del Popolo with his face turned towards Weimar.

Some of those he left behind him he was to meet again. He was in Venice once more in 1790 but he had left Rome for ever. Meyer, like Kayser, remained a lifelong friend. Schütz, his cheerful companion in the lodgings, he ran across in Frankfort twenty-six years later. Bury turned up in Venice during his second visit, and they met again in Karlsbad in 1808. Goethe found real pleasure in welcoming Moritz as a visitor to Weimar in 1788 and again in 1791, but he died prematurely two years later. On the other hand Kniep, who had combined youthful and enthusiastic hero-worship with much helpful service during the Sicilian holiday, lived out his life in Italy. Angelica Kauffmann died in Rome in 1807. The letters she wrote to Goethe after his departure seem to indicate that the feelings he had aroused in her were warmer than he realized. The beauty and unselfishness of her character, universally recognized, are shown nowhere more clearly than in her relations with him.

Finally, Tischbein. After the arrival of Kayser in December 1787 Goethe no longer felt any need for him, and Tischbein remained working in Naples for the Prince of Waldeck and more particularly for his patron the Duke of Gotha. Goethe hoped that he would come to Rome in order to say good-bye to him, but he failed to do so, and Goethe took it very much to heart, though he sent messages to Tischbein through Meyer. They corresponded but they never met again. Tischbein, when occupying a teaching post in Olten, was invited to Weimar. He frequently sent gifts of sketches to Goethe, which are to be seen to-day in Weimar as Goethe himself arranged them. 'Tischbein', Goethe has said, 'is like Jehovah, what is and is to be. If you do something for him, he pushes you back.' Elsewhere he says: 'Tischbein tried to be lovable and clever, but he did not work out his life from a right angle. One must thank him for enlivening the study of the antique, and it is he who brought the Etruscan vases to public notice.' These are sayings of Goethe in extreme old age, and the praise is certainly guarded. It is pleasanter to remember a remark made in 1800, when he recognized some studies of Tischbein and called him his old friend and a sculptor poet. It would have been interesting to hear Tischbein's side of the story, but, as we know, he did not keep letters. Most people have found right on the side of Goethe, but the short record of their relations given here seems to induce the inevitable conclusion that Goethe demanded too much of him. At least it is certain that Tischbein could have made out a case for himself had he chosen to do so, and it is to his credit that he was content to be silent. Therein at least we may find evidence of respect for genius and a personal loyalty which remained unimpaired to the last.

V

There is no account of the return journey in the *Italienische
Reise*. It covered a period of eight weeks. From Rome Goethe
proceeded to Florence, where on his way outward he spent but
a few hours, and in Florence he remained twenty-one days.
During his stay he worked, as has been said, at *Tasso* in the
Boboli Gardens. The Venus de' Medici of all the treasures of
the city most aroused his enthusiasm, but he remained insensible
to the beauty of the Italian Primitives or to the Florentine
painters of the thirteenth and fourteenth centuries. The spirit
of devotion which inspired their art was incomprehensible to
him, and he still found it impossible to reconcile himself to the
portrayal of so many scenes of horror and of agony. For all that,
he systematically worked his way round the sights like any other
tourist, and then proceeded to Parma, where in S. Giovanni and
elsewhere he could admire the work of Correggio. In Milan he
had no appreciation for the gothic of the cathedral—its over-
elaboration was bound to be distasteful to him. Da Vinci's
Cenacolo in the refectory of S. Maria delle Grazie he regarded
with an enthusiasm seldom aroused during his stay in Italy. He
bought a mineralogist's hammer to be made use of on his journey
home through the mountains. His letters continued to repeat
with what sorrow he had bidden farewell to Rome, and it was
with a heavy heart that he prepared to cross the Alps. Having
reached Italy by the Brenner, the least awe-inspiring of the
Alpine passes, he returned by the Splügen. The road that exists
to-day was only constructed some thirty years later, and the
journey up through Chiavenna at the head of Lake Como must
have been an uncomfortable one, though Goethe, who never
shirked discomfort, says nothing about it. At the top of the
pass he bade farewell to Italy and found himself in Canton
Grisons. He must have been interested to see Coire, for it was
at Battazatta in the immediate neighbourhood of that town that
Angelica Kauffmann had been born. At a point rather above
Coire the road joins the Rhine valley, and the sight of the Rhine
and the reappearance of the German tongue must have induced

in Goethe the feeling that he was indeed nearing home. The road passes Feldkirck and reaches Lake Constance at Bregenz, and from there Goethe made his journey to Constance by water. It was at Constance that he wrote to Herder, mistakenly believing him to be in Rome. The letter shows with what depth of feeling he continued to look back on his stay there: 'Travel in happiness', he says, 'and open my letter where for the first time in my life, I was entirely happy. I do not know whether I am awake or whether I dream while I write to you these lines. Mine is a heavy burden. Farewell. Make the most of your time.' There had been some idea before he left Rome that he would visit his mother on his way home, and after so much travelling and hardship it need not have taken very long to make the comparatively easy journey between Constance and Frankfort. His mother's loyal devotion to her son knew no bounds. Of this he had good evidence not long afterwards in the matter of Christiane Vulpius, but, devoted though he was to her, he was at all times content to go for long periods without seeing her. He was bound for Weimar, and to Weimar he was impelled to hurry forward. From Constance his route is variously given as through Stuttgart or through Augsburg to Nuremburg.[1] Thence by Gotha to Weimar, which he reached on the night of June 18th.

It remains only to add something upon the effect of his Italian journey upon Goethe's life and ideas. He returned a free man, determined to maintain his freedom from office. The Duke with his usual good-natured complaisance accepted the situation, but at the same time retained for him a seat on the Council which was his whenever he should choose to attend. Their relations with one another remained close, and Goethe was frequently consulted behind the scenes. A year or two after his return he found himself invested with the position of Director of the Court Theatre, and even for a time found pleasure in the exercise of his responsibilities. But for the most part his time was his own.

---

[1] Duntzer gives Augsburg, but the road Bregenz–Augsburg goes nowhere near Constance. The fact that Goethe went to Constance appears to justify the view of Lewis and others that he passed through Stuttgart.

Another change was in regard to Frau von Stein. One of his reasons for undertaking the journey to Italy had been the strained relations into which they had drifted with one another; and only as the months had passed did her bitter resentment of his flight die down, and her letters display once again something of the old warmth. Goethe returned cured of his passion for her. There was constraint on both sides, and when she became aware of his relations with Christiane their friendship came to its natural end. There was no quarrel. Goethe as we know, wrote to Frau von Stein about Christiane with a strange disregard of her feelings. Passionate lover though he was, once his passion had cooled he could always show a curious insensibility; but though there was no breach, Frau von Stein faded out of his life, and with Christiane he found ease and peace at home such as he had never known before. Indifferent to public opinion, he endeavoured to settle down to work. He was the more ready to do so since he discovered, as returned travellers so often discover, that his experiences were of more interest to himself than to others. The next few years, until the period of his friendship with Schiller, opened rather a disappointing chapter in his life, a period which accounts for relatively little creative effort, and was occupied by collecting his work already published and by desultory attention to further work in process of achievement. Largely owing to his own fault he was out of touch with many who had previously made up his circle, and he seems to have found most of his pleasure in the visits of those whom he had met in Italy. After about 1796 matters improved, largely owing to the warm-hearted Grand Duchess. The liaison with Christiane was condoned, and the period of his association with Schiller marks a new phase of productivity.

It was given to Goethe to see Italy again, but he saw it with different eyes. His journey to Italy in fact had come when he was in the very middle of his journey through life. Behind him lay tender memories of happy days in the dignified old house at Frankfort with his grave father, his beloved sister, and his kindly, cheerful, understanding mother, his idyll with Kathe,

whom as a youth he wanted to marry, the happy times at
Leipzig, Gretchen his first real love, his university life, the gay
society of the town, his early efforts in prose and verse, his illness. Then had come Strassburg and his meeting with Herder,
who opened new worlds to him; his introduction to the works
of Winckelmann, his hopes so tragically disappointed of meeting
him, Friederike the gentle Alsatian from whom he fled, certainly
the least creditable of his adventures, the beginning of his professional life. There followed the return to Frankfort and the
appearance of *Götz von Berlichingen*, the visit to Wetzlar,
Werther, and fame. During these years there had come into his
life Lotte, perhaps the most beautiful and the most intelligent
of all the girls who aroused his fancy, and Lili, the type that had
always attracted him most, whose temperament had induced in
him the serious desire for marriage, even though it had passed
like the others. To all this had succeeded the happy, busy years
at Weimar, years of service to the duchy and of devotion to
Frau von Stein; and finally the conviction that the great projects
he had in mind could only be completed if he were away from
both the one and the other. In effect when he returned in 1788
his travelling days were done, and in the years after he came
back from Italy his existence was bound up with Weimar alone.
During those years there were to follow in splendid succession
Tasso, *Roman Elegies*, *Wilhelm Meister*, *Hermann und Dorothea*,
Elective Affinities, and finally *Faust*. And side by side with them
are the names of those who during all these years played their
parts in his life: Christiane, always 'my child'; Bettina, who
worshipped him with a sentimental devotion which became an
embarrassment; Minna, whose youth inspired in him such
intense emotion; August, the source of such bitter disappointment borne with such dignity; Ottilie, who did what a daughter-
in-law could do to sweeten his later years, and so on to that last
phase so well portrayed by the youthful discipleship of Eckermann. Enthusiastic youth had merged into disillusioned middle
age, and middle age faded into the serenity of an old age which
so splendidly fulfilled all the tasks with which he had dallied
through the long years.

As an event in the life of Goethe there can be no question of
the importance of the Italian journey. When we turn to consider its influence on his work and philosophy of life it is not
possible to write with the same measure of certainty, and, as we
might expect, different authorities interpret its influence in different ways. Professor Herford has already been quoted. Professor Dowden roundly declares that Italy effected no change
in him, and that Rome was only the flowering of what had long
been in process of growth. The practical and the ideal side of
him could now meet in harmony, and the 'strain upon his affections' was relaxing in its intensity. Professor Hume Brown[1] on
the other hand quotes three authorities as to the changes which
in their view Italy had wrought. There is the testimony of
Caroline Herder. On his return she did not know whether to
like him or not. She found him less than frank, and the days
of close friendship were already over between them when she
wrote to her husband in this sense, though it is fair to add that
she praised him as a manly soul. 'He feels himself a being of a
higher order' no doubt sums up correctly the impression he
made upon her. The Olympian Goethe of his final phase was
already making its appearance to the mind of this highly intelligent observer. Von Knebel noted his concentration upon
himself and upon his own opinions. It certainly seemed to von
Knebel that the views Goethe had formed in Italy had changed
him. Schiller also at first felt that it was difficult to know the
real Goethe behind the mask, and that the happiness he had
sought and claimed to have found had in fact not made him
happy. To Goethe, on his side, the little world of Weimar
seemed narrow and provincial. They had learnt to get along
without him, and he realized that some of his old friends were
wounded, some were puzzled, and most of them were uninter-
ested in his new attitude of mind. His Italian journey left
Goethe dissatisfied and uneasy at Weimar, and it needed a
second journey to enable him to settle down at home under new

---

[1] *Life of Goethe*, vol. i, p. 396. I would here also express my indebtedness to
Goethe's most recent biographer, the late Professor J. G. Robertson, *Life and
Work of Goethe*, 1932.

conditions, happy and contented, ready to take up his life once
again. When he was in Italy in 1790 he was joined at Venice by
Meyer and by the Duchess accompanied by Bury. In their society
he revisited Padua, Verona, and Vicenza, and the fragmentary
remarks on Venetian painting attached to the *Italienische Reise*,
already noted, date from this visit. They show that Goethe's
real interest in Italy remained almost exclusively classical. From
this visit he returned cured of his yearning and passion for the
south, and he settled down contentedly in the home in which
he had installed Christiane. Italy had encouraged the breadth
of his interests even though botany, mineralogy, drawing, painting, and anatomy had all occupied his mind from early days.
When he returned they remained with him, and the house at
Weimar, which has become a place of pilgrimage, is no mere
poet's residence but the home of a many-sided genius. Dr.
Edward Caird, late Master of Balliol, has pointed out that it was
Goethe's philosophy of life that each must know himself in the
sense of knowing his work, and that nobody should 'allow himself to be drawn away to interests and pursuits which lie beyond
the range of his faculty'. This explains much in his conduct in
Italy that appears strange; it explains also his attitude in later
years to the political storms which passed over his country, and
more especially his attitude towards Napoleon. According to
Caird's interpretation of Goethe he held that 'activity that does
not advance our own self culture will be useful to no other man'.
Goethe returned in 1788 a Roman and a pagan. His journey
to Italy can in fact account for little more than the completed
Tasso and the *Roman Elegies*. The years which immediately
followed were occupied largely with scientific study and investigation. To Goethe art and nature were always of equal
interest: just as his knowledge of anatomy helped him in his
study of art, so in his literary work he is the sculptor and the
painter.

The full force of the influence of the Italian journey passed.
The old Goethe sunned himself in the atmosphere of love and
veneration which Weimar gradually came to develop, and the
romantic who became a classicist evolved an artistry in which

appeared once more something of the warmth and colour which had characterized the productions of his early years. We return once again to Professor Herford's essay, where it is pointed out that Goethe, unlike Wordsworth, unlike Shelley, is 'the poet of nature that evolves'. His life, which he made an harmonious evolution, reproduces itself in his work. In this evolution the most important single element is his journey to Italy.